HISTORY OF THE JATS

A contribution to the History of Northern India

HISTORY OF THE JATS

A contribution to the History of Northern India

By

KALIKA-RANJAN QANUNGO, M.A.,

Assistant Professor of Hisotry, Lucknow University,
Author of Sher Shah.

WITH A FOREWORD BY

JADUNATH SARKAR, M.A., I.E.S.

VOL. I

To the death of MIRZA NAJAF KAHN, 1782

ISBN: 978-93-5128-513-7

First Published in 1925
Indian Reprint in 2017

Published by

Kalpaz Publications
C-30, Satyawati Nagar,
Delhi – 110052
E-mail: kalpaz@hotmail.com
Website: kalpazpublications.com
Ph.: +91-9212142040

Cataloging in Publication Data—DK
Courtesy: D.K. Agencies (P) Ltd. <docinfo@dkagencies.com>

Kānūnago, Kālikā Rañjana, author.
    History of the Jats : a contribution to the history of northern
India. Vol. 1, To the death of Mirza Najaf Kahn, 1782 / by
Kalika-Ranjan Qanungo (M.A.) ; with a foreword by Jadunath
Sarkar (M.A., I.E.S.).
    pages cm
    "First published in 1925"—Title page verso.
    Includes bibliographical references.
    ISBN 9789351285137

    1. Jat (Asian people)—India—History. 2. India—History—
1526-1765.   I. Title. II. Title: To the death of Mirza Najaf
Kahn, 1782.

DS432.J3K36 2017   DDC 305.800954   23

CONTENTS

iv

———

FOREWORD

The Jats are one of the most important races among the Indian population today, as during the Muslim period, and their traditions go back to dim antiquity. A critical study of the past history of such a race on the basis of all the available materials cannot fail to be a subject of deep interest and instruction to all Indians. Such a study is presented in this book.

It represents the loving and devoted labour of Professor Kalika R. Qanungo for years together. He has denied himself holidays and worked at this history in my library by sacrificing his vacations. All known sources, printed and manuscript, Persian, Marathi, French and English, (besides Sanskrit for the mythical age), have been utilised here, and this History of the Jats represents a synthesis never attempted before, and leaving (so far as I can see) nothing for future workers unless new materials are discovered hereafter. Professor Qanungo has already proved his sound critical powers and true historical spirit in his first book, *Sher Shah*, which at once leaped into the position of the standard work on the subject.

In his *History of the Jats,* he has not been
content to be a closet student of written records.
He has lived and worked among the Jat boys
of his former college at Delhi, he has won their
love and confidence (as I was pleased to learn
when I spent a day there three years ago), and
has visited their historic places and tribal gather-
ings and talked with old Jats whose memories
are richly stored with the past. The information he has thus gathered by a personal quest
spread over a wide field is concentrated in this
book and gives it a unique value.

As will be expected from the high quality
of his earlier work, he has here sifted the
evidence impartially and reviewed events and
characters from the broad point of view of
India as a whole, instead of narrowing his
vision to a single tribe. This wider outlook,
this philosophical detachment from the particular dynasty or community dealt with, is
specially necessary in any history of India in
the 18th century that deserves to live as a true
history. For, the Jats were only one out of the
many threads that made up the tangled web
of North Indian history during the decline of
the Mughal empire. The Jats, Ruhelas, Sikhs,
Marathas, Rajputs, Oudh Nawabs, English
Company, French adventurers, besides the Delhi

Emperors and their semi-independent nobles,—
all entered into the criss-cross of Indian politics
during that one century which saw the rise
maturity and downfall of the Jats as the makers
of Indian history; and, therefore, Professor
Qanungo has done wisely in studying the contemporary history and interplay of *all* of these
Powers, before he felt himself competent to
write this account of the Jats alone,—though
very little of his labour appears on the surface
to the reader of the following pages.

Here is a first-rate contribution to the
critical study of the Fall of the Mughal Empire.
The Jat people may be congratulated on having
secured such a historian. Possibly the ignorant
among them may grumble that their tribal prejudices have not been flattered; but truth is
great and will prevail, and Qanungo has sought
truth with singleness of aim and backed by all
the resources available to scholarship in his
day.

JADUNATH SARKAR

May, 1925.

AUTHOR'S NOTE

This volume owes its inception to the enthusiasm of my Jat pupils at Delhi for a history of their race which I promised to them four years back. The task proved more formidable than had appeared to me at the outset. The political history of the Jats is inextricably interwoven with the general history of the Mughal Empire in the eighteenth century ; and their origin is still a mystery to themselves as well as to scholars. I ventured into the dark and unfamiliar realms of Indian antiquity and ethnology to search for the lost pedigree of the Jat ; but I do not pretend to have discovered the right one. I am painfully aware of the many imperfections of this volume. Through my bad hand-writing or inadvertence, I have failed to preserve consistency in the spelling of proper names and allowed several regrettable errors to creep in for which a revised list of errata has been found necessary.

I take this opportunity to acknowledge with gratitude the generosity of Chaudhuri Chhajju Ram of Alakhpura, Hissar, who has borne a considerable portion of the expenses of publishing this volume. Sentiment and duty alike impel me to thank my beloved pupils Chaudhuri Sadi Ram, B.A., Pandit Mukhyaram, B.A., and others for their devoted services during our historical tours and investigations. It is hardly necessary for me to reiterate the extent of my obligations to my master, Professor Jadunath

Sarkar, without whose constant help and guidance I could have hardly hoped to traverse so confidently this strange and obscure field of Indian history.

Lucknow University,
  30th April, 1925. }   **KALIKARANJAN QANUNGO**

HISTORY OF THE JATS

CHAPTER I.

ORIGIN AND EARLY HISTORY

Country and the people.

The Jats are a tribe so widespread and numerous as to be almost a nation by themselves, now numbering about nine million souls. The region mainly occupied by them may be roughly defined as bounded on the north by the lower ranges of the Himalayas, on the west by the Indus, on the south by a line drawn from Haidarabad (Sindh) to Ajmir and thence to Bhopal, and on the east by the Ganges : the Jat country spreads, so to say, in a fan-like form with Sindh as its base. Beyond the Indus there is also a sprinkling of the Jat population in Peshawar, Balochistan and even to the west of the Sulaiman range.* This race

---

* In Karmán and Irak there is a mixed Jat and Gipsy population of about 20,000 souls, and in Makrán and Afghanistan about 50,000. See *Asia* by A. H. Keene, ed. Sir Richard Temple, pp. 210, 218.

forms the backbone of the agricultural community in the Panjab, Sindh, Rajputana and
the western portion of the Gangetic Doab. Up
to the beginning of the thirteenth century the
Jats had been a compact people, having community of blood, community of language, and
a common religion. But at present about one-
third of them are Muslims, one-fifth Sikhs, and
the rest are Hindus. The Jat is a Jat after all,
whether he be a Hindu, Sikh or Muslim; he
tenaciously clings to his tribal name as a proud
heritage, and with it the tradition of kinship.

They are indeed a bold peasantry, their
country's pride, accustomed to guide the plough-
share and wield the sword with equal readiness
and success,—second to no other Indian race
in industry or courage. In physique, they
belong to the same ethnic group as the Rajput
and the Khatri, and represent a type, which
"approaches most closely to that ascribed to
the traditional Aryan colonists of India. The
stature is mostly tall, complexion fair, eyes
dark, hair on face plentiful, head long, nose
narrow and prominent but not very long".*

In character the Jat resembles the old
Anglo-Saxon and the ancient Roman, and has
indeed more of the characteristics of the Teuton

* Risley's *People of India*, p. 8.

than of the Celt in him. He is tough, slow, unimaginative and unemotional, lacking brilliance, but possessed of great solidity, dogged perseverance and an eminently practical turn of mind. He is hardly ever convinced by words without concrete facts. Sturdy independence and patient vigorous labour are among his good points, as Ibbetson has noted. Another trait of the Jat character which has been marked by good observers, is his strong individualism. "The Jat is of all the Panjab races the most impatient of the tribal or communal control and the one which asserts the freedom of the individual most strongly. In tracts where, as in Rohtak, the Jat tribes have the field to themselves, and are compelled, in default of rival castes or enemies, to fall back upon each other for somebody to quarrel with, the tribal ties are strong. But as a rule a Jat is a man who does what seems right in his own eyes and sometimes what seems wrong also, and will not be said nay by any man . . . . . . He is independent and he is self-willed; but he is reasonable, and peaceably inclined if left alone."*

The Jat is still in the tribal stage of social evolution, knowing no caste distinction or

* Ibbetson, quoted in the *Punjab Glossary*, ii. 366.

kulinism (*i.e.,* social precedence based on birth). All the tribesmen are on a dead level of equality, modified only by habitual respect to elders. The Jat invariably marries the widow of his elder brother, and this alone stands in the way of his being recognized as a pure Kshatriya. But it is a custom which obtained in the Vedic* age among the pure Aryans of the three higher castes.

"The distinction between the Jats and Rajputs both sprung from a common stock, is marked by the fact that the former practises and the latter abstains from a usage [*karewa*] which more than any other is regarded as a crucial test of relative social position."† In the government of their villages, they appear much more democratic than the Rajput; they have less reverence for hereditary right and a preference for elected headmen. The clanish feeling is very strong among them. Hereditary feud is carried on as a sacred duty. An old Jat would hardly die in peace until he has unloaded his breast by telling his heirs the good and the evil done unto him and his ancestors by his

* A passage in the *Rig Veda* quoted by Zimmer shows that in some cases, at any rate, the widow married her husband's younger brother.

(Macdonell's *History of Sanskrit Literature,* p. 126.)

† Ibbetson, *Census Report,* 1881, para 446.

neighbours and enjoining upon them revenge
for injury and return of good services. Family
[*kunbha*] may fight against family; one sept
against another, but when it is a question of
tribal honour, or quarrel with a rival caste,
every member of the clan, capable of wielding
a *lathi* (quarter-staff), will loyally assemble to
carry out implicitly the order of the tribal elders,
laying aside for the moment their own differences.

The origin of this interesting people is
enveloped in the mist of obscurity, which the
light of scientific research has yet to dispel. In
physical features, language, character, sentiments, ideas of government, and social insti-
tutions, the present-day Jat is undeniably a
better representative of the ancient Vedic Aryan
than any member of the three higher castes of
the Hindus, who have certainly lost much of
their original character in the course of evolution
through many centuries. But the Jat's tribal
designation, is supposed to point to a foreign
and less exalted origin, *viz.* Indo-Scythian.
The European pioneers of Indian antiquities
and ethnology apparently started with the pre-
sumption that fine and energetic martial peoples
like the Rajput and the Jat must have been com-
paratively new-comers from the north-west into

India who overcame the effete descendants of the
Vedic Aryans and pushed them eastward and
southward; because within the known historic
period from Alexander to Ahmad Shah Durrani
the foreign immigrants have invariably imposed
their rule upon the children of the soil. Besides,
it is a known fact that several foreign hordes,
such as the Sakas, Yuehchis, Kushans, and
Hunas from Central Asia, the reputed home of
the Parthian races, entered India successively
during the period 100 B.C.—600 A.D. and
were absorbed by Hindu society. If so, where
are their modern representatives? The Rajput
and the Jat with their warlike habits, unorthodox
customs, and confused traditions about their
origin, tempted the ingenuity of the scholars,
who at once identified them with the Sakas and
Hunas. The fanciful theory of Col. Tod, who
suggested kinship among the Indian Jats, the
Goths of the Roman Empire, and the Juts of Jut-
land, cast a mighty spell upon several generations of scholars. The *Jat* tribe's name sounded
in the scholarly ear like that of the *Gaete, Yuti*
and *Yetha* of the Oxus region. The philologist
for the first time raised his note of protest against
this. Dr. Trumpp and Beames* very strongly

---

*He remarks :—"The theory of the Aryan origin of the
Jats, if it is to be overthrown at all, must have stronger

claimed a pure Indo-Aryan descent for them
both in consideration of their physical type and
language, which has been authoritatively pronounced as a pure dialect of Hindi, without the
slightest trace of Scythian. But they were
silenced by the progressing science, which
established the unassailable dictum "Language
is no proof of race."

Next, the anthropologist appeared in the
field armed with his scientific apparatus to
measure the skulls and noses of the various
peoples of India for the purpose of restoring
their lost pedigree. This investigation resulted
in the sevenfold classification of the races of
India by Sir Herbert Risley, who declared the
Rajput and the Jat to be the true representatives
of the Vedic Aryans. This was the first scientific assault upon the Indo-Scythian theory.*

arguments directed against it than any that have yet been
adduced. *Physical type and language are considerations
which are not to be set aside by mere verbal resemblance,
especially when the words come to us mingled beyond recognition by Greek and Chinese.* [Elliot's *Memoirs of the Races
of North-Western Provinces of India,* i. 135—137.]

* Risley says :—"Of the people themselves [Scythians]
all traces seem to have vanished and the student who
enquires what has become of them finds nothing more
tangible than the modern conjecture that they are represented
by the Jats and Rajputs. But the grounds for this opinion
is of the flimsiest description and consists mainly of the
questionable assumption that the people who are called Jats

But science does not stand still. Since then
Risley's theory and classification have been
attacked by many scholars* on different
grounds.

Whatever may be the difference of opinion
as regards the validity of the test of anthropometry, or language, each considered by itself,
none can at the present state of our knowledge,
disagree with Sir Herbert Risley in his remarks :
—"In India where historical evidence can
hardly be said to exist, the data ordinarily available are of three kinds—physical characteristics,
linguistic characteristics and religious and social
usages. Of these the first are far the most
trustworthy. Most anthropologists indeed, are
inclined to adopt without much question, the
opinion of the late Sir William Fowler who
wrote to me some years ago, that physical
characters are the best, in fact the only true test
of race; language, customs etc. may help, or
give indications, but they are often mislead-

at the present day must have something to do with the people
who were known to Herodotus as the Gatæ." [*People of
India*, 60-61.]

  * Anthropometry is about to share the fate of philology
as a test of race. Prof. Ridgeway says :—"As the physical
anthropologists cannot agree upon principles of skull measure-
ment, the historical enquirer must not at present base any
argument on this class of evidence." (Quoted in Mr. Chanda's
Indo-Aryan Races, p. 62).

ing.'* The Jat has been declared by all eminent authorities, to pass successfully the combined test of the physical type and language† of a true Aryan.

As regards religious and social usages, all observers generally agree that in these points the Jats do not differ much from other Hindu communities of admittedly Aryan origin. Science may be said to have succeeded fairly well in establishing the Indo-Aryan origin of the Jats, but this cannot meet with much acceptance till they are definitely identified with some Aryan tribe of old mentioned in Sanskrit literature. Accurate scientific data for such investigation having almost disappeared, scholars have been compelled to proceed in this direction rather in an unscientific way, viz., relying mainly upon the similarity of sounds. The Mahabharat contains several chapters, devoted to the description of the different tribes of the Panjab and Sindh—the home of the Jat people within historic times. A people known as the

---

* Risley's People of India, p. 6.

† Grierson notices some Pisáca peculiarities in the Sindi and Panjabi, spoken by a considerable section of the Jat community. But "these peculiarities are probably not derived from invaders of Pisáca speech, but from the stock language spoken by the invaders akin to the Homo-Alpinus of Eastern Turkestan." [R. P. Chanda's Indo-Aryan Races, p. 78.]

Jartrikas is mentioned therein along with the *Madrakas*,—both called Bahikas or outlanders. Sir James Campbell and Grierson consider this to be the earliest notice of the Jats in Sanskrit literature.* The acrimonious reply of Karna to Shalya, king of Madrakas contains a graphic though distorted picture of the habits and character of these people. "The Madras are always false to their friends......without affection, always wicked, untruthful, and cruel. That wicked people eat fried barley and fish and in their house father, son, mother, mother-in-law, father-in-law, uncle, daughter, son-in-law, brother, grandsons, with friends and guests, menial and maidservant, *male and female together, drink wine with cow's flesh,* and sometimes cry, sometimes laugh and delight in indecent talk and songs.........Their women, overcome with wine, dance naked...... They are of *fair complexion* and tall stature,

---

* Sir James Campbell holds them to be foreigners who entered India along with the Kush horde (about B. C. 150—100) whose greatest representative was Kanishka [*Bom. Gaz.* Vol. IX, part 1, p. 459]. Grierson considers them as degraded Aryans and not *infidels ab initio.* Baraha Mihir mentions two peoples, *viz. Jatāsuras* in the *north-east,* and *Jatadharas* in the *south* near the Kaveri, whose names may sound like that of the Jats in the scholarly ear of Grierson.

See *Brihat Samhita,* Sans. text ed. by Sudhakar Dwivedi, Vol. X, part I. pp. 293,289.

wearing blankets, eating large quantities of food, shameless and lax in the observance of the laws of purity. The Bahikas, who *have been expelled* from the region of the Himalayas, the Ganges, the Jamuna, the Saraswati and Kurukshetra should be avoided. The Bahikas are not created by Prajapati, the creator of the orthodox Aryans; they are the offspring of a *Pishach* couple, named Bahi and Heek who dwelt on the bank of the Bipasa (the Beas). There is a town named Sakala and a river named Apagā where a section of the Bahikas, *known as the Jartrikas*, dwell. Their character is very reprehensible. These people, eat contentedly a large quantity of meat and boiled barley, or barley-bread, cow's flesh with garlic and fried barley. Their women drink wine, laugh and dance in public, sing indecent songs in a loud shrill voice like that of a camel or an ass; they become very unrestrained and boisterous specially on festive occasions when they dance and shout, calling one another, ''Thou ill-fated one; husband-slayer etc.'' A Bahika who had to sojourn for a time in the Kuru-jangal country sang the following song about the women of his country: ''Though a Bahika, I am at present an exile in the Kuru-jangal country; that *tall and fair-complexioned* wife of mine, *dressed in her fine blanket* certainly remembers me when she retires to rest. Oh! when shall I go back to my country crossing again the Satadru (the Sutlej) and the Iravati and see the beautiful females of fair complexion, wearing stout bangles, dressed in blanket and skins, eye-sides coloured with the dye of *Man-shila*, forehead, cheek and chin painted with collyrium [tatooing]? When shall we eat under the pleasant shade of the *Shami*, *Peelu* and *Karir*, loaves and balls of fried barley powder with waterless churned curd [*kunjik*], and gathering strength, take away the clothes of the wayfarers and beat them?" Among the Madrakas and Shakalas, young and old both drink heavily and sing aloud, "Vainly are they born who do not eat the flesh of boars, cocks, kine, asses, camels and sheep."

The above sketch brings vividly before us a picture of the Land of the Five Rivers and its people in the classic age. Its first impression almost leads one to suppose that these Jartrikas were the ancestors of the modern Jats. But on closer examination this identification of the two peoples proves most illusory. The above extract that the Bahikas were not created by Prajapati, clearly indicates the belief of the dwellers of the Vedic Aryandom that the outer nationalities originated from an ethnic stock or stocks that were quite different from the stock or stocks from which they themselves originated.* These people were apparently the ancestors of the speakers of what Grierson calls the modern Pisáca languages,—the Kashmiris, the Dards, and the Kafirs of the Hindukush. The later or outlandish Aryans were broad or medium headed and therefore were least likely to be the ancestors of the long-headed Jat people. The fact that the Bahika women wore fine blankets and skins, perhaps shows that they were immigrants from some colder countries. The tall, fair, debauched and filthy women of Kashmir are perhaps the truer representatives of the ancient Bahika females.† The Jats observe some, though not all the ten customary ceremonials of the Hindus. The *Upanayana* ceremony does not indeed take place at the usual time, but at the time of marriage. It is the custom for *purohits* to place on them at their marriages the *janeo* or sacred

---

* R. P. Chanda's *Indo-Aryan Races*, i. 42.

† The Jat women nowhere in the Panjab wrap round a blanket or even cotton cloth. They wear *ghāghrās* generally. They do not ease themselves half bent, but sitting on the ground, with the *ghāghrā* spread out in the form of a circle by giving it a clear flap.

thread, removing it a few days after marriage.* The Bahikas married within the same *got* [*vamsa*], which the Jat does not. The Jats observe the same law of succession as that of the other Hindus, and in no case is the sister's son regarded as the lawful heir in preference to their own sons—a custom attributed to the Bahikas. No doubt the orthodox Hindus of Sindh still contemptuously call the Jats of that province *Baheka*† or aliens; but it is least likely that the name of one insignificant tribe *Jartrika*, not known for morality, character, power or purity of conduct, should be adopted by many millions of people, inhabiting the large stretch of country from Afghanistan to Malwa. Besides *no Jat tribe remembers any connection with Sakala;* almost all of them believe their ancestors to have been immigrants from the interior of India. This suggested identification based on similarly sounding tribal names alone cannot therefore be accepted as valid.

Jatharas and the Jats

As the European scholars have ransacked Greek and Latin literatures to establish the Indo-

---

* *Hoshiarpur Dist. Gaz.* 1883, p. 56. The Brahmans who have taken to agriculture rarely perform the investiture ceremony separately at the prescribed time. Boys are given *janeo* at the time of marriage, in cases of early marriage.

† *Asia* by A. H. Keene, p. 296.

Scythian origin of the Jat, so some educated leaders of Jat society were also engaged in proving their undoubted Kshatriya origin by identifying the Jats with some one of the numerous warrior clans of our classic age. Pandit Giribar Prasad, a Jat Sanskrit scholar of Aligarh, employed a Shastri named Angad Sharma to investigate the origin of the Jats in the light of the orthodox literature. The Shastri, also depending mainly on the similarity of sound, lighted upon the Jatharas, as the hypothetical ancestors of the Jats. He propounded a learned theory in a little Sanskrit pamphlet, *Jatharotpatti*. It is a *catena* of all the ancient texts mentioning the tribe of Jatharas, whose origin is related as follows in the *Padma Purán* :—"When the son of Bhrigu [*i.e.*, Parashuram] exterminated the warrior-class, their daughters, seeing the world empty of the Kshatriya and being desirous of getting sons, laid hold of the Brahmans and carefully cherishing the seed sown in their womb [Jathara] brought forth Kshatriya sons called Jatharas."*

---

* क्षत्रशून्ये पुरालोके भार्गवेन यदाक्रते ।
विलोक्याचव्रियो धार्वीं कन्यास्तेषां सहस्रश: ॥
ब्राह्मणान् अग्रहुस्तस्मिन् पुत्रोत्पादन लिप्सया ।
जठरे धारितं गर्भं संरच्छ्य विधिवत् पुरा ।
पुत्राम् सुषुविरे कन्या जाठरान् चचर्षभजान् ॥

Growse remarks that "there is no great intrinsic improbability in the hypothesis that the word *Jātharas* has been shortened into *Jat*, but if one race is really descended from the other, it is exceedingly strange that the fact should never have been so stated before. This difficulty might be met by replying that the Jats have always been, with very few exceptions, an illiterate class, who were not likely to trouble themselves about recording their mythological pedigrees; while the story of their parentage would not be of sufficient interest to induce outsiders to investigate it. But a more unanswerable objection is found in a passage, which the Shastri himself quotes from the *Brihat Samhita* (xiv. 8). This places the home of the Jatharas in the south-eastern quarter, whereas it is certain that the Jats have come from the west. Probably the leaders of Jat society would refuse to accept as their progenitors both the Jatharas of the Beswa Pandit and Sindhian Zeths of Genl. Cunningham; for the Bharatpur princes affect to consider themselves as of the same race as the Yadavas."*

The second Jat attempt at solving the mystery of his origin is found in a small booklet entitled *The Ethnology of the Jats*, written

---

* Growse's *Mathura* (1874), pp. 21-22.

by Chaudhuri Lahiri Singh, a Jat pleader of
Meerut, at the request of the Census officials of
1883. This author also derives the word *Jat*
from *Jathara;* but he differs from the author of
the *Jatharotpatti* by making the Jatharas a
foreign people deriving their name from the
mountain Jathara, mentioned in the *Mahabharat,
Vishnu Puran* and *Bhagavat.* The first two
mention the country of the Jatharas along with
Kalinga, Kashi, and Aparkashi.

However, the Jats cannot be held to be the
same people as the ancient Jatharas, because
the doubtful testimony of the similarity of
sounds breaks down in the face of the significant absence of any tradition whatsoever, con-
necting the two peoples. This claim is strange
enough even to startle the majority of the Jats.
One might close his eyes against the absurdity
of the case, if the Jatharas had been altogether
an extinct people. But they still survive in
Southern India, without claiming any connection with Jats. These Jatharas belong to a sub-
section of the Deccani Maratha Brahmans called
Karhadas.＊

＊ Mr. G. B. Jathar has kindly supplied me with this
valuable piece of information in a letter, dated 8th August
1924, Deccan College, Poona.

2

The alleged Yadava origin of the Jats.

The foregoing dissertation has left the Jat, so to say, hanging in the mid-air. We know this much that there is no scientific ground, philological, or ethnological, for rejecting his claim to the Indo-Aryan blood, and that·he is neither a Scythian, nor a cross between a Brahman and a Kshatriya widow [Jathar]. He is not a foreign invader either from the plains of Central Asia or the fictitious Jathar mountain, but a true son of India, who points to Malwa and Rajputana as the home of his ancestors before they migrated to the Panjab and the trans-Indus region. The Jats are difficult to persuade that they are not descended from the ancient Yadavas, though they cannot produce any evidence in support of this claim. Now that all fantastic theories as to their origin have exploded at the touch of science, we cannot with justice refuse to accept the alleged Yadava origin of the Jats, at least tentatively, so long as it is not positively disproved. It is only fair to put this tradition to the test of historical investigation, and see whether there is any rational ground for believing in it.

Al-Beruni, who wrote at the beginning of the eleventh century, thus relates the story of

Sri Krishna's birth: "Then there was born a child in the city of Mathura to Vasudeva by the sister of Kansa, at that time ruler of the town. *They were a Jatt family, cattle-owners, low Shudra* people." The Yadus, as we learn from the *Vishnu Purán*, though somewhat above the Jat status of "low Shudra" of the eleventh century, were well-nigh approaching it, being little esteemed by the more orthodox Aryan tribes with monarchical constitution. (Wilson's *Vishnu Puran*, pp. 602-603.) There is no greater improbability in deriving Jat, Ját or Jut, —as the tribal name is pronounced in various forms in the different provinces—from the Indian Yadu or Yadava than from the Chinese Yuti or Ye-ta-li-to. If the phonetic difficulty alone stands in the way of recognising the Yadava origin of the Játs, there cannot be any objection in identifying the Jats with the *Jatas* or *Sujatas*, a branch of the great Haihaya Yadavas.* "The Sujatas" says the *Vishnu*

---

* Of the hundred sons of Kartavirya, the five principal were Sura, Surasena, Vrishana, Madhu and *Jayadhwaja*. From the last sprang up the five great divisions of the Haihaya tribe, the Talajanghas, Vitihotras, Avantyas, Tundikeras, and *Jatas* also called *Sujatas from the prolific number*. (Wilson's *Vishnu Puran*, pp. 417-418). Wilson seems to entertain a doubt whether the Haihayas are not the Huna and Saka tribes engrafted upon the great genealogical tree of the Aryans by the clever Puranic ethnologists. *The Jats were known by the*

Puran, "*are not commonly specified for their great number.*" (Wilson, p. 418, foot-note 20). So, we need not wonder if the *Brihat Samhita* or any other later Sanskrit work does not mention the *Jatas* by their particular tribal designation. It may be argued that the Haihayas were a southern people inhabiting the region of the Narmada, and were therefore little likely to be the ancestors of the modern Jats, who are mainly found in Sindh and the Panjab. We may point out that the Jats are not, even to this day, rare in the Narmada Valley, in Bhopal and other places, and that the Haihayas are also mentioned among the *Western Peoples* in the *Brihat Samhita* (Sans. text, chap. 14, p. 291). The tribe of Yadu gradually shifted towards the north-west. The Jat clans of Bal, Bhular, Chahal, and Kahlon point out to Malwa, Dharnagar [Dhar], and the Deccan as their original home. (Rose's *Punjab Glossary,* ii.)

The ancient Yadavas, like the modern Jats, were not a homogeneous tribe but a composite race, rather a confederacy of tribes, consisting of Andakas, Bhojas, Kukkuras,

___

name of *Sus, Abars,* and many other names, as Beames says. We shall meet these contentions in the appendix "*The Yadus.*"

Dasharnás etc. Prolific were the progeny of
Yadu; so are the Jats to-day. But it will be
too far from the truth to maintain that this multi-
plication is due to birth alone. The affiliation
of one tribe into another was a common phenomenon in the tribal stage of society. The facts
that there are conflicting traditions about the
origin of the different Jat *gots* and that even
the Babbars of Dera Ghazi Khan claim to be
Jats, clearly illustrate this. These were
apparently an out-landish people affiliated to
the Yadu clan. This is supported by a passage
in the *Bhagavat Puran* which says that King
Sagara, after exterminating the Haihayas,
turned his arms against the Saka, Yavana, and
Barbaras who had fought as the allies of the
Haihayas, against his ancestors (Sans. text,
skanda ix, chap. 8). The *Harivamsa* describes
a long standing hereditary feud between the
descendants of Puru and Yadu,—which was
also a struggle between orthodoxy and heterodoxy, a struggle between the pure Indo-Aryans
and the out-landish peoples headed by the
Yadavas. A similar phenomenon of a tribal
feud in which even aliens range themselves
under one faction or another has not altogether
disappeared in the Rohtak and Delhi districts,
where the country-side is divided into two

factions—Dahiya and Ahulanas : *"the Gujars
and Tagas* of the tract, the Jaglan Jats of *thapa*
Naultha, and the Látmár Jats of Rohtak joining
the Dahiyas, and the Huda Jats of Rohtak...
joining the Ahulanas. This division runs right
through Sonepat and more faintly through Delhi
tahsil, and is so firmly rooted in the popular
mind that Muhammadans even class themselves
with one or the other party. Thus the Muhammadan Gujars of Panch-i-Gujran call themselves Dahiyas, and so do all the neighbouring
villages" (Rose's *Punjab Glossary*, ii. 220).
Modern history does not contain a more faithful
picture of the tribal feuds of the bygone ages.

The race of Yadu suffered a fearful retribution at the hands of Parashuram who had all
but exterminated the ungodly and tyrannical
warrior-caste. The few fugitives from his
terrible battle-axe took shelter in mountains or
concealed themselves among the lower classes.
Without instruction and without ceremonials
they grew up like Shudras. The liberal-minded
Rishi Kashyapa reclaimed them and restored
them to the rank of Kshatriyas. This was
perhaps the first creation of a class of Neo-
Kshatriyas, like that of the Agni-kulas in the
subsequent ages. The Kassab [Kashyap]
Gotri Játs with pretensions to Rajput blood may

thus owe their kinship with the ancient Yadavas, to the good services of their patron saint.

The Jat community has been, within historic times, the great refuge of the high caste victims of Hindu social tyranny, and the up-lifter of the depressed and untouchables to a more respectable status, transforming all recruits to a homogeneous Aryan mould both in physique and sentiment. If the origin of the Jat is to be correctly traced we must ascend the main stream and not the tributaries. To say that the Jat is of foreign origin, because some out-landish tribes were admitted into his community is as absurd as to say that the Ganges descends not from the Himalayas but from the Vindhya because the Son brings some waters of the latter mountain to swell her stream.

Migration of the People.

There is no authentic history of how the Jats migrated to the north-west, beyond the boundary of India; because even at the dawn of Indian history, they were found in occupa-tion of the country between Kirman and Mansura, and other tracts, bordering on Persia by the early Arab geographers and historians.*

* Elliot's *History of India* i. 14, 449; ii. 247.

They were the first Hindu people with whom
the Arabs came into contact, and all the Hindus
were known to the Arabs by the name *Jat* only.
They formed the rear of the far-flung Hindu
dominion then beginning to retire to the east
of the Indus before the impetuous onset of
Islam. This eastward retreat of a section of
the Jats has to a great extent lent colour to the
theory that they were barbarian invaders of
India. It is likely that the Jats, always enterprising and eager for military service, migrated
beyond the Indus as mercenaries of the Persian
and Maurya Emperors. They suffered a good
deal in the subsequent ages for their heresy
against orthodox Brahmanism. In Sindh they
were reduced from the status of rulers to that
of helots by the Brahman usurper Chach. And
this defiance of orthodoxy was greatly responsible for the social degradation of the Jats during
the Middle Ages.

The Jats and their early history.

The various waves of migration from
Central Asia in the early centuries of the
Christian era partly submerged, and partly
swept the Jats and other Indian races back upon
the shores of the Indus. The inaccessible
desert of Sindh became the new home of the

Jats. They had lost their caste, owing to their intercourse with impure races, their unreformed ways of life, and indifference to the rules of caste and Brahmanical teaching. They had become half *Mlechchas** just like the poorer section of the Hindus of Kabul, who are but half Muhammadans in the eyes of the orthodox. It was perhaps for this reason that Yuan Chwang calls the king of Sindh in the seventh century A.D. a Shudra (Beal, *Buddhist Records of the Western World*, ii. 272) and Al-Beruni found the Jats in no higher social grade in the eleventh century. There they settled as agriculturists and lived under their old tribal organization, which, however, was replaced later on by a monarchy.

The author of *Mujmal-ut-Twarikh* records an interesting legend that a joint embassy was sent by the Jats and Meds of Sindh to the Court of king Duryodhana, asking for a ruler to govern them. "The Jats and Meds......dwelt in Sindh and on the banks of the river which

---

* One modern writer remarks : "These Jats of the Indus Valley have never adopted the institution of caste in its integrity, and are regarded by the rest of Hindus *with a feeling which embodied* in the expression *Baheka* or aliens. (*Asia*, by A. H. Keene, p. 296). This is undoubtedly the same terms as *Baheeka* of the *Mahabharat* applied to Jartrikas, Madras, and peoples of Sindhu-Sauvira.

is Bahar (mouth of the Indus?)......The Meds
held the ascendancy over the Jats, and put
them to great distress, which compelled them
to take refuge on the other side of the river
Paban (Panjnad river?), but being accustomed
to the use of boats, they used to cross the river
and make attacks on the Meds, who were
owners of sheep. It so came to pass that the
Jats enfeebled the Meds, killed many of them
and plundered their country. The Meds then
became subject to the Jats.

"One of the Jat chiefs (seeing the state to
which the Meds were reduced) made the people
of his tribe understand that there was a time
when the Meds attacked the Jats and harassed
them, and that the Jats in their turn had done
the same with the Meds. He impressed upon
their minds the utility of both tribes living in
peace, and then advised the Jats and Meds to
send a few chiefs to wait on king Dajushan
(Duryodhana), son of Dahrat (Dhritarashtra),
and beg of him to appoint a king to whose
authority both tribes might submit......After
some discussions they agreed to act upon it,
and the Emperor Dajushan nominated his sister
Dassal [Dushala], wife of king Jandrat [Jaya-
dratha] a powerful prince to rule over the Jats
and Meds. Dassal went and took care of the

countries and cities......There was no Brahman
or wise man in the country. She therefore
wrote a long letter to her brother for assistance,
who collected 30,000 Brahmans from all
Hindustan, and sent them with their goods and
dependents to his sister" (Elliot, i. 104.)*

Though the story cannot be literally true,
it seems to be a vague reminiscence of an
immigration into Sindh of a colony of pure
Aryans, mostly Brahmans, from the middle
country. These were perhaps invited by some
enlightened prince who thought of reclaiming
his subjects and clansmen from ignorance and
heresy. Perhaps the name of the famous city
of Brahmanabad points to the place where the
Brahman immigrants first settled. They prospered under the patronage of the native princes
till they became so powerful that about 10 A. H.
Chach, the Brahman father of Dahir,—usurped
the throne of his master, King Sahasi Ray II
through the influence of the fair but faithless
queen Suhandi, who had fallen in love with

---

* This is no doubt a legend which is not even countenanced by the *Mahabharat*. However, we have a striking
twelfth century parallel to it in the history of Bengal. Adisur,
the reputed founder of the Sur dynasty invited five Brahmans
from Kanauj to officiate as his priests, who afterwards revived
Brahmanism in Bengal and became founders of orthodox
Brahman families there.

him. He married the widowed queen formally and reigned vigorously for 40 years, leaving behind him the reputation of a wise and enlightened prince. But he was an implacable foe of the Jats, the bulk of whom were reduced to serfdom. He degraded the Jats and Luhanas and bound over their chiefs. He took hostages from them and confined them in the fort of Brahmanabad.

He obliged them to agree to the following terms: "That they should never wear any swords but sham ones; that they should never wear undergarments of shawl, velvet, or silk; that they should put no saddles on their horses, and should keep their heads and feet uncovered; that when they went out they should take their dogs with them; that they should carry firewood for the kitchen of the chief of Brahmanabad; they were to furnish guides and spies, and were to be faithful when employed in such offices." (*Chach Nama*, Elliot, i. 151). When Muhammad Bin Qasim invaded the territory of Dahir the Jats of the western border joined the invader, while those of the eastern countries fought for Dahir. (See *Chach Nama*, Mirza Kalich Beg's translation, pp. 124, 137.)

After the completion of the conquest, Muhammad Bin Qasim asked the ex-minister of Dahir who was made wazir by the conqueror, what was the position of the Jats in the time of his late master. He replied that "they were not allowed to wear soft clothes, used to wear a black blanket beneath (*lungi?*), and throw a sheet of coarse cloth over their shoulders...... They used to take their dogs with them when they went out of doors, so that they might by these means be recognised......It was their business to conduct parties from one tribe to another......the caravans used to travel day and night under their guidance. *There is no distinction among them of great and small. They have the disposition of savages, and always rebelled against their sovereign.* They plunder on the roads, and within the territory of Debal all join with them in *their highway robberies.* (Elliot, i. 187). The change of rulers brought no improvement of their lot; Muhammad Bin Qasim maintained the former rules regarding them. The Jats were in independent possession of the country of Kaikan (supposed to be in south-eastern Afghanistan,— Elliot, i. 383), which was conquered from them by the Arab general Amran Bin Musa in the reign of the Khalif Al-Mutasim-bi-llah,—A. D. 833-811, (Elliot, i. 448). During the same reign another expedition was sent against the

Jats who had seized upon the roads of Hajar (?)
.........and spread terror over the roads and
planted posts in all directions towards the desert.
They were overcome after a bloody conflict of
twenty-five days. Twenty-seven thousand of
them were led in captivity to grace the triumph
of the victor. It was a custom among these
people to blow their horns when marshalled
for battle. (Elliot, ii. 247.)

Other scanty notices of the Jats in Persian
histories prior to the reign of Aurangzib are not
of any political importance, but they are
eminently illustrative of their national characteristics. They have shown in all periods,—
whether against Sultan Mahmud of Ghazni, or
against Nadir Shah and Ahmad Shah Abdali—
the same propensity to fall upon the rear of a
retreating army undeterred by the heaviest
odds, or the terror-inspiring fame of great con-
querors. When encountered they showed the
same obstinate and steady courage, unmindful
of the carnage on the field or of the miseries
that were in store for them after defeat. They
seem to have a wonderfully short memory as
regards the terrible lessons taught by the merci-
less sword of their enemies.

The Jats had the audacity to attack the
army of Mahmud of Ghazni on his return from

Somnath. His seventeenth expedition was undertaken for chastising them. He had to fight a great naval battle in which his genius shone no less splendidly than on land. "He led a large force towards Multan, and when he arrived there he ordered fourteen hundred boats to be built each of which was armed with three firm iron pikes, projecting one from the prow and two from the sides, so that anything which came in contact with them would infallibly be destroyed. In each boat were twenty archers, with bows and arrows, grenades, and naphtha; and in this way he proceeded to attack the Jats, who having intelligence of the armament, sent their families into the islands and prepared themselves for the conflict. They launched, according to some four, and according to others eight thousand boats, manned and armed, ready to engage the Muhammadans. Both fleets met, and a desperate conflict ensued. Every boat of the Jats that approached the Muslim fleet, when it received the shock of the projecting pikes was broken and overturned. Thus most of the Jats were drowned and those who were not so destroyed were put to the sword. The Sultan's army proceeded to the places where their families were concealed and took them all prisoners''. (*Tabakat-i-Akbari*, quoted in Elliot, ii. 478).

After the defeat of Prithviraj in 1192 A.D., the Jats of Hariana raised the standard of tribal revolt, and under a capable chief, named Jatwan, besieged the Muslim commander at Hansi. On receiving this news Qutb-ud-din marched twelve *farsakhs* i.e., about 40 miles during one night. Jatwan raised the siege of Hansi and prepared for an obstinate conflict. "The armies attacked each other" says the author of Taj-ul-Maasir "like two hills of steel, and the field of battle [on the borders of the Bager country] became tulip-dyed with the blood of warriors......Jatwan had his standards of God-plurality and ensigns of perdition lowered by the hand of power" (Elliot, ii. 218). About 1530, the Jats formed *mandals** round Sunam and Samana with the Bhattis, Minas, and kindred tribes, withheld tribute and plundered the roads. Sultan Muhammad Bin Tughlaq marched against them, destroyed their *mandals*, and they were torn from their old lands, and

---

* *Mandal*, is not a *stronghold*, as Elliot supposes. It means a confederacy, union of several villages or tribes for a common object and mutual assistance. Such organisation, though rare is not unknown even now in that part of the country, formed either for communal interests or for resisting unjust demands and making their grievances felt.

scattered (*Tarikh-i-Firozshahi*, Elliot, iii. 245).
Timur dwells with considerable satisfaction on
his suppression of the Jats, whom he describes
as a robust race, demon-like in appearance and
as numerous as ants and locusts, a veritable
plague to the merchants and wayfarers.
(*Malfuzat-i-Timuri*, Elliot, iii. 429).

Babur found the Jats living amongst the
mountains of Nil-áb and Bhera, where they
acknowledged the ascendancy of the Gakkar
chiefs (*Memoirs of Babur*, A. S. Beveridge,
p. 387). They still retained their old turbulent
and predatory habits. He says: "If one go
into Hindustan the Jats and Gujārs always pour
down in countless hordes from hill and plain
for loot in bullock and buffalo. These ill-
omened peoples are just senseless oppressors !
......When we reached Sialkot, they fell in
tumult on poor and needy folks who were
coming out of the town to our camp, and
stripped them bare. I had the silly thieves
sought for, and ordered two or three of them
cut to pieces." (*Ibid*, p. 454).

During the period of confusion intervening
between the death of Babur and the accession
of Sher Shah to the throne of Delhi, one bold
robber chief Fath Khan Jat of Kot Kabulah
devastated the whole tract of Lakhi Jungle, and

3

kept in ferment the high roads from Lahor to
Panipat. Haibat Khan Niazi, governor of the
Panjab on behalf of Sher Shah, crushed him
after a severe campaign.* The Játs had little
scope for their lawless activity under the strong
government of the Surs and the Mughals down
to the accession of Aurangzib. They remained
quiet till the religious persecution of that
Emperor and the misrule of the provincial
viceroys goaded them into rebellion.

CHAPTER II.

JAT HISTORY IN AURANGZIB'S REIGN

Hindu reaction and the Rise of the Jat Power.

After the enchanted sleep of a century, administered successivley by the hypnotic spell of Akbar, the genial indifference of Jahangir, and the mild pattings of Shah Jahan, Hindu India woke to life again in the second half of the seventeenth century, being rudely shaken by the pious activity of the saintly Emperor Aurangzib. Accustomed to look upon the occupant of the throne of Delhi, though of an alien faith, as the Shadow of God on earth, (दिल्लिश्वरो वा जगदीश्वरो वा) the awakened Hindus found to their surprise and sorrow that the impartial Ruler of Hindustan had changed into a militant missionary of Islam. He reverted to the old and forgotten ways. *Jaziya* (poll-tax) was reimposed; temple destruction and image-breaking went on briskly under strict imperial supervision; cart-loads of broken idols came in from all quarters, and were buried under the stair-cases of the Jama mosques of Delhi and Agra. Hindus were excluded from public offices, and an ordinance was issued to dismiss all Hindu clerks from the revenue department.

Hindu religious fairs were abolished and
public celebration of their festivals prohibited.
Custom duty was altogether abolished in the
case of Muslim traders while that on the Hindus
was retained at the old rate. Hindus were
tempted out of heathenism by the grant of State
subsidies. In short "Every device short of
massacre in cold blood was resorted to in order
to convert heathen subjects."* We are not
inclined to attribute this, either to Aurangzib's
deliberate wickedness, depravity of heart, or
short-sighted policy. This was rather the outcome of the severe and uncompromising pursuit
of an idea, neither eccentric nor vicious. His
fault lay in his failure : he carried to his grave
his unfulfilled dream of an Islamic India.

However, by this open enmity, Aurangzib
unknowingly revived Hindu Nationalism,
which the cruel kindness of his predecessors
had well-nigh succeeded in killing. From the
far-off Maharashtra came the pulsation of a new
life which moved northwards stirring the paralysed limb of Hindu society. In the Panjab,
persecution turned a humble sect of sentimental
devotees into ferocious warriors. The Sikhism
of Guru Govind was a veritable counterblast to
Islam. Fanaticism was met with fanaticism ;

---

* Sarkar's *Hist. of Aurangzib*, iii. 290.

Sikhs went out to fight Muslim armies singing, "He is of the *khalsa* who fights in the Van, *who slays a Khan*." Aurangzib's attempt to imprison Jaswant's wives and infant son opened the eyes of the Rajputs. The brave Durgadas led the way and the Rathor blades were unsheathed for the defence of liberty and religion. His countrymen paid a tribute to his memory, saying "Had not Durga been born in the house of *Askarn, all would have been circumcised."

In 1669, another sturdy race, the Jats living almost under the very shadow of the imperial capital rose in revolt. This was but one flare of the mighty conflagration, kindled throughout India, by the missionary zeal of the Emperor. The Jat peasants of the Mathura and Agra districts had long been the victims of oppression and misrule. Their religious susceptibilities were shocked by the destruction of the Hindu temples of Mathura, whose lofty spires seemed to mock the edifices of Agra. They saw their fields devastated and their wives and daughters carried off to gratify Muslim lust.

---

* It is said once a Jat carried off the palm of poetic victory from a *charan* by reciting the following extempore lines :—

ढमक ढमक ढोल बाजे दंदे ठोर् नाग्राकी ।

भासी घर दुगा नड़ीं हीतो सुघ्रत ह्री जाती ख्वाराकी ॥

Marwar Census Report (vernacular) 1892, vol. iii. p. 56.

One faujdar of Mathura, Murshid Quli Khan used to make raids upon the villages to procure beautiful women. Another infamous practice of his was this : at the time of Hindu fairs and festivals, "the Khan, painting his forehead and wearing a *dhoti* like a Hindu used to walk up and down in the crowd. Whenever he saw a woman whose beauty filled even the Moon with envy, he snatched her away like a wolf, pouncing upon a flock, and placing her in the boat which his men kept ready on the bank (of the Jamuna) he sped to Agra."*

Aurangzib appointed as governor of Mathura, Abdun Nabi, "a religious man" in the sense understood by his master. He entered heartily into the Emperor's policy of "rooting out idolatry, and fell in fight against the Jats (about 10th May 1666). The victorious rebels, under the leadership of Gokla, the zamindar of Tilpat, looted pargana Sadabad. So serious was the menace that the Mughal Government offered him pardon on the condition of giving up his booty. The rebel refused to come to terms. Aurangzib sent a very strong army under Radandaz Khan, Hassan Ali Khan and other high officers, and himself marched

---

* Sarkar's *History of Aurangzib*, iii. 332.

from Delhi to the affected area. Hassan Ali
delivered an attack upon three fortified villages
of the Jats and won a very costly victory. The
peasants fought long and steadily, displaying
that cool obstinate valour which has ever
characterised them. When resistance became
hopeless, many of them slew their women and
rushed upon the Mughals to sell their lives
dearly. Gokla mustered 20,000 men and
offered fight to the imperial forces at a place 20
miles from Tilpat, charging their lines most
gallantly. But courage could hardly make up
the deficiency in discipline and equipment.
After a very long and bloody contest, they had
to give way before the superior discipline and
artillery of the Mughals. They fell back
upon Tilpat, and there held out for three days.
The Mughals lost 4000 men in killing 3000
rebels. Gokla was taken prisoner; his limbs
were hacked off one by one on the platform of
the police office of Agra. [Sarkar's *Hist. of
Aurangzib*, iii. 330-336]. Gokla's blood did
not flow in vain; it watered the newly-sprouted
seedling of liberty in the heart of the Jats.

Rajaram Jat (1686-1688).

Fifteen years after the death of Gokla Jat,
a more capable leader appeared among the Jats

in the person of Rajaram, son of Bhajja Singh, laird of Sinsani.* He united his own clan, the Sinsinwar Jats, with the Sogorias under their chief Ramchehra, who owned the castle of Sogor.† He gave the disorderly host of tribesmen the appearance of a regular army, embodied in regiments, equipped with firearms, and trained to obey their captains. Small forts (*garhi*) were built at advantageous positions, amidst the almost trackless jungles of the Jat country, and strengthened by mud walls that could defy artillery.

Rajaram soon put an end to the authority of the Mughals in the Agra district, closing the roads to traffic and plundering many villages. Safi Khan, the governor of Agra, became practically besieged in the city, and it was after a very severe fighting that Mir Abul Fazl, the faujdar of the place, succeeded in saving Akbar's tomb at Sikandra, from being sacked by Rajaram. The Jats soon showed greater audacity. Near Dholpur they surprised the

---

* Sinsani, 16 miles n. w. of Bharatpur.

† Sogor is spelt as *Sogghair* in the French MS. of Wendel. It lies four miles to the south-east of Bharatpur. Rustam Sogoria and Khemchand Sogoria were the prominent leaders of their *got*. Suraj Mal captured Bharatpur from the last-named chief. Ramchehra, rather an awkward name, occurs nowhere except in the French MS.

camp of the renowned Turani warrior Aghar
Khān and carried off his carts, horses and
women.   The Khān while pursuing the raiders,
was killed with his son-in-law, and 80 followers.

Worn out with the unending chase of
the Maratha fox in the south, the unhappy
Emperor was startled at the yell of the Jat
wolves howling for their prey under the
very walls of his capital.   As early as
May, 1686, Aurangzib had recognised the
gravity of the situation by detaching against the
Jats a great general, Khan-i-Jahan Kokaltash
Zafar Jang. Now the success of Rajaram and
the failure of Khan-i-Jahan thoroughly alarmed
him, and in December he ordered his son
Azam to go there and command the operations
in person.   But the prince had only reached
Burhanpur, when he was recalled to the
Emperor's side by the more pressing need of
retrieving Mughal prestige before Golkonda
(July 1687). The prince's eldest son, Bidar
Bakht, a gallant lad of 17, was however sent
(in December 1687), to assume the supreme
command in the Jat war, while Khan-i-Jahan
was to continue as his adviser and chief officer.

But before the prince could arrive, the Jat
leader committed more atrocities.   Early in
1688, Mir Ibrahim of Haidarabad (newly

entitled Mahabat Khan) was marching to his viceroyalty of the Panjab. Near Sikandra, he was encamped on the bank of the Jamuna, when Rajaram attacked him, but was repulsed after a long and stubborn fight with the loss of 400 men, while the Mughals lost 190 in killed and wounded. Rajaram soon returned to the scene, and profiting by the delay in the coming of Shaista Khan, the new subahdar of Agra, he plundered Akbàr's tomb,* taking away its carpets, gold and silver vessels, lamps, etc. and damaging the building. Khan-i-Jahan did nothing to check him.

Bidar Bakht, on his arrival, infused greater vigour into the Mughal operations. At this time an internecine war was raging between the Shekhawat and Chauhan clans of Rajputs for lands in the Bagtharia and some other parganas. The Chauhans enlisted the support of Rajaram, while the Shekhawats gained the armed help of the Mughal faujdar of Mewat. A severe battle was fought between them near

---

* Ishwardas, 132b. Manucci (ii. 320) adds "They began their pillage by breaking in the great gates of bronze which it had, robbing the valuable precious stones and plates of gold and silver, and destroying what they were not able to carry away. Dragging out *the bones of Akbar, they threw them angrily into the fire and burnt them.*"

the village of Bijal. The Rajputs grappled with one another in deadly animosity, and many were slain on both sides. In the thick of the contest, Rajaram was shot dead by a Mughal musketeer hiding in a tree (4th July 1688).

Rajah Bishun Singh's campaign against the Jats.

After the death of Rajaram, the leadership of the Jats was assumed by his old father Bhajja Singh of Sinsani. "Bishun Singh Kachhwa, the new Rajah of Amber (Jaipur), was appointed by the Emperor as *faujdar* of Mathura with a special charge to root out the Jats and take Sinsani as his own jagir [Ishwardas, 133a]. He gave the Emperor a written undertaking to demolish the fort of Sinsani (Ishwar, 139a, 135b), as he was burning to distinguish himself and win a high *mansab* like his father Ram Singh and grandfather Mirza Rajah Jai Singh. Bidar Bakht laid siege to Sinsani. But the campaign in the jungles of the Jat country severely taxed the invading army.

The Mughals before Sinsani had to undergo great hardship from scarcity of provisions and water, as the enemy by frequent attacks cut off the grain-convoys and watering parties. Incessant night-attacks kept the siege-camp in perpetual alarm. "The men were prostrated by hunger, and the animals perished in large numbers through weakness." But the besiegers held tenaciously on, and in four months carried their trenches to the gate of the fort, mounted guns on raised platforms, and laid mines. The jungle round the fort was cleared. One mine under the gate was fired, but the Jats having previously detected it and blocked its further side with stones, the charge was driven backwards, destroying many of the artillerymen and supervising officers of the Mughal army. A second mine was then laid and carried under the wall in a month's time. It was successfully fired (end of January, 1690), the wall was breached, the Jat defenders lining it were blown up, and the Mughals stormed the fort after three hours of stubborn opposition. The Jats disputed every inch of the ground and were dispersed only after losing 1500 of their men. On the imperial side 200 Mughals fell and 700 Rajputs were slain or wounded. The remnant of the garrison was put to the sword [Ishwardas, 136b-137a; *M. A.* 334; Hamid-ud-din's *Ahkam,* § 26].

Next year (21st May, 1691) Rajah Bishun Singh surprised the other Jat stronghold of Sogor. "The Rajah hastened there with the imperial army. By chance, as the gate of this little fort was kept open at the time for admitting grain, the invaders entered it at the gallop, slaying all who raised their hands and taking 500 of the rebels [Ishwar]. The result of these operations was that the new Jat leaders went into hiding in 'nooks and corners' unknown to the imperialists. The tribesmen returned to the peaceful work of cultivation and the district enjoyed peace for some years.*

Churaman Jat (1695-1721).

Churaman, the younger brother of Rajaram, assumed the leadership of the Jats after the death of his father Bhajja Singh of Sinsani. "He had a genius for organization and making clever use of opportunities,"† combining in his character the stubbornness of a Jat with the cunning and political sagacity of a Maratha. His moral maxim was that of the sixteenth century Muslim theologians like Sayyid Rafi-ud-din Safavi, who assiduously preached to the faithful that no faith should be kept with the

---

* This section is partly a summary, and for the most part quotation *verbatim* from Prof. J. N. Sarkar's article "The Breaking-up of the Mughal Empire: Jats and Gaurs" published in the *Modern Review*, October, 1923.

† Prof. J. N. Sarkar's article "Jats and Gaurs"—*Modern Review*, October, 1923.

infidel.* Churaman served many a Muslim master, but he was never faithful to any for faithfulness' sake. He was a hard, practical politician, who could boast of never losing his head under the impulse of any noble sentiment like fidelity, honour or compassion, which had indeed no room in his cold heart : yet this was the man who built up the fortune of the Jats and made the Jat Power an important political factor to be reckoned with in the eighteenth century politics of Northern India.

The author of *Imad-us-Saadat* gives the following account of the early career of Churaman. "He began his career as the leader of a gang of highwaymen, plundering caravans and wayfarers. Within a short time he collected under his command 500 horse and one thousand footmen. Nanda Jat, the father of Bhure Singh, and grandfather of Daya Ram and Bhup Singh, the notorious castellans of Hathras and Mudsan, also joined him with 100 horsemen. As his establishment became too large to be maintained by the plundering of merchant caravans, he began to loot parganas. At this time he built a place of refuge in a low marshy and thickly wooded tract about 48

---

* Dorn's translation of *Makhzan-i-Afaghana*, p. 137.

kos from Agra, digging a deep moat around it. There he used to deposit his booty, and, by gradual additions, it was turned into a mud fort which afterwards became known as Bharatpur. He brought some Hindu Chamars from the neighbouring villages, and settling them there, entrusted its defence to them. When his army grew to 14,000 men, he left one of his trustworthy brethren with sufficient men and materials of war in charge of Bharatpur, and himself started on a plundering expedition towards Kota and Bundi where he looted many caravans and acquired a rich booty.* Being more enterprising than those who had preceded him, he not only increased the number of his soldiers, but also strengthened them by the addition of fusiliers (musketeers) and a troop of cavalry whom he shortly after set on foot......and having robbed many of the ministers of the Court on the road, he attacked the royal wardrobe and the revenue sent from the provinces [Fr. MS. *f.* 41.].....About 1704 he recovered Sinsani from Mughal possession, but lost it again in Oct. 1705. [Prof. J. N. Sarkar, *Modern Review,* Oct., 1923.]

Greater opportunities came to the robber-

---

* *Imad-us-Saadat,* Pers. text p. 55.

chief, when Aurangzib closed his weary eyes
in the Dakhin in 1707. Bahadur Shah and
Azam prepared for a decisive fight at Jajau, not
far from Samugarh, where Fortune had placed
the crown of Hindustan upon their father's
brow, Churaman collected his tribesmen, and
hung about the neighbourhood of both armies,
looking out for an opportunity to attest his
timely zeal for the victor by falling upon the
camp and baggage of the vanquished. He
became eminently successful, securing at the
end a very rich booty as well as a *mansab* of
1500 *zat*, 500 horse, bestowed upon him by
the victorious Bahadur Shah. Churaman made
an intelligent investment of his vast wealth by
building forts, collecting men and winning
over his enemies. But as the government of
Bahadur Shah was fairly strong, he chose to
be faithful to it, and render good services to
justify his newly acquired rank as an imperial
commander. He accompanied Bahadur Shah
to Lahor in 1711 and there witnessed the
battle of succession among his four unworthy
sons in 1712.

Jahandar Shah, the eldest son of the late
Emperor, a profligate fool, now disgraced the
throne of Aurangzib. He was old in years

(about fifty at this time), but worse than a child in frivolity and frolicsomeness, a slave to his sweet-voiced concubine Lal Kunwar, and passing the few inglorious days (ten months) of his reign in midnight revelry and morning slumber, preferring fiddlers to soldiers, and loving to play at night the part of the Great Monkey, Hanuman, by setting fire to a mimic city of Lanka. A successful rebel who had carved out a principality for himself, could scarcely entertain any fear or respect for such a sovereign. Accordingly, Churama retired to his own estates and gathered resources to make a fresh bid for fortune. When the news of Farrukh-siyar's march from Patna reached Delhi, Jahandar Shah induced Churaman by many fair promises to join his army. Churaman had become the *de facto* ruler and law-giver of the Jats and other Hindu peoples, inhabiting the western bank of the Jamuna from Delhi to the Chambal, owing to the weakness of the imperial Government to provide security of life and property to the inhabitants. So, he was a man to be reckoned with in those troubled times;—his attitude practically determining the friendship or hostility of the whole rural population towards a particular candidate for the throne of Hindustan. He came with a large

4

number of Jats and was present with Jahandar
Shah's army at the battle which was fought
outside Agra city. But, instead of rendering
any help to the unfortunate Jahandar Shah, he
rather contributed to his defeat by falling upon
the imperial baggage at a critical moment of
the fight. (January, 1713).

Churaman marched away from Agra after
plundering the baggage of both sides impartially. He seemed to have been aiming at
independence, at least deferring his submission
till the new Emperor should show more energy.
He felt himself strong enough to hold out,
because the Emperor was weak-minded and his
Court corrupt and divided against itself. The
majestic beauty and splendid physique of
Farrukh-siyar, ill-suited his cowardly and
vacillating nature: never did a more magnificent body clothe a poorer spirit. Early in
Farrukh-siyar's reign Chabela Ram, the then
subahdar of Agra, made strenuous but unsuccessful efforts to humble the stiff-necked
Jat chief. Samsam-ud-daulah (Khan-i-Dauran),
the next governor of Agra, reluctant to risk his
reputation in a doubtful enterprise, tried con-
ciliation. He secured Churaman's pardon
from the Emperor, who summoned him to the
Court. Churaman marched at the head of

4000 horsemen and was escorted with honour, befitting a rajah, from Barahpula into the city. He was conducted to the Dewan-i-khas by Khan-i-Dauran himself, and appointed by the Emperor to the charge of the royal highway (shah-rah) from the neighbourhood of Delhi to the crossing on the Chambal ! A wolf was left to watch over the flock : thereby loot was only legalised and made more methodical.

Churaman had been allowed by the Mughal Government to levy a toll on traffic along that portion of great road which was left in his charge. He made his collections so harshly and arbitrarily that an outcry soon arose against him from every quarter. A Jat tax-collector, as the proverb says, is indeed a sign of God's wrath; his penny breaks a head while the Baniya's hundred rupees hardly touch the skin. He behaved as if he were the absolute master of the whole tract traversed by this portion of the road. Even the jagirdars could not get their dues from the villages, except what Churaman pleased to dole out to them. The Emperor and his courtiers burned with rage, but no one was willing to undertake the task of punishing the rebel.

The rapid growth of the Jat power on the immediate border of his own State caused alarm

as well as hatred of the ruler of Jaipur.
Aurangzib had employed Rajah Bishnu Singh
Kachhwa to crush the ancestors of Churaman;
since that time a hereditary feud had continued
between the Jats and their Rajput neighbours.
Now Rajah Jai Singh Sawai came forward to
take command against Churaman, to the great
joy of Farrukh-siyar. The Rajah was liberally
supplied with men and money; Maharao Bhim
Singh Hada of Kota, Rajah Gaj Singh Narwari,
and Maharao Budh Singh Hada of Bundi also
accompanied him. The campaign (November
1716—April 1718), opened with the siege of
Thun in which Churaman was said to have
gathered grain, salt, ghee, tobacco, cloth and
fire-wood for twenty years! The prudent Jat
had turned out empty-handed all merchants
and traders—useless consumers of bread, with
their families, before the siege began. The
besieged made a sally and led by Churaman's
son, Muhkam Singh, and his nephew, Rupa,
gave battle in the open. The Jaipur Rajah
claimed a victory which only enabled him to
resume the blockade. But as success seemed
doubtful, Abdus-samad Khan, the brave and
energetic governor of Lahore who had won
great fame by crushing the Sikhs, was recalled
from the Panjab to reinforce Rajah Jai Singh.

However, owing to Court intrigue, he was not sent. Churaman had also allies outside, *viz.*, the *zamindars* and villagers who kept the imperialists in perpetual alarm by pillage and plunder. The siege dragged on for twenty months without any definite result. Party strife at the Court between the Hindustani faction headed by the Sayyid brothers, and the Turani faction led by the Nizam-ul-mulk proved the salvation of Churaman. The wazir Sayyid Abdullah was hostile to the Jaipur Rajah, whose success, therefore, he did not wish. Through a relation and agent of the wazir, Churaman made offers of submission by promising to pay a tribute of 30 lakhs of rupees to the imperial treasury, and another 20 lakhs to the wazir himself. Farrukh-siyar was helpless, like Sindbad the Sailor, with the two Sayyids upon his shoulders; so he reluctantly and ungraciously granted pardon to the rebel, brought before his presence, under the safe conduct of the wazir. From this time Churaman became an active and trusted partisan of the all-powerful Sayyids.

Churaman and the Sayyid brothers.

In February 1719, Farrukh-siyar was ed, blinded, and put to death by the

Sayyids who raised a consumptive youth, Rafi-ud-darjat, to the throne. The new Emperor was deposed after three months, and his elder brother Rafi-ud-daulah succeeded him. This man was so fortunate as to die a natural death after four months. Then the throne was given by the Sayyids to Muhammad Shah in September 1719. However, the end of the Kingmakers was drawing near. A woman's curse rested upon one, and extreme insolence drew down Heaven's vengeance upon the other. Sayyid Abdullah had fixed his licentious gaze on Inayat Banu Begam, wife of the Emperor Rafi-ud-darjat. The unhappy queen, feeling her husband unable to protect her, cut off her beautiful locks and sent them to her tempter in order to escape dishonour. The vanity and infatuation of Sayyid Husain Ali had also gone beyond limit. He once boasted that upon whomsoever he cast the shadow of his shoe that man would become the equal of the Emperor Alamgir! Churaman followed the Sayyids like a shadow; he was with the army of Husain Ali at the time of Farrukh-siyar's deposition. Later on he accompanied him to Agra in the expedition against a pretender, Neku-siyar, who had been proclaimed Emperor by the enemies of the Sayyids. He was assigned an important post in the siege of that fort,* and it was through his influence with the garrison that the fort was surrendered. After that he started for the Dakhin with Husain Ali when he marched against the Nizam-ul-mulk (May 1720). For his faithful services, the Sayyid promised him the title of Rajah, but this promise could not be fulfilled as Husain Ali was soon afterwards murdered by the Mughals with the connivance of Muhammad Shah. Large rewards were offered to Churaman to induce him to desert the cause of the Sayyids. Considering it foolish to incur the enmity of the Emperor for nothing, he accepted them and joined Muhammad Shah's army. The cunning Jat persuaded the Emperor to change his route which would have passed through his villages. Leaving his own villages at a distance, he led the army of the Emperor across the territories of his enemy Rajah Jai Singh, and took it over high hills, thorny

---

* Another instance of Churaman's heartless treachery is given by Father Wendel :—"There, having made an agreement with Neku-siyar to allow his brother Ali Záfar to pass with a large sum of money to Rajah Jai Singh's country for raising troops and marching, when he would be summoned, to his succour, Churaman turned traitor to that unfortunate prince, seized the money (50 lakhs in gold), and sent by perfidious hand, Ali Zafar, to Husain Ali." [Orme MSS. p. 73 of Prof. J. N. Sarkar's transcript].

jungles, and waterless waste (Irvine's *Later Mughals*, ii. 68-69).

When Sayyid Abdullah advanced at the head of a large army against Muhammad Shah, Churaman went over to the minister with all his Jats. In this he was not certainly actuated by sentiments of devotion and gratitude to his old patron. The cynical Jat argued that "in case of the Sayyid's defeat, it would be much easier to secure pardon from Muhammad Shah, than it would be, in the reverse case, to save himself from the Sayyid's vengeance." (*Later Mughals*, ii. 81).

On the day of the battle (Nov. 1720), fought in the neighbourhood of Hodal, Churaman* with his Jats was employed to make diversion by attacking the camp and baggage of Muhammad Shah. He threw himself heartily into this congenial task which meant a maximum of gain with a minimum of loss. Like a pack of wolves, the Jats fell upon the baggage camp from the west, south, and east in succession, and though driven back with difficulty, they carried off many oxen and horses

---

* According to another account "Churaman with his band fell on the baggage of Emperor and that of Abdullah also, and took a considerable booty in the very heat of the action." [Fr. MS., p. 73].

and created much confusion among the camp-
followers. But in actual fighting, the day had
ended in the virtual destruction of Abdullah's
army. So, next morning, Churaman without
caring for the favour or frown of either party,
plundered both sides with strict impartiality,
and made off with the booty to his own country.

Churaman now openly acted as an independent Rajah though he did not assume that
title for fear of exciting the jealousy of his
kinsmen. He strengthened himself against the
Kachhwas by making an alliance with Rajah
Ajit Singh Rathor of Marwar and he sent
assistance to the Bundelas to keep the Mughal
Government busy in the east. But he committed an indiscretion and injustice by throwing
his nephew Badan Singh into prison.

Badan Singh was released by the intervention of other Jats who began to be suspicious
of Churaman's design. Family dissension
afforded fresh opportunities to his enemies.
Badan Singh fled for protection and assistance
to Saadat Khan, subahdar of Agra, who had
already begun a campaign against the Jats.
Muhkam Singh, son of Churaman, inflicted a
crushing defeat upon Nilkanth Nagor, deputy
of Saadat Khan. The Khan himself fared no
better, and was accordingly removed from his

office. Again Rajah Jai Singh took the command against the Jats, to wipe off the disgrace of his previous failure. But by this time, old Churaman had committed suicide by taking poison. (Sept.—Oct. 1721).

The story of his death runs as follows :— "One of his relations, a wealthy man died childless. The brethren sent for Muhkam, the eldest son of Churaman, and made him head of the deceased's zamindari, and gave over to him all his goods. Zul Karan, the second son of Churaman said to his brother, "Give me too a share in those goods and admit me as a partner." A verbal dispute followed and Muhkam made ready to resist by force. Zul Karan determined to have the quarrel out, gathered men together, and attacked his brother. The elders of the place sent word to Churaman that his sons were fighting which was not well ....Churaman spoke to Muhkam. The son replied to his father in abusive language, and showed himself ready to fight his father as well as his brother. Churaman lost his temper, and from chagrin swallowed up a dose of deadly poison which he always carried with him, and going to an orchard in that village lay down and gave up the ghost. After a long time had elapsed, men were sent to search for him and they found his dead body." (*Later Mughals*, ii. 122).

Again did Rajah Jai Singh Sawai appear on the scene to subdue the Jats. He began his operations with 14,000 horsemen, and the number by subsequent reinforcements rose to 50,000. The sons of Churaman were besieged in Thun, whose chief defence was a belt of impenetrable jungle. The imperialists gradually closed upon the fort by cutting the trees. Badan Singh who was with the army of Rajah Jai Singh pointed out the weak spots and helped in the reduction of two fortified outworks. After conducting the defence for about two months, Muhkam Singh lost heart, and secretly fleeing from Thun, took refuge with his father's ally Rajah Ajit Singh Rathor. On November 18, 1722, the imperialists entered the place. Badan Singh was installed as the chief of the Jats with the title of Thakur, by the ruler of Jaipur.

CHAPTER III.

EXPANSION OF THE JAT POWER

Thakur Badan Singh, founder of the ruling house of Bharatpur.

Thakur Badan Singh, father of Suraj Mal, started his career as a feudatory of Maharajah Sawai Jai Singh of Amber (Jaipur), who had given him the lands and title of Churaman Jat in the reign of the Emperor Muhammad Shah. Unlike his notorious uncle, he was a quiet and politic man, having no taste for a predatory life. He set up as a legitimate ruler, sincerely desirous of promoting the arts of peace. He believed more in the steady expansion and consolidation of his dominions than in erratic and slippery conquests. The task which he took upon himself was not a light one; it meant transforming a robber-chief's "sphere of influence" into an orderly principality with a regular government. In this however, he succeeded eminently after years of patient toil and tactful administration. We do not hear of any diplomatic activity or brilliant exploit of arms on his part. Nevertheless, it is clear that within a few years of his accession, he grew powerful enough to shake off his dependence upon

Amber. Badan Singh, then uniting himself with the rebels of Mewat, carried raids into the territories of the Rajah of Jaipur, who had to conciliate him by a grant of lands, yielding 18 lakhs of Rupees a year.* Taking advantage of the confused state of affairs, he made some acquisitions in the Biana district and built a fort at Wair, which was given to his youngest son Pratap Singh. His greatest achievement was the establishment of the authority of his house over almost the whole of the Agra and Mathura districts, partly by posing as the protector of the Hindus against Muslim misrule, but mainly by clever matrimonial alliances with some powerful Jat families of those places. He married the daughter of a wealthy and influential Jat of Kamar,† Chaudhuri Maha Ram [Mohan Ram?], and took another wife from the laird of Sahar. These marriages made him virtually the master of the entire Mathura district.

In the eyes of the Mughal Government, Badan Singh was still a plebeian rebel, who

---

* *Imad-us-Saadat,* p. 55.

† *Kamar* [lat. 27° 50″; long. 77° 30″] is near Kosi in the Mathura district about 33 miles n.w. of Mathura. *Sahar* 18 miles n.w. [lat. 27° 40″; long. 77° 44″]. Crowse's *Mathura,* p. 23.

deserved the severest punishment, if only the
corrupt and effete Court of Delhi could inflict it.
Had Nadir Shah decided to stay in Hindustan
a few months more, or made his intended
pilgrimage to Ajmir,* the Jat Chief would have
been the first to feel the weight of the Persian's
arm. Since his departure the timid gaze of the
Mughal Court was mainly fixed on the north-
west. In the meanwhile, Thakur Badan Singh
silently consolidated his authority over many
outlying districts, without much difficulty.
People welcomed him because he meant to rule
and not plunder them like his predecessors.
His one dear object was to secure the title of
Rajah, and for this, he was even ready to bow
before the imperial throne, which he could
otherwise have safely defied. But he was not
successful, perhaps owing to the jealousy of
the ruler of Jaipur, who affected to look down
upon the Jats as his subjects. It was perhaps
from this time that the ruling house of Bharatpur openly laid claim to the Yadava lineage
and the title of *Braj-Raj*, a claim if not sanctified
by past tradition, at least justified by their
complete sway over what is known as *Braj-
mandal* or the Mathura region. Ajit Singh

---

* Irvine's *Later Mughals*, ii. 374.

and Abhai Singh of Marwar, it is said, used to
address Badan Singh as *Rajah*. His ambition
was certainly flattered, when he was invited to
the *Ashvameda** sacrifice of Maharajah Sawai
Jai Singh, and the honour of a prince was
accorded to his son Suraj Mal. Undoubtedly,
Badan Singh worked and lived in a manner to
deserve that title. He kept Court with adequate
grandeur. Several Muhammadan officers whom
he had taken in service brought the requisite
polish and dignity into his Court and served
there as models of Court-life and teachers of
etiquette to his rough tribesmen. His growing
predilection for Islamic culture and aristocratic
training becomes prominent in the education of
his youngest and most beloved son, Pratap
Singh.†

Badan Singh had some aesthetic sense and
a taste for architecture too, which is testified by
the remains of his numerous buildings and

---

* Jawala Sahai's *History of Bharatpur*.

† The author of *Imad-us-Saqdat* tells us that this young
man grew up (in airs and graces) a high-bred Muslim grandee
with good manners and elegant speech. In the style of tying
his turban, the fashion of his dress as well as his favourite
dishes, he imitated the manner of Delhi. Bahadur Singh, son
of this Pratap Singh, went a step ahead of his father. He
took to the study of the *Quran* and read up to the Shura Jami.
Imad. 55.

garden-palaces.   He beautified the fort of Deeg
with handsome palaces, which are known as the
Purana Mahal.   At Wair in the Biana district,
he planted within the fort a large garden with
a beautiful house and reservoirs in the centre,
now called *Phul-bari.*   He also built palaces at
Kamar as well Sahar, which are now in ruin,
and dedicated a temple at Brindaban, known
by the poetic name of *Dhir Samir.**

Badan Singh lived to a ripe old age, which
he spent in happy retirement at Sahar, leaving
the management of his State to his most capable
son Suraj Mal.   He died on the 9th of Ramzan,
1169 A.H. = 7th June, 1756 (*Waqa,* 133) under
the usual suspicion of being poisoned, though
there was no imaginable ground for it.

Rajah Suraj Mal : his character and early career.

Rajah Suraj Mal, the successor of Thakur
Badan Singh, was a strongly built man of
"above the medium height, with a robust frame,
inclining to corpulence in his old age, and a
very dark complexion. His eyes were unusually
sparkling, and all his appearance indicated
more fire than one could notice in his conduct,
which was very sweet and supple."†   He had

---

* Growse, p. 139.
† Father Wendel, Orme MS., p. 51.

little of book-learning, and none of the courtly grace of his youngest brother, being plain and unassuming in dress and manners. He possessed great political sagacity, a steady intellect and a clear vision. "Though he wore the dress of a farmer, and could speak only his own *Braj*-dialect, he was", says the author of *Imad-us-Saadat*, "the Plato of the Jat tribe. In prudence and skill, and ability to manage the revenue and civil affairs he had no equal among the grandees of Hindustan except Asaf Jah Bahadur* (the Nizam). He possessed pre-eminently all the nobler qualities of his race, energy, courage, shrewdness, dogged perseverance and an in-domitable spirit that would never accept a defeat. But in the pursuit of an exciting game, whether in war or diplomacy, he was of no more delicate conscience than most of his con-temporaries. In an age of intrigue and unscru-pulous diplomacy, he equally baffled the dis-sembling Mughal and the cunning Maratha. In short, he was a wary old bird that picked up grain from every net, without getting entangled in the noose.

Suraj Mal's first exploit, during his father's lifetime, was the capture of the fort of Bharat-

---

* *Imad*, p. 55.

5

pur, in 1732, by a daring night-attack upon its
lord, Khem Karan Jat Sogoria. At that time,
the place was only a small mud-fort without
any of the formidable fortifications with which
its name was afterwards associated. His un-
tutored genius turned it into an impregnable
stronghold, and around it grew up a prosperous
city vying in grandeur with the imperial capitals
of Delhi and Agra. The fame of his just and
wise rule attracted men of all classes, profes-
sions and creeds to his principality, which was
the only spot where peace and security reigned
in the midst of the chaotic plains of Hindustan. He early attached himself to Maharajah
Sawai Jai Singh, the most powerful Rajput
ruler of his time, in order to disarm the Rajput
jealousy and allow the infant Jat Power to grow
unhampered under the shadow of Amber.
Besides policy, an inherent sentiment of loyalty
to the throne of Amber moved him to act thus.
Suraj Mal's sincere devotion to the Maharajah
was repaid with fatherly affection by that great
ruler. After the death of the Maharajah, Suraj
Mal, true to the dying wish of his beloved
patron, stood faithfully by his eldest son Iswari
Singh whose rightful claim to the throne was
unjustly disputed by his younger brother Madho
Singh in pride of the Sisodia blood derived from

his mother. To sweep Iswari Singh off the throne of Amber Malhar Rao Holkar, Gangadhar Tatiya and the Maharana of Mewar advanced upon Jaipur with a huge army of Marathas and Sisodias, swelled by Rathor and Hada contingents from Jodhpur and Kotah. Rajah Iswari Singh, accompanied by Suraj Mal started from his capital with the levy of Amber and his Jat auxiliaries.

On Sunday, 20th August, 1749 both armies joined in dreadful conflict at Bagru;* the contest was an unequal and unfair one: seven confederated rulers having combined against one prince. The Van of the army of Amber was led by Shiv Singh, the barve feudatory chief of Sikar; Suraj Mal was posted in the centre, and Rajah Iswari Singh himself commanded the rear. The first day ended in an indecisive artillery duel. The second day closed gloomily for Amber, because the valiant Lord of Sikar, leading the Van died after an obstinate encounter. With the break of dawn on the third day, the eager enemy, confident of success, appeared in battle array. The army of Amber came out to meet them: the honour

---

* Bagru is a town on the Ajmir—Agra Trunk Road about 18 miles south-west of Jaipur. (*Rajputana Gaz.* ii. 155).

of leading the *harawal* (Van) devolved on Suraj
Mal on this fateful day. The battle raged
furiously throughout the line in spite of an
autumn shower which failed to cool the ardour
of the combatants. The clever Maratha chief
Malhar sent Gangadhar Tatiya with a strong
division to surprise the rear of Rajah Iswari
Singh. Gangadhar marched stealthily and fell
upon Rao Sardar Singh Naruka, vassal of
Uniara, who commanded the rear of the Amber
army. He threw the rear division into confusion and pressed vigorously upon the artillery
posted in the centre. The gunners were cut
down and the cannon spiked : defeat stared
Rajah Iswari Singh in the face. Seeing
everything lost, the Rajah commanded Suraj
Mal, his last hope to charge Gangadhar. The
Jat chief bowed his head and without a
moment's pause delivered a flank charge
upon a stronger enemy. An obstinate struggle
between the half-victorious Maratha and the
stubborn Jat lasted for two hours. At last
Gangadhar turned his back, and Suraj Mal
restoring the broken rear, and leaving Sardar
Singh Naruka in command there, returned to
the Van to breast the surging tides of the hostile
army. In that supreme hour of peril, the Jat
chief fought with superhuman valour, "killing"

says the enthusiastic native chronicler, "50 and wounding 108 of the enemy with his own hand. At last the darkness of night parted the combatants. Suraj Mal triumphantly led back the army of Amber, after having snatched a victory from the jaws of defeat. The Rajput bard did not grudge the heroic Jat his due on this memorable occasion. The Bundi poet Suraj mal commemorates the deed of his Jat namesake in the following spirited couplets :—

" सच्चौ भलेकौ जट्टिनौ, जाय अरिष्ट अरिष्ट ।
जाठर तस रबिमल्ल ड्रव, आमेरन कौ इष्ट ॥ "

" बहुरि जह मलहार सन, लरन लग्यो हरवक्ष ।
अंगद है हुआर, जाट, मिहर मल्ल प्रतिमल्ल ॥ "

i.e., The Jatni did not in vain bear [the pain of travail.

The issue of her womb [Jathara] was Suraj [Rabi] Mal, the scourge of enemies, and the well-wisher of Amber.

Turning back [from the rear] the Jat began to fight with Malhar in the Van.

Holkar was the shadow [of night], and he the sun: the two champions well matched [in conflict].

Daylight brought the hostile armies again
into conflict on the fourth day. In this way
fighting continued for two days more, till at
last the arduous struggle wore out the patience
of the less persevering Maratha. Holkar proposed peace and Madho Singh had to content
himself with the five parganas given to him as
his appanage.*

Suraj Mal's first encounter with the Mughals.

In the reign of the Emperor Ahmad Shah,
Saadat Khan, Amir-ul-umra Zulfiqar Jang,†
had been appointed governor of Agra and
Ajmir. He entered into a league with Rajah
Bakht Singh Rathor, who had usurped the
throne of Marwar by ousting his nephew, Ram

---

* Life of Maharajah Iswari Singh *in Hindi* (pp. 69-73)
by Thakur Narendra Singh Varma, Vaidic Press, Ajmir.

† In the original text of the *Siyar-ul-Mutaqharin* we do
not find the name Saadat Khan [see original text, ii. 38],
imported in the translation. This Saadat Khan has been
confounded by the translator with his namesake, the uncle
and father-in-law of Nawab Safdar Jang [*vide* vol. iv., index,
p. 63]. Burhan-ul-mulk Saadat Khan died during Nadir
Shah's stay at Delhi [*Siyar*, i. 316]; the exact date being 10th
March, 1739. The second Saadat Khan (Zulfiqar Jang) was
appointed governor in the reign of Ahmad Shah who
ascended the throne on Wednesday, 2nd Jamada I., 1160 H.
(1st May, 1747; *Waqa*, p. 35). He was created *Mir Bakhshi*
by the Emperor Ahmad Shah on Thursday, Rajab 14, 1160 H.
(11th July, 1747) on the very same day that Rajah Bakht
Singh was appointed subahdar of Gujrat (*Waqa*, p. 38).

Singh. Though driven out of the capital, Ram Singh, with the support of the Rajah of Jaipur, held out near Ajmir, waiting for the arrival of his Maratha allies. So the situation was full of danger for Bakht Singh who, therefore, sought the help of Saadat Khan. The Khan also required his assistance against the Jats for recovering the greater portion of his subah of Agra from their clutches. An understanding seems to have been entered into, to the effect that Saadat Khan, instead of marching to Agra by the Delhi-Agra royal road, should strike south-west from Delhi, through Mewat, unite his forces with those of Bakht Singh somewhere on the frontier of his principality, and thence turn towards Ajmir to crush Ram Singh : after the conquest of Ajmir, the subjugation of the Jat country would become easier,—so the Khan was made to believe. He began his march (1162 H.)* with an well-equipped army of 15,000 horse, and arrived at a place, Nimrani, on the northern boundary of Suraj Mal's

---

* *Siyar's* date 1163 H. is wrong [*Siyar*, iii. 312]. In that year Suraj Mal was, according to better authorities, fighting as an ally of Safdar Jang against the Ruhelas. The correct date seems to be *Safar 1162 H.* The translator of *Siyar*, iii. 311, 20th line, omits the date, "the end of the year 1162" (text, ii. 38). The text is also wrong. This should be the end of 1161, as is evident from *Waqa-i-Shah Alam Sani*.

dominion. The Jat Rajah was watching the movements of the Mughal army, without any intention of showing his hand first. But some soldiers of Saadat Khan picked a quarrel with the Jat garrison of a small fort and drove them out. This was construed by the Khan as a great victory, and he ordered his drums to be beaten in rejoicing. He became over-confident of his strength, and the sudden elation of an insignificant success changed his whole plan of campaign. He made a halt there, and recalled his advanced guards from the direction of Narnol. In spite of the earnest remonstrances of some of the officers of his army, he decided to conquer the Jat country first and then go to Ajmir. Saadat Khan ordered Fath Ali Khan to go out on a forage in force. The party started in the morning from their camp near Sobha Chand's *sarai*. While at noon the foragers with their convoy were about to return, the Jat army commanded by Rajah Suraj Mal himself appeared. Fath Ali Khan, who was at a distance of two or three *kos** sent urgent requests for reinforcement, but it came tardily towards the sunset.

Thinking a retreat by night before a

---

* This is omitted in the translation of the *Siyar*.

stronger enemy dangerous, they sent word to Saadat Khan proposing to pass the night on the spot, expecting him to march with the whole army to their relief in the morning. This was objected to, and their immediate return was insisted upon by the Khan. The Jats surrounded the retreating column; their mounted matchlockmen closed in small bodies and discharged volleys upon the confused Muslim troopers without dismounting. Such a mobile force as Suraj Mal's mounted matchlockmen could hardly be brought to the grapple in the darkness of night. A great many of the Mughals died helplessly, and the rest lost heart when Hakim Khan was shot dead and Ali Rustam Khan wounded—the two gallant officers who had brought reinforcements. The retreat became a panic-stricken flight. The main camp was also thrown into confusion by the rush of fugitives and the appearance of the advanced party of the enemy, close on their heels. A greater disaster was averted by the firmness and decision of Saadat Khan's more discreet captains, who did not hesitate to prevent by force their master's flight. The Lord of Lords writhed in agony in their grip till the panic subsided. "Luckily", says the author of the *Siyar*, whose uncle was an eye-witness of the affair, "as the Jat chief, for his own safety, did not wish to gain the evil repute of having captured or slain an Amir-ul-umra, he contented himself with besieging the camp for two or three days together, at the end of which he offered terms through Fath Ali Khan, an officer with whom he was acquainted. The Amir-ul-umra, considering it to be a great gain, consented to them." Suraj Mal sent his own son Jawahir Singh, to the Amir-ul-umra and concluded an agreement on several conditions, two of which were, that the dependents of the viceroy should not cut any *pipal* tree, nor offer any insult or injury to the Hindu temples in the country.* This victory over the Amir-ul-umra of the empire brought great prestige and self-confidence to Rajah Suraj Mal. Soon afterwards he entered the political arena of Hindustan to play a bolder and more honourable role.

Suraj Mal's marriage with Rani Kishori.

Rajah Suraj Mal followed his father's policy of extending the dominion of his house by politic marriages. He had his son Newal Singh married to a daughter of Sardar Sitaram,

---

* For this campaign, see *Siyar*, iii. 313-315=Pers. text, Part II., pp. 38-39. The translation is wrong in many places.

the powerful castellan of Kotman,* and himself married a daughter of Chaudhuri Kashi, the head of a strong and prosperous Jat family of Hodal, 53 miles north-west of Mathura. This lady was the gifted queen Rani Kishori,† commonly known by her pet name, Hansia (the Smiling One), who figures prominently in the history of the house of Bharatpur. The story goes that one day while Rajah Suraj Mal, mounted on a huge elephant, was passing through a street of Hodal, a group of girls, returning from the well, ran away terrified at the sight of the mighty beast; only one girl refused to move and stood gazing with unshaken nerve upon the strange animal and the gorgeous equipage of the princely retinue. The Rajah, struck at the intrepidity of the girl, enquired about

---

* Situated in the Mathura district on the Agra-Delhi Trunk Road about three furlongs to the south of the boundary line dividing the Gurgaon and the Mathura districts.

† I have not been able to find out the date of Rani Kishori's marriage. The descendants of Chaudhuri Kashi still occupy a respectable position at Hodal. Some of them, e.g., Chaudhuri Ratan Singh, still serve in the Bharatpur State. The magnificent palaces, built by their ancestors, are now in ruins. Chaudhuri Devi Singh Zaildar, Daulat Singh, Ratan Singh and Hari Singh are the most prominent living members of this house. The last-named gentleman is a personal friend of mine and entertained me very hospitably in the *mahal* or inner-apartment of his ancestral palace.

her, and demanded her in marriage from her relatives. Whatever may be the element of truth in this popular story, her courage and constancy in the face of grave disasters in later life are testified by authentic history. Her genius and resourcefulness saved the fortunes of Bharatpur many a time from almost inevitable ruin.

———

CHAPTER IV.

RAJAH SÜRAJ MAL, AN ALLY OF NAWAB SAFDAR JANG.

Suraj Mal helps the Jats of Ballamgarh against the Nawab Wazir Safdar Jang.

Already master of the Mathura district, Suraj Mal cast his eye upon the neighbourhood of Delhi and was waiting for an opportunity to extend his authority further south. The Jats of Ballamgarh, hard pressed by the faujdar of Faridabad, sought his help, and this embroiled him further with the Mughal Government. We may here briefly trace the history of the Jat feudal house of Ballamgarh. One Gopal Singh Jat of the Tawatia *got* (sept) settled in Sihi, a village three miles north of Ballamgarh, about 1705 and became wealthy and powerful by highway robbery on the Mathura-Delhi road. He allied himself with the Gujars of Tiagaon (8 miles east of Ballamgarh; long, 77°30″, lat. 28°25″) and with their help killed the Rajput Chaudhuri of the neighbouring villages. Murtaza Khan, the local Mughal officer of Faridabad, instead of punishing the rebel, made peace with him by appointing him

as Chaudhuri of Faridabad pargana, entitled to
a cess of one anna in the rupee on the revenue
in 1710. After the death of Gopal Singh, his
son Charandas succeeded him, and seeing how
weak the imperial grasp was growing even in
the nearer districts, withheld the revenue and
set the authority of Murtaza Khan at defiance.
However, Charandas was captured and thrown
into prison at Faridabad. After some time, his
son Balaram, duping* the Khan by a false
payment of ransom, set him at liberty. Father
and son fled to Bharatpur, and securing the aid
of Suraj Mal, killed Murtaza Khan. (*Delhi
Gazetteer*, p. 213).

This act of rebellious aggression remained
unpunished till the accession of Emperor
Ahmad Shah (1747). The wazir wrote repeatedly to Balaram and Rajah Suraj Mal to give up
the above-mentioned parganas, but was put off
with false pretences and evasive replies. This
was sufficient to kindle the wrath of the wazir

---

* The story goes that Balarm promised to pay a large
amount in cash directly his father was freed. According to
previous stipulations, Charandas was brought guarded to the
side of a tank near Ballamgarh, and when the cart bringing
the treasure had come up, and one or two bags of rupees had
been examined, Charandas was let go. He immediately made
off on a fleet horse with his son. The other bags were found
to contain copper coins (*paisa*) only. (*Delhi Gazetteer*, foot-
note, p. 213).

and to make him swear the utter destruction of the Jats. So he took the field against them in 1162 H. (January, 1749), almost simultaneously with the Amir-ul-umra, and captured Faridabad. Suraj Mal, elated with his recent success over one imperial army led by the commander-in-chief of the Mughal empire, was not in a mood to hear the proposals of the wazir to resign peacefully the places in dispute. He prepared to back the Jats of Sihi with all his resources and putting the forts of Deeg and Kuhmir in a state of defence, marched against the wazir (June, 1749). Fortune befriended Suraj Mal; the wazir, on receiving the news of a formidable Ruhela rebellion in the immediate neighbourhood of his subah of Oudh, had to put off the settlement of his score with the Jats and return to Delhi. He fought these Afghans, and after quelling their disturbance, left his deputy Nawal Ray in charge of the districts wrested from them (beginning of 1750). Then he resumed his operations against the Jats, and sent an army against them. The Jats having got ready for fight, the wazir started against them during the rains (July 1750) and advanced as far as Khizirabad. About this time the news of a great disaster, viz., the defeat and death of Nawal Ray at the

hands of Ahmad Khan Bangash, induced the
wazir to make up his quarrel with Suraj Mal.
A compromise was effected through the mediation of the Maratha vakil. In order to save
appearances, Balaram,* with his wrists bound
together, accompanied the Maratha envoy to
the presence of the wazir, who graciously
pardoned him and gave an implicit sanction to
his illegal acquisitions. Rajah Suraj Mal was
given a khilat of 6 pieces, and his bakhshi one
of two pieces. Mutual appreciation of merit
and ability laid the foundations of a true friendship between the Nawab wazir and the great
Jat, who ever after stood faithfully by his ally,
even under most desperate circumstances.

Rajah Suraj Mal joined the wazir in an

---

* This Balaram is the builder of the fort of Ballamgarh or
Ballabgarh. He is not the same man as his namesake, who
was the brother of Suraj Mal's wife, Hansia. This Balaram
was killed on the 29th November, 1753 by one Aqibat Mahmud
Khan as appears from the follwing entry (p. 83) in the
Waqa-i-Shah Alam Sani: "On the 2nd Safar [1167 H.] Aqibat
Mahmud Khan, who went to Ballu Jat [Balaram] to settle the
affair of his jagir, had an exchange of harsh words with Jat.
He cut off the head of the said Jat and brought his head
to His Majesty [Ahmad Shah]." This Aqibat Mahmud was
the son of Murtazá Khan, whom Balaram had slain. However, Ballamgarh and Faridabad remained in possession of
Suraj Mal who appointed Kishan Singh and Bishan Singh,
sons of Balaram, as the qiladar and nazim of Ballamgarh.
They retained their office till 1774. (See Delhi Gazetteer,
p. 213). This date, like all others, in the Gazetteer is doubtful.

expedition* against Ahmad Khan Bangash and the Ruhelas. The Nawab started on the 29th Shaban, 1163 H. = Monday 23 July, 1750 with an army of 70,000 horse. Suraj Mal with his Jats, occupied Farrukhabad, the capital of Ahmad Khan. A severe battle was fought at Pathari on Monday 22nd Shawwal 1163 H. (13 Sept., 1750). The wazir stood in the centre, mounted on an elephant; his right and left wings were commanded respectively by Suraj Mal Jat and Ismail Beg Khan. Both wings vigorously charged the enemy at a gallop and drove away Rustam Khan Afridi and some other Ruhela commanders, killing 6,000 or 7,000 Afghans. The battle began at nine and raged till the afternoon, the advantage being on the side of Safdar Jang. Ahmad Khan Bangash, seeing all lost, summoned his tribesmen and urged them to make a last effort to retrieve their honour; "Otherwise", he said to them in the characteristic Pathan style "every Afridi [their braver comrades] will make water upon the beard of the Bangashes."† The

---

* *Waqa*, pp. 57-58; Harcharan Das; *Imad*, 49.

† *Imad*, p. 49; *Siyar*, p. 295. The author of *Gulistan-i-Rahamat* says that Rustam Khan Afridi had actually been killed by Suraj Mal, and that Ahmad Khan concealed this fact from his followers.

6

Afghans assembled in a grove of *palash* trees, and made a sudden rush upon the wazir's party. The wazir had dangerously weakened his division by sending reinforcements to his wings. But he neither pushed forward to keep touch with his commanders nor recalled them from pursuit. Nawab Safdar Jang severely wounded was brought into the camp. Next morning he began his retreat towards the imperial capital. The Afghans occupied almost the whole of his territories; the city of Allahabad was plundered; and its citadel besieged: Lucknow was saved only by the stubborn courage of the citizens. In the meanwhile, when the news of his defeat had reached Delhi, his enemies had turned the heart of the Emperor against him, and were plotting for his overthrow. But his timely arrival disconcerted their plan. The wazir again summoned Rajah Nagar Mal, Rajah Lachmi Narayan, Rajah Suraj Mal Jat, Ismail Khan Kabuli and others who were his well-wishers, to discuss the plan of a new campaign against the Ruhelas. He took into his pay the Maratha army of Malhar Rao Holkar for Rs. 25,000 per day, and the Jats of Suraj Mal* on a daily allowance of Rs. 15,000.

---

* *Ibratnama*, p. 41; *Bayan-o-Waqa*, p. 262; *Waqa-i-Shah Alam Sani*, p. 61.

On the 6th Rabi I., 1164 H. (Tuesday, 22 Jany. 1751) he started a second time against Ahmad Khan Bangash. Farrukhabad was sacked and the whole Ruhela country was devastated with fire and sword. A thorn was planted in the side of the Ruhelas to torment them perpetually by giving the tract of country from Koel (Aligarh) to Korah Jahanabad to the Marathas* as jagir. He sent greetings to the Emperor on his victory over the Afghans on 9th Jamada II. 1164 H. = April 24, 1751 [*Waqa*, p. 62]. This shows that this campaign was a short but sharp one, everything being finished within three months.

About a month after the wazir's departure from the capital, a great calamity had befallen the empire. Ahmad Shah Abdali invaded the Panjab, entered Lahor on the 3rd of Rabi II. 1164 H. = Monday, 18 Feby. 1751 and threatened to march upon Delhi. The Emperor, as a compliment to Suraj Mal conferred a mansab of 3,000 zat, 2,000 horse, and the title of *Rao* upon Ratan Singh, and that of 1,000 zat, 1,000 horse upon Jawahir Singh (13th Jamada I. = 29 March 1751) in addition to his

---

* *Waqa*, p. 62. A good account of the Maratha activity during this campaign is to be found in Sardesai's *Marathi Riyasat Panipat Prakaran*, pp. 10—14.

former rank, making him in all a mansabdar of
4000 *zat*, 3500 horse [*Waqa*, p. 70]. Repeated
and urgent messages were sent to the wazir to
come with all haste, bringing Malhar Rao
Holkar and other Maratha chiefs with him.
During the wazir's absence a lady of the harem,
an eunuch, and a supple intriguer had acquired
complete control over the Emperor's fickle mind.
They induced him to accept the terms of the
Durrani invader, who consented to retire on
getting the subahs of Lahor and Multan. On his
return to the capital, the wazir justly resented
this ignominious treaty made in his absence and
without consulting him. He was bent upon
punishing the evil-doers. The eunuch was to
be the first victim of the wazir's wrath. Jāvid
Khan was invited to a feast in the wazir's house
and there poisoned.

The Emperor Ahmad Shah, instigated by
the queen-mother and the nobles of the Turani
faction, dismissed Nawab Safdar Jang, from
the office of the wazir, confiscated his estates,
and removed him from the viceroyalties of
Oudh and Allahabad. A civil war broke out
between them; the ex-wazir, stung with the
ingratitude of his sovereign, and unwilling to
yield to him so tamely, laid siege to the capital
and sent for Rajah Suraj Mal Jat. The

Afghans, the natural enemies of Safdar Jang, joined the imperial army under young Ghazi-ud-din Imad-ul-mulk. The Jats, instigated by the angry Nawab, so thoroughly sacked old Delhi and its neighbourhood that the people still remember it as *Jat-gardi** or Jat loot which takes rank in their memory, with two other classic loots the *Shah-gardi* of Ahmad Shah Abdali, and the *Bhao-gardi* of the Marathas before Panipat. But the Mughals in the service of Safdar Jang deserted him to a man, and joined their Turani brethren under Ghazi-ud-din. His only hope now rested upon Rajah Suraj Mal, and the Jat proved no broken reed to him in this hour of supreme need. Promises of high honours and threats of vengeance were treated with equal scorn by that faithful chief, who was determined to fight to the last for his ally, though his was clearly a lost cause. In order to terrify him, Ghazi-ud-din sent for Malhar Rao Holkar from the south. But this was equally unavailing; the clever Jat took advantage of the jealousy of the new wazir Intizam-ud-daulah towards his ambitious nephew Ghazi-ud-din, whose motive he suspected and whose ability he dreaded. So successful was the

---

* *Imad,* p. 63.

diplomatic move of Suraj Mal that before the
Marathas could arrive, offers of peace were
made from the Emperor's side; Maharajah
Madho Singh Kachhwa, who came to Delhi
about the end of 1753, was asked to mediate.
The Jat Rajah refused to sheathe his sword unless the Emperor restored the viceroyalties of
Oudh and Allahabad, if not the office of wazir
also, to Safdar Jang.   At last peace was concluded on the above conditions; and the Nawab
departed to rule his subah.   Suraj Mal had
saved his ally from almost inevitable ruin by
drawing upon himself the implacable enmity
of Ghazi-ud-din, the full force of which he was
made to feel very soon.*

---

* For a detailed account of this civil war, see *Tarikh-i-
Muzaffari*, pp. 65-75; *Bayan-o-Waqa*, pp. 270-280. Harcharan
Das also describes this civil war in five pages. The general
narrative given in *Tarikh-i-Muzaffari* is more authentic.

CHAPTER V.

SURAJ MAL'S STRUGGLE WITH THE MARATHAS

Maratha invasion of Bharatpur.

The Jats and the Marathas had met together for the first time in 1749, but then it was as auxiliaries fighting on opposite sides in the Kachhwa War of Succession after the death of Maharajah Sawai Jai Singh. Three years later (1752) Rajah Suraj Mal and Malhar Rao Holkar had fought shoulder to shoulder as hired allies of Nawab Safdar Jang in his war against the Ruhela Afghans. During the civil war between the Emperor Ahmad Shah and the ex-wazir Safdar Jang in 1752, Ghazi-ud-din Imad-ul-mulk had invited the Marathas to aid him against Rajah Suraj Mal and Nawab Safdar Jang. In Oct. 1753, Raghunath Rao, with a large army under renowned chiefs, started on his first expedition to Northern India, having for its main object the plunder of the flourishing Jat principality, yet unvisited by them. Rajah Suraj Mal had not given them the least provocation to justify a war. They crossed the Chambal at the ford of

Dholpur and entered the territories of Bharatpur.
The Jat Rajah sent his *purohit* Rupram Katari
as an envoy to Raghunath Rao to negotiate for
terms, and in the meanwhile hurriedly put
Bharatpur, Ramgarh (modern Aligarh) and his
other forts in a state of defence, stocking them
with provisions and war materials. He concentrated his main army at Kuhmir, midway
between Deeg and Bharatpur, the best strategic
position imaginable for the defence of the heart
of his dominion. Raghunath Rao demanded
the extravagant ransom (*khandani*) of one
krore of rupees; Rupram agreed to forty lakhs
at the utmost. The Marathas resumed their
advance, and the envoy came back promising
to procure a reply from his master. Suraj Mal
wrote to Raghunath either to accept peacefully
forty lakhs or to take to war; and with the latter
he sent five cannon-balls and some gun-powder
as samples of the hospitable fare he might
expect in the Jat country. In January 1754 the
invaders appeared before Kuhmir and the
frowning look of that giant fort dispelled their
delusion. Raghunath in his avarice had over-
shot the mark, and now regretted his injudicious demand. Somewhat cast down, he
ordered batteries to be erected against the fort.
With the imperial *risalah* and *topkhana*, Ghazi-

ud-din* joined the Maratha army and infused
more vigour into the camp of the besiegers.

Siege of Kuhmir (Jan. 1754—May 1754).

The Maratha batteries failed to make any
impression upon the walls of Kuhmir and their
main army was held at bay by the resolute
enemy. One day, young Khande Rao Holkar,†
the only son of Malhar, after taking his meal
went, drawn by fate as it were, to an advanced
battery and was struck down by a stray bullet
from a Jat swivel-gun (*jazail*). Revenge nerved
the arm of the Maratha, and the Jats began to
feel its weight. Three months thus passed
away, and every day the prospects became
gloomier for Suraj Mal. There was no power
in Hindustan, bold enough to lift a finger to
help him openly against the Marathas. Rajputana lay prostrate at their feet; the Emperor
of Hindustan was hostile and powerless, and
even the ally Safdar Jang was too afraid of the
Maratha lance to move alone. The destruction of Suraj Mal appeared to be only a question

---

* He made a forced march of 22 *kos* from Hodal to
Mathura in one day, (15th Rabi II. 1167=Feb., 1754). See
Waqa, 85.

† He was about thirty years of age at this time. The *Waqa*
makes an entry, recording his death under the date 4th Jamada
I., 1167 A.H.=Wednesday, Feby. 27, 1754. This corresponds
with the time "*About a month and half* after the beginning of
the siege" given by *Bhao Bakhar*, p. 4.

of time. Like a Rajput, the Jat calmly waited
for that awful hour when the smoke of the
horrible sacrifice of his females (*Jauhar*) would
ascend to heaven, giving signal to him to rush
forth sword in hand to find an honourable
death. Though equally indifferent to death
the Jatni, bred in a freer atmosphere, with a
wider outlook of the world and a deeper
penetration of human character than the Rajput
lady, proved to be more optimistic and resource-
ful. Hansia* (the 'Smiling One', wife of
Suraj Mal) roused the drooping spirits of her
husband, telling him to trust her and banish
despair from his mind. She had heard of
Jayaji Appa Sindhia, as a man, generous,
straightforward, and chivalrous, who could be
trusted more than any other Maratha chief; the
mutual jealousy among the Maratha leaders,
and their accessibility to bribe were also not
unknown to her. In order to create division
in the enemy's camp, she one night sent Tej-
ram Katari, son of Rupram, with a letter
from Suraj Mal and his turban to Jayaji Sindhia,
to implore his protection and friendship by an

---

* The editor of *Bhao Bakhar* (p. 5, foot-note 17) sanskritises
the name as *Anasua*, with unnecessary philological discussion.
For a Jat girl, this is, however too learned and poetic a name
beyond the comprehension of the countryfolk.

exchange of head-dress. Jayaji made a noble response, accepted the pledge of Suraj Mal and sent him his own turban in exchange with an encouraging letter, and a leaf of the sacred *Bel* tree, taken from the offerings to his patron deity (*Bel Bhandar*), as the most solemn proof of his sincerity. The news of the incident leaked out and Holkar became despondent.*

Suraj Mal himself, spurred to exertion by his energetic wife, began to intrigue with the Emperor and the wazir Intizam-ud-daulah, who had viewed with misgivings the junction of Ghazi-ud-din with the Marathas. The timid Emperor also feared the dictatorship of Ghazi-ud-din no less than that of Safdar Jang. A mighty wicked spirit had been conjured up which might as well break the neck of the con-jurers. He wrote letters to the Emperor as well as to the new wazir that Ghazi-ud-din by allying himself with the Marathas was bringing the empire to ruin. Who would stand across his path when he chooses to push aside his old uncle from the wazirat or deal harshly with His Majesty, if no bridle is now put on his ambition and no check upon his sinister activities? Ghazi-ud-din had sent for some heavy cannon

* *Bhao Bakhar*, p. 6.

from the citadel of Delhi. But Intizam-ud-
daulah, who did not desire the success of his
nephew, advised the Emperor not to send them.
He shrewdly remarked that if the warlike
resources of the Marathas, the vast wealth and
strong forts, conquered from Suraj Mal, and
the imperial topkhana were placed at the disposal of the turbulent and unscrupulous Ghazi-
ud-din, his ambition would exceed all the
bounds of imagination.

Suraj Mal and Intizam-ud-daulah were
busy in weaving a net of diplomacy round the
Marathas and Ghazi-ud-din. The Emperor
himself became a party to the conspiracy.
Under the royal seal letters were sent to
Maharajah Madho Singh of Jaipur, the Rajah
of Marwar; and Safdar Jang—who had all
suffered much at the hands of the Marathas—
asking them to unite their forces under the
imperial standard and relieve Hindustan of
these southern pests. Assurances being given
by all, the actual plan of the intended attack
was left to be devised by Suraj Mal. He
suggested that the Emperor, under the pretence
of hunting and visiting the crownlands in the
Doab should reach Koel [Aligarh], and halt
there till Nawab Safdar Jang joined him. On
the arrival of the Oudh troops he was to march

rapidly to the city of Agra where the Kachhwa
and Rathor Rajahs would meet him with their
armies. The plan was to form a cordon on the
Chambal, so that the enemy might not escape.
If the Marathas raised the siege of Kuhmir and
marched upon Agra, Suraj Mal was to come
close behind them and join the Emperor.

The Emperor started from the capital with
his army, Court and harem, and by leisurely
marches reached the neighbourhood of Sikandra. Nawab Safdar Jang also arrived at
Mehdighat on the Ganges and encamped there
expecting the Emperor at Koel. But the
Emperor, instead of marching to Koel and
putting himself in the shelter of its strong fort,
delayed at Sikandra, enlisting new troops. In
the meanwhile Malhar Rao secretly left the
siege-camp at Kuhmir with five thousand horse,
intending to swoop down upon the unsuspecting
royal quarry and appropriate the gain alone.
The imperial camp was surprised; its treasures
and equipages, and some of the ladies of the
harem and the whole park of artillery fell into
the hands of the Marathas. The imbecile
Emperor and his cowardly minister fled in
disguise. The Marathas chased them towards
Delhi and besieged the capital. Intizam-ud-
daulah put the city in some sort of defence,

foolishly expecting help from the Rajput princes, Safdar Jang and Suraj Mal.* Ghazi-ud-din withdrew his army from the siege of Kuhmir and joined the Marathas. Still suspecting a combination of enemies, he invited the Ruhela chief Najib-ud-daulah to his assistance, promising him a high post and a liberal subsidy.

The fort was captured; the Emperor with his mother and other relations was made prisoners. Intizam-ud-daulah was dismissed from office and the eyes of the Emperor were blinded by the order of Ghazi-ud-din. He himself became wazir and raised to the throne another prince Aziz-ud-din with the title Alamgir II. (10th Shaban, 1167 A. H.=2nd June, Sunday, 1754), [Waqa, 91]. It was now too late for Suraj Mal to retrieve the situation. Safdar Jang was being watched by Najib-ud-daulah, who was in league with Ghazi-ud-din. The rajahs of Rajputana did not move, seeing that the plan had miscarried. Suraj Mal cannot be held responsible for the miserable fate of the Emperor,

---

* The best account of the counter-plot against Ghazi-ud-din and the intrigues of both parties are to be found in the *Tarikh-i-Muzaffari* [MS. 84-94] which differs considerably from the *Siyar* (text, ii. 48-49).

which the latter owed solely to his own negligence and want of discretion. Had he reached Koel and encamped within its strong walls, surprise would have been impossible and his junction with Safdar Jang, who was waiting at Mehdighát, would have been easily effected. Such deplorable carelessness and lack of discipline prevailed in the Emperor's camp, that when Holkar fired some rockets at a distance to feel the pulse of the enemy, none in the imperial camp cared to go out and reconnoitre. Worse still they surmised that perhaps Aqibat Mahmud, a lieutenant of Ghazi-ud-din might be burning some village! They contentedly went to repose, but lo! the thieves broke in and the brave lords and princes were soon in headlong flight. At any rate the immediate object of Rajah Suraj Mal's diplomacy, viz., to turn away the Marathas from Kuhmir, was eminently successful. This unexpected success opened more alluring vistas of aggression to the Marathas. Standing behind the throne of the Great Mughal, the heart of the Maratha nation throbbed with a nobler impulse and they cast their wistful eyes upon the glimmering waves of the far-off Indus. The siege was practically raised when Malhar Rao and Ghazi-ud-din marched off towards Sikandra.

The Maratha army had already eaten up the supplies of the neighbouring country, and scarcity pressed the besiegers more than the besieged. They dispersed in small bodies, leaving Jayaji Appa Sindhia before Kuhmir. Malhar Rao and Ghazi-ud-din, who still found themselves beset with many difficulties, forgot their old animosity and tried to win over so steadfast a friend and so redoubtable an adversary as Suraj Mal. Through the mediation of Sindhia, peace was concluded with him on the condition of the Jat Rajah paying an indemnity of 60 lakhs. The Marathas evacuated the Jat territory, Raghunath Rao starting for home and Jayaji Sindhia for Marwar* (June 1754).

---

* *Bhao Bakhar*, p. 10. It is doubtful whether the stipulated sum was paid at all. Persian authorities and French MS. are silent about it.

CHAPTER VI.

AHMAD SHAH DURRANI'S CAMPAIGN AGAINST THE JATS
1169 A.H. (Nov. 1756—April 1757).

Suraj Mal's struggle with the Abdali.

Rajah Suraj Mal was left undisturbed by the new Government of Delhi for about a year, as Ghazi-ud-din and the Marathas were busy in the Panjab. The Afghans were driven across the Indus, and again that province became a part of the empire. A quarrel soon sprang up between the wazir Ghazi-ud-din, and Najib-ud-daulah (the Amir-ul-umra), who resented the dictatorship of his rival. The Emperor Alamgir II. being a nonentity, whose movements were swayed by the will of his keeper, the imperial camp had no room for two such equally ambitious and powerful grandees. Najib-ud-daulah feared the alliance of the Marathas with Ghazi-ud-din, who might some day bring him to account with their help. He looked for protection to the Durrani Shah, and opened treasonable negotiations with him. Ghazi-ud-din made peace with Rajah Suraj Mal as a counterweight to the alienation of the

7

Ruhela chief. In the second year of Alamgir
II.'s reign, Ahmad Shah Durrani again crossed
the Indus (Rabi I., 1169; Nov. 1756), and
marched rapidly upon the capital to punish
Ghazi-ud-din. Antaji Mankeshwar and other
Marathas in the pay of the wazir anticipated the
Afghan freebooters, and after thoroughly looting the old fort, and the suburbs of the capital,
fled at midnight. Ghazi-ud-din surrendered
himself to the Shah in his camp at Narelah.
On his arrival at Delhi he was utterly fleeced,
having to pay about one krore of Rupees and to
lose the office of wazir. Ahmad Shah sat on
the throne of Delhi and issued coins in his own
name (8th Jamada I., = Saturday 29th January
1757). Rajah Suraj Mal being nearest among
the refractory chiefs, the wrath of the Shah
turned upon him first with all its pent up fury.
Jawahir Singh, son of Suraj Mal, was watching
the movements of the Afghan army from
Ballamgarh* with five or six thousand troops.
He cut off a foraging party of the Afghans, who
had gone towards Faridabad. The Shah was
extremely enraged, and that very night sent
Abdus Samad Khan, with instructions to decoy

---

* Ballamgarh is written Ballabgarh in the modern atlas,
22 miles south-west of Delhi on G. I. P. Ry.; Faridabad,
16 miles south-west of Delhi.

the infidels into an ambush. The Jat prince almost fell into the trap, by chasing a squadron of the enemy's cavalry to their hiding place. He made his escape losing some followers and a part of the booty. The Afghans looted some villages and beheaded as many men as they could capture. On the 22nd Jamada I., = Saturday 12th Feb. 1757 Ahmad Shah left Delhi and marched against the Jats with the determination of conquering Deeg, Kuhmir and Bharatpur. A strong division of the army was sent ahead under the command of Jahan Khan, (the Durrani general), and Najib-ud-daulah, with these instructions, "Move into the boundaries of the accused Jat, and in every town and district held by him slay and plunder. The city of Mathura is a holy place of the Hindus, and I have heard Suraj Mal is there; let it be put entirely to the edge of the sword. To the best of your power leave nothing in that kingdom and country. Up to Akbarabad (Agra) leave nothing standing". Not satisfied with this command to his generals, the Shah directed the mace-bearers "to convey a general order to the army to plunder and slay at every place they reached. Any booty they acquired was made a free grant to them. Every person cutting off and bringing in heads of infidels should throw them down before the tent of the chief minister, wherewith to build a high tower. An account would be drawn up and five Rupees per head would be paid them from the Government funds." This was not a war but a scalp-gathering expedition on a big scale, worthy of a Red Indian Chief.

The campaign began with the siege of Ballamgarh,* as Jawahir Singh had taken his post there with two Maratha chiefs, Shamsher Bahadur and Antaji Mankeshwar. The fort was bravely defended for two days. On the third night the son of Suraj Mal and the Maratha leaders fled in disguise; a few men left in the fort to cover the flight were put to death by the Afghans. Twelve thousand Rupees, some horses, and camels fell into the hands of the victors. Ahmad Shah at once sent out parties for making a vigorous search for the fugitives in the neighbouring places. But Jawahir Singh and the Maratha leaders, dressing themselves in Qizzilbash [Persian] clothes had gone through an underground chamber into the ditch of the fort, threaded their way through the Shah's troops, and hidden in some ravines near the Jamuna. For two days and

---

* This was not originally intended by the Shah. He was prevailed upon by Ghazi-ud-din to besiege it.

nights they did not come out, even to drink water from the river.

The Shah halted for two days and ordered a general slaughter and plundering. An eye-witness, a Sayyid who was in the Afghan camp, thus describes their raids : "It was at mid-night when the camp-followers went to the attack. It was thus managed : one horseman mounted a horse and took ten to twenty others, each tied to the tail of the horse, preceding it, and drove them just like a string of camels. When it was one watch after sunrise I saw them came back. Every horseman had loaded up all his horses with the plundered property, and atop it rode girl-captives and slaves. The severed heads were tied up in rugs like bundles of grain, and placed on the heads of the captives, and thus did they return to the camp ....Daily did this manner of slaughter and plundering proceed. It was a marvellous state of things, this slaying and capturing, and no whit inferior to the day of the Last Judgment. All those heads that had been cut off were built into pillars, and the men upon whose heads bloody bundles had been brought in, were made to grind corn, and then, when the reckoning was made up, their heads too were cut off. These things went on all the way to the city of Akbarabad, nor was any part of the country spared." [Irvine's translation of a Persian MS., *Indian Antiquary*, vol. xxxvi. p. 60.]

Jahan Khan had also carried out to the letter his master's instructions. On the 28th February 1757, two days after the *holi*, he suddenly appeared before the doomed city of Mathura. The inhabitants had little apprehension of the terrible fate which was to overtake them in the midst of the gay rejoicings of the spring season. Mathura was an unfortified city, without walls and ditches, easily accessible on all sides. Suraj Mal had left there about 5000 troops, to defend the city against the Durrani generals. Though taken by sunprise, they gave a good account of themselves. After an obstinate fight in which three thousand Jats fell in the defence, the holy city was taken by the Afghans and an awful carnage began. A detachment of the Shah's troops attacked Gokul lying to the south of Mathura. About four thousand warlike Naga sannyasis, ever ready to die for their religion, assembled there; two thousand of them fell after killing an equal number of Pathans. Gokul was saved;* the Musalmans turned back terrified by militant

---
* See Sardesai's *Panipat Prakaran*, (in Marathi), p. 77.

Hindu fanaticism. But they met with no resistance at Brindaban, the earthly paradise of an
effeminate cult—the resort of females and un-
sexed males. And a terrible treatment was
meted out to it by the followers of a sturdier
faith.

That year the *holi* was played afresh by
the Durranis with the blood of the Hindus; the
whole city of Mathura burnt like a huge bonfire
such as was never lighted on the merry moonlit
night of the *holi*. Groans of outraged women
and cries of mothers from whose bosom the
fiendish soldiery tore away their children for
slaughter, echoed through the burning streets.
The blue current of the Jamuna of the poet's
imagination flowed blood-red for seven days
and yellowish for a week more. The devotees
of the degenerate Vaishnavism, who lived in
bowers beside the stream, dreaming of the
frolics of the Divine Cowherd and hearing in
ecstasy the tune of his amorous flute, met with
a fit retribution. The throats of the meek
babajis were cut in the exact manner of
Muhammadan butchers, in their dwelling
places.* In each hut lay a severed head
[of a *bairagi*], with the head of a slaughtered
cow applied to its mouth and tied to it with a

* *Bhao Bakhar*, 34.

rope round its neck.' [*Ind. Ant.* Vol. 36,
p. 62}. The Musalman inhabitants of the city
also did not fare much better at the hands of
their co-religionists. They saved their heads,
but not their honour and property. The soldiers
of the Shah so scrupulously enforced his order
that those who declared themselves Musalmans
had to strip themselves naked and show the sign
of circumcision, before they were let off. At
Mathura, about 14 days after massacre, a stark
naked figure crept out of a heap of ruins and
stood before the Mir Sahib, who penned this
horrible account, asking for a little food. On
being questioned he related the following story :
"I am a Musalman; I was a dealer in jewellery,
my shop was a large one. On the day of
slaughter...............a horseman, drawn sword
in hand, came at me and tried to kill me. I
said I was a Musalman. He said "Disclose
your privities." I undid my cloth. He continued "Whatever cash you have, give to me that
I may spare your life. I gave him my 4,000
rupees. Another came and cut me on the
stomach with his sabre. I fled and hid in a
corner" (*ibid,* p. 62). Brindaban met with a
worse fate, as the Mir Sahib's description bears
out. "Wherever you gazed you beheld only
heaps of slain. You could only pick your way

with difficulty, owing to the quantity of bodies lying about and the amount of blood spilt. *At one place, we saw about two hundred dead children in a heap. Not one of the dead bodies had a head*............The stench and fetor and effluvium in the air were such that it was painful to open your mouth or even draw a breath. Every one held his nose and stopped his mouth with his handkerchief while he spoke" [*Ibid.* p. 62].

About the middle of March, Ahmad Shah reached Mathura and was gratified to see what his generals had done. Jahan Khan and Najib-ud-daulah were exalted by the gift of *khilats* and commanded "to move on to Akbarabad where there are many wealthy men who were subjects of the Jat." The city of Agra was also depopulated by a general slaughter and the fort invested. Fortunately an epidemic broke out in the Shah's army,—150 men dying every day. It took one hundred rupees to purchase one seer of tamarind. The Shah made up his mind to march back to his country. Jahan Khan was called back from the siege of the citadel of Agra. His return march began on the 27th of March and by the 29th the Jat country was cleared of enemies. [*Ind. Ant.*, vol. xxxvi, pp. 64-65.] The campaign of Ahmad Shah was a failure from the military point of view : Suraj Mal's strength remained almost unimpaired. Deeg and Bharatpur were not taken, nor was their proud owner brought to his knee. Only two or three undefended towns were captured and the civilian population massacred. He had failed to draw out Suraj Mal and make him fight. Suraj Mal's tactics were to play a waiting game till the heat of the Indian plains would drive the Abdali away or bring upon the scene the Marathas, who were reported on the banks of the Narmada. When the Durrani threatened to advance from Mathura upon Kuhmir, he amused him with the offer of a krore of Rupees as *peshkash*, if the Shah would postpone his march. A few days after, Suraj Mal now grown bolder at the Shah's distress, wrote to him bluntly, as advised by Rupram Katari, "I cannot pay more than ten lakhs as *peshkash;* let there be peace and amity between us by your acceptance of this ; otherwise continuation of hostilities is decided upon."* Shah was glad to agree to this little, as his brave Afghans were dying by hundreds every day. A written agreement for paying ten lakhs was

---

* *Bhao Bakhar*, p. 38. For another version, see Wendel, 39 : "His good fortune so willed it that he had no need to give a penny of what he had promised."

executed by Suraj Mal, and the Durrani army retreated to Delhi. But of this sum the Jat Rajah did not pay a single penny.

Suraj Mal's alliance with Ghazi-ud-din and the Marathas.

Scarcely had the Northern tempest abated its fury, when a deluge came from the south to overwhelm Hindustan. It stopped only at the foot of the Himalayas and the bank of the Indus, threatening to engulf Islam in India; sweeping off momentarily all vestiges of the Durrani conquest, and submerging all the Muslim principalities in Northern India. The victory of the Shah was a triumph of Ghazi-ud-din's rival, the Ruhela chief Najib-ud-daulah, whom the conqueror left as his deputy in charge of the person of the titular Emperor Alamgir II and the imperial city. The office of the wazir had been taken away from him and restored to his intriguing uncle Intizam-ud-daulah. Ghazi-ud-din burnt with the thirst of revenge against the Emperor, the wazir, and the Amir-ul-umra, and to gratify it he invited the Marathas again. Raghunath Rao came to Hindustan second time (Nov. 1756—Oct. 1757), and infused a new life among the despondent Maratha chiefs. Delhi was recaptured and Ghazi-ud-

din reinstated as wazir. Najib-ud-daulah
escaped the terrible vengeance of his trium-
phant rival by throwing himself upon the mercy
of Malhar Rao Holkar, whom he called his god-
father [Dharma Pitá]. Raghunath reconquered
the Panjab, defeated the Durrani's general
Jahan Khan, and his son Taimur Shah, and
drove them across the Indus. A de facto
Maratha dominion was established throughout
Northern India.

Rajah Suraj Mal swam cautiously with
the current. He had now to make choice
between the Abdali and the Marathas : between
an enemy of his faith and his own unscrupulous co-religionists. His Pan-Hinduistic ideal
inclined him to the Maratha cause, though
their conduct inspired little confidence. But
he was too prudent to join them in their offensive
campaigns and thereby diminish his resources
and earn the enmity of his Muslim neighbours.
This informal Jat-Maratha alliance was of a
purely defensive nature against the foreign
Afghan invaders. The political views of the
great Jat chief, expressed on many occasions
during this period, deserve high admiration,
and had the Maratha Government acted upon
them their de facto sovereignty in Hindustan would have remained long unshaken.

Suraj Mal in the first place recognised the supreme necessity of doing away with the traitor Najib-ud-daulah and crushing thoroughly the colonies of Ruhela Afghans before the Durrani should find time to come to their relief: in short, the prospect of any assistance from the traitors within to the invader from Afghanistan must be cut off. Raghunath Rao and Dattaji Sindhia were also of the same view, and would have killed Najib-ud-daulah, but for the unwise and interested intervention of Malhar Rao Holkar. Secondly, Suraj Mal's desire was to make Nawab Shuja-ud-daulah the wazir of the empire in the place of Ghazi-ud-din. This was not at all dictated by personal prejudice. Ghazi-ud-din was an isolated figure in Northern India; having neither territorial nor family influence, his position was extremely weak. On the other hand Nawab Shuja-ud-daulah was practically the independent and hereditary ruler of a large and wealthy kingdom. This would bring the requisite strength for the maintenance of the dignity of the wazirat, without making him independent of the support of the Marathas. His family being of Persian origin, and of the Shia faith, he had no extra-territorial attachment like that of the Ruhela Afghans to the Abdali, so as to make him dangerous and formidable like Najib Khan.*

The inevitable crash came a couple of years later. Najib-ud-daulah, besieged for about a year at Sakkar-tal, remained unsubdued owing to the scarcely veiled enmity of Holkar to other Maratha leaders. The racial sympathy of Ruhela leaders like Hafiz Rahamat Khan, Dundi Khan, and others, was with Najib-ud-daulah and the Abdali. But they could not hitherto move owing to the fear of Nawab Shuja-ud-daulah. The designs of Holkar against Oudh having now become known, the Nawab became extremely alarmed and was driven to form a coalition with them to help Najib-ud-daulah, though he was strongly averse to their proposal of inviting the Sháh from Kabul. The unhappy Emperor Alamgir II found the throne of his ancestors not even the softest of chairs under the humiliating dictatorship of Ghazi-

---

* Malhar Rao Holkar advocated and acted upon a contrary policy, viz, to uphold the power of his *dharma-putra* Najib Khan, and with Najib's help crush Nawab Shuja-ud-daulah and conquer the kingdom of Oudh. This would, he thought, bring the whole of India from Attock to Rameshwar under the shadow of the Peshwa's umbrella, i.e., sovereignty1 (*Panipat Prakaran*, p. 103). With leaders, so much deficient in farsight and statesmanship, no nation, however brave in war, did ever succeed in building up an enduring empire.

ud-din. He sent secret letters to the Abdali entreating him to rescue him from the galling yoke of his cruel wazir and restore to him Najib-ud-daulah, the best of his gaolers. The Shah, in order to wipe off the past disgrace and avenge the defeat of his son and his generals, crossed the Indus for the fourth time. (Thursday, 25th Oct., 1759).* The wazir had his uncle Intizam-ud-daulah and the Emperor, murdered, as they were suspected of being in secret league with the invader, and raised another prince to the throne under the title of Shah Jahan II (8th Rabi II, 1173 H. = Thursday, 29th Nov. 1759). The Shah steadily marched towards Najib Khán's territory and was there joined by all the Ruhela chiefs and the Nawab Shuja-ud-daulah. But there was no unanimity in the Maratha camp. They were defeated in several small engagements; a panic set in among them. Dattaji Sindhia raised the siege of Sakkartal on 11th Dec. 1759, and came to Delhi. Consternation and dismay prevailed everywhere; the imperial capital became deserted. Those who had anything, either honour or wealth, to lose, fled southward, to the territory of the Jats, which became the hospitable asylum of both Hindu

---

* 3rd Rabi. I. 1173 H.; (*Waqa*, p. 135).

and Muhammadan fugitives. The Maratha chiefs also sent their wives and children to the protection of Rajah Suraj Mal. And with them came the harem of the wazir of Hindustan, who did not hesitate to trust the honour of his ladies to the custody of his generous foe. Suraj Mal had hitherto maintained an attitude of suspicious aloofness while the fortunes of the Marathas were in the ascendant. But at this critical stage, he was not deterred by the fear of the Abdali's vengeance from coming forward and standing by their side. The Jat had not forgotten the good done to him by Jayaji Appa Sindhia during the siege of Kuhmir, and was on the look out for an opportunity to return it. While Dattaji Sindhia was yet before the fort of Sakkartal, and Delhi was without adequate Maratha troops, Suraj Mal sent 5,000 Jats to reassure the people and aid in the defence of the city. Seeing the overwhelming superiority of the enemy, every one advised Dattaji to retreat beyond the Chambal and wait for the arrival of reinforcements. But that noble hero, conscious of the responsibility of the new rôle which his country aspired to play, resolved to demonstrate in the open field that Maharashtra would not shrink from paying the necessary price in blood for the dominion of India. He reached Delhi on the 3rd January 1760 and told Jankoji Sindhia to go home with the ladies. But the latter firmly refused, having resolved to stay and share the fate of his chief. Rupram Katari conducted the ladies to Suraj Mal's territory for safety. On the plain of Badli, about 8 miles from Delhi, Dattaji gave battle to the Abdali in the first week of Jamada II, 1173.* Long and fierce was the conflict. Inspired by their brave leader, the Marathas, reckless of life, fought with a dashing valour and perseverance never displayed before by that people in Hindustan. But the superior generalship of the Durrani and the greater staying power of the Ruhelas won the day. The Marathas left ten thousand men by the least computation dead on the field. The Jats carried Jankoji, wounded and disabled, and other survivors to the fort of Kuhmir.

The wazir Ghazi-ud-din Imad-ul-mulk, divining the probable issue, had left Delhi before the battle. Fallen from fortune he stood a suppliant at the gate of Suraj Mal's fort for an asylum which he despaired of getting any-

---

* All Persian histories including *Siyar*, say that this battle took place in the month of *Jamadi-ul-Akhir* which begins on Jan. 20, 1760. *Waqa* makes no exact entry. It took place in the last week of January.

8

where else against the wrath of the victorious
Shah. This was the same Ghazi-ud-din who,
as Father Wendel and Ghulam Ali (author of
Imad-us-Saadat) remind us, had shortly before
armed all Hindustan to destroy Suraj Mal and
sat as an implacable foe before those very walls
whose protection he now sought. Suraj Mal
came out and conducted his honourable guest
in "with all attention and respect befitting his
rank."* We are told that he richly furnished
his best palace at Bharatpur for the use of
Ghazi-ud-din, amply provided for the comfort,
security and honour of the wazir and his family,
and treated him rather like a master on a visit
to the house of a servant. In the meanwhile,
the Shah after making himself master of the
capital, demanded one krore of Rupees from
Suraj Mal as fine for his disloyal conduct. The
Jat Rajah was too prudent to supply the sinews
of war to his enemy, whose next demand, as
he knew would be the surrender of the fugitives.
He banished all idea of peace with the perfidious invader and made up his mind to spend
that sum more honourably in carrying on a war
of defence. All Hindustan rejoiced over the
fall of the Marathas, and the joy was shared
even by the Hindus who had suffered rather

---

* Wendel 51; *Imad*, 73.

more severely from their rapine than the Musalmans had done. Their character and conduct
created no confidence among the peoples of
Northern India. Their hand had been against
everybody and now everybody's hand was
against them. Rajputana had suffered so much
at their hands, that Rajput princes, like Madho
Singh of Amber, and Bijoy Singh of Marwar,
greeted the victory of the Abdali with as much
joy as their unhappy descendants evinced forty
years after, at the victory of Lord Lake over the
same race.*

But Rajah Suraj Mal who had suffered
equally at their hands, viewed the situation in
another light, and acted with greater foresight
to gain higher political ends. It was not
merely the sentiment of gratitude to the Jayaji
Appa Sindhia that determined his conduct
during this critical period. To him the annual
Maratha raid appeared to be a lesser evil than
the revival of a strong Muhammadan empire
under a new dynasty, viz., that of the Durrani.

---

* The situation is graphically described in the contemporary Maratha letters :

कारावांचा हर्ष उड़न गेला, बहुत फिकिरींत पेड़ली, काळ फिरला,
जंगीम आले जाटमाए जथाजी शिन्द्याचा कुभरील उपकार मानन वरचेवर
साह्य करीत इाने बाकी सर्व्व रजपुत सुद्धां मराठांवर उड़न आंचा वदनत्र
झालावद्दल आनन्द मानु लगले ।

He regarded the presence of the Marathas in
Northern India as a great political necessity to
keep out all foreign invaders and hold the
balance between the Hindu and the Muhammadan powers. He was too much of a practical statesman to think of an exclusive and
intolerant Hindu *swaraj* like the short-sighted
Bhao. No one was more conscious—as we shall
see hereafter—of the value of preserving the
dignity of the Mughal imperial throne, as the
only centre of attraction and the sole bond of
union among newly risen Hindu and Muhammadan principalities. So far as we are in a
position to infer from his attitude towards his
neighbours, his aim was to establish a confe-
deration of several practically autonomous
States under the headship of the Mughal
Emperor, having no other obligation than to
combine under the imperial banner in times of
common danger. He was willing to give the
Mughal empire a new lease of life, *but not of
power,* being averse to the idea of riviving the
tradition and the formidable power that it had
been in the days of Akbar and Aurangzib,
when aspiring smaller nationalities were merci-
lessly crushed under the dead-weight of the
despotic imperialism of Delhi. Any attempt in
that direction, he knew full well, could begin

only with the destruction of the Jat Power. In his scheme, the Emperor was to remain only the dignified figurehead, all initiative and lead remaining with the wazir, who should not be allowed to become powerful enough to be independent of the support of the confederates or overthrow the house of Taimur. Suraj Mal fixed his choice upon Shuja-ud-daulah, the wise and tolerant ruler of Oudh, to be the constitutional wazir of this confederated empire.

Ahmad Shah Durrani, after having put the affairs of Delhi in some order, started on 2nd February 1760 (14 Jamada II., 1173 H.), against Rajah Suraj Mal, and on 7th February invested the fort of Deeg. But this seems to have been a mere demonstration, because we find him marching away towards Mewat on the 27th (*Waqa*, 170-171). Suraj Mal came out of his stronghold and made incursions into the Doab. The Jats plundered half of Koel and stormed the citadel of the town (March 17, 1760). The daily entries in the *Waqa-i-Shah Alam Sani* about the movements of the Durranis, Jats and the Marathas give us some idea of their tactics. While the Durrani was before Deeg, a Maratha detachment advanced from the direction of Rewari in order to draw away the Afghans in pursuit. Ahmad Shah

chased them through Mewat, but they vanished
in the desert tracts beyond Rewari, and another
division of the Marathas appeared before
Bahadurgarh (about 20 miles w. of Delhi), in
the rear of the Abdali. When the Shah made
one march towards Delhi they crossed the
Jamuna and plundered Meerut and Sikandra.
The Abdali started in pursuit and chased them
towards Mathura and Agra. Again the Jats
appeared in the Doab, plundering and conquering; in short they carried on a brilliantly
planned running fight in concert with the remnants of the Maratha army (*Waqa*, 173).

Holkar and Suraj Mal, forgetting their old
animosity, had become friends under the stress
of adversity. Malhar Rao, who perhaps did
not desire that his rival Dattaji should win the
glory of defeating the Durrani, appeared tardily
on the scene after the disastrous battle of Badli
and asked Rajah Suraj Mal to join him in
giving another battle to the Afghans. But
Suraj Mal refused to move until reinforcements
came from the Peshwa. Holkar was once so
completely surprised by the Abdali general
Shah Pasand Khan at Sikandra in the Doab that
his whole detachment was cut off, and he himself managed to flee with only his clothes on,
riding upon a mare (*Siyar*, iii. 381). He never

ventured to issue out again from Deeg where
he had taken refuge in fear of the Abdali.

Aware of the impending danger that
awaited him in Hindustan, the Shah hearing
the reports of the vast Maratha preparation in
the South, busied himself in forming a coalition
of all princes, Hindu and Musalman, of
Northern India, who had suffered so much at
the hands of the southern robbers. He tried
to convince them that his mission was that of
their emancipation from the Maratha pest, and
not one of conquest and new enslavement. He
wished to detach Rajah Suraj Mal and Ghazi-
ud-din from their alliance with the Marathas,
and for that purpose sent the esteemed Ruhela
chief Hafiz Rahamat Khan with proposals of
peace* [*Tarikh-i-Husaini,* 537]. The fickle-
minded Ghazi-ud-din wavered, and Suraj Mal
gave his guest complete liberty of action.
News reached Delhi on 19th February (2nd
Rajab, 1173 H.) that peace had been concluded
between the Shah and Ghazi-ud-din Imad-ul-

---

* In the month of Shawwal 1173 H., Hafiz Rahamat Khan
went to Mathura to talk of a compromise with the Jat and
Ghazi-ud-din. *Negotiations were cut off by the Jat* on the
23rd of Shawwal (8th June, 1760), when the Marathas approached [*Waqa,* 175]. This corroborates the statement of
the *Tarikh-i-Husaini,* the only Persian history which mentions
the embassy of Hafiz-ul-mulk.

mulk, the latter having been confirmed in the
office of wazir [*Waqa,* 171]. Throughout the
eventful year of 1760 Suraj Mal fought the
Shah not only with arms but also the subtler
weapon of diplomacy and intrigue. The
Durrani wanted to invest a sordid quarrel
between himself and the Marathas over the
carcase of the Mughal empire with the more
attracting character of a Hindu-Musalman conflict for the dominion of India. The credit of
Rajah Suraj Mal lies in baffling this aim of
Afghan diplomatic activity. He carried on a
counter-intrigue with the son of his old ally,
the Nawab of Oudh. Shuja-ud-daulah did not
like the permanent establishment of the Durrani
Power in India, because it would only make his
natural enemies (the Afghans) too formidable
for his safety. Suraj Mal almost achieved his
end, but fortune befriended the Abdali. Those
who follow the complicated threads of diplomacy, and the movements of the Nawab of
Oudh during this period, cannot but hold that
the junction of the Nawab with the Shah was
a pure accident (*vide* Kasi Rao, *Asiatic Researches,* vol. iii). Suraj Mal had at first
allowed Ghazi-ud-din to swallow the bait of the
Shah, but he now made him reject it by playing
upon his fear. Though Ghazi-ud-din was a

fugitive, poor and powerless, his adhesion was anxiously sought by both parties, as it carried a great moral value, and Suraj Mal bid as high as the Shah to secure it for the Marathas.   He promised in a most solemn manner to procure his restoration to the office of wazir after the repulse of the Afghans.   Ghazi-ud-din broke the newly made treaty with the Shah and waited for the arrival of the Bhao.

———

CHAPTER VII.

SURAJ MAL'S GREAT DISAPPOINTMENT

The prelude to Panipat.

India held her breath in painful suspense for the last six months of the year 1760. The two mighty war-clouds which had so long darkened the political horizon, were now gathering impetus for a more tremendous shock. A struggle between the foreign Afghan invader and the Marathas for ascendancy in Northern India was given the appearance of a great communal and religious war by the Durrani and the Peshwa. The Afghan monarch claimed the support of all Muhammadans as the champion of decaying Islam against the aggressive Hindu reaction; while the Maratha declared his mission to be to rescue his co-religionists from their age-long servitude under oppressive Muslim rule. Agents of the Peshwa visited the Court of every Hindu prince of Rajputana, but received a cold reception and evasive replies. If the periodical visits of the Marathas when moving under the shadow of the Mughal throne meant such misery and ruin to them,—so the princes argued—what would be their fate under the undisputed sovereignty of the Southerners, relieved of the fear of the Abdali? No Rajput prince responded to the Peshwa's appeal; so little was the faith reposed in them even by their Hindu allies that Rajah Suraj Mal dared not visit the camp of the Bhao without taking beforehand from Holkar and Sindhia the most solemn pledges of his safety.

The Peshwa Balaji Baji Rao sent his brother Sadasiva, and his son Biswas Rao at the head of the largest and best-equipped army, numbering about two lakhs, that had ever crossed the Narmada to contend for the dominion of India. His parting words to his brother were: "Take this nephew of yours to Hindustan and win over all non-Afghan nobles of the empire to our side. I shall soon follow you with another strong army; through the blessings of Shri Bhawaniji, I shall make Qandahar empty of living beings, and leave no seed of the Afghan race on earth. After that only one or two Musalmans like Shuja-ud-daulah and Jafar Ali Khan [Mir Jafar of Bengal] would remain to be dealt with. If they show hostility, their existence would be wiped out; if they submit, we shall keep them like pigeons stripped of their feathers (manand kabutaran par buridah). Then placing Biswas Rao on the throne of Delhi I shall go on a pilgrimage" [*Imad*, 78]. How far these high hopes were realised is now a notorious fact in the history of India.

After his arrival on the bank of the Chambal, the Bhao sent a high-flown letter to Rajah Suraj Mal, requesting him to come without delay to the Maratha camp and unite [*Imad*., 78, 178]. Malhar Rao Holkar and Sindhia persuaded him to meet the Bhao at Agra. Suraj Mal went to the Maratha camp and was honourably received by the Bhao and other Maratha generals. From Agra they marched together to Mathura where the sight of Abdun-nabi's mosque inflamed the anger of the Bhao. He turned upon Suraj Mal and said to him, "You profess to be a Hindu; but how is it that you have kept this mosque standing so long?" Suraj Mal mildly replied : "Maharaj ! of late, the Royal Fortune of Hindustan has become fickle in her favours like a courtesan; to-night she is in the arms of one man and the next in the embrace of another. If I could be sure that I should remain master of these territories all through my life, I would have levelled this mosque down to the earth. But of what use will it be, if I to-day destroy this mosque, and to-morrow the Musalmans come, and demolish the great temples and build

four mosques in the place of this one? As
Your Excellency has come to these parts the
affair is now in your hands." The Bhao
rejoined, "After defeating these Afghans I
shall everywhere build a temple on the ruins
of mosques." However, a holy bath in the
Jamuna, after the capture of Delhi, cooled his
temper; the faqirs of the Jama Mosque shared
his charity equally with the Brahmans (*Waqa*,
178).

Everything went on well for a few days
and it was all love and cordiality between the
Jats and the Marathas. But a coolness soon
sprang up owing to a difference of opinion as
to the plan of campaign against the Abdali.
The Maratha commander-in-chief called a
council of war at Agra, and there, Suraj Mal
was asked to give his opinion as to the proper
method to be followed in the impending campaign. The Jat chief replied: "I am a mere
zamindar [peasant], and Your Highness is a
great prince; every man forms his plan according to his capacity. Whatever appears advisable in my opinion, I shall submit to you. This
is a war against a great emperor, assisted by
all the chiefs of Islam. Though Shahán-i-Shah
is a sojourner in Hindustan, his adherents
are all inhabitants of this country and lords of

large estates. If you are clever, the enemy is
cleverer....Undoubtedly it is proper that you
should act with great caution and reflection in
conducting this war. If the breeze of victory
breathes upon the cow's tail [on your standard]
it should be considered as written by the pen
of destiny on your auspicious forehead. But
war is a game of chances, holding out two
alternatives................It is wise not to be too
confident and rest in too much tranquillity. It
seems proper that your ladies, the unnecessary
baggage, and large cannon which will be of
little use in this war, should be sent off beyond
the Chambal, to the fort of Jhansi or Gwalior,
and you yourself with light-armed war-like
troops, meet the forces of the Shah. If victory
is won, much booty would come to our hands;
if the case is the reverse, we shall have our
legs [unfettered by females and other impedi-
menta] to flee away on. If you are opposed
to the idea of sending them to such a distance
or consider it impracticable, I shall vacate any
one of my four iron-like forts according to your
choice where you may keep in safety your
women and baggage, stocking it well with
provisions, so that at the moment of decisive
action your heart may not be weighed down
and your hands fettered by anxiety about the

honour of your ladies. And in this time of
famine, the road for the supply of grain must
be kept open, so that scarcity of grain may not
cause hardship to the army. I shall wait upon
your stirrup with my troops; and as my country
has been free from the depredations of the
enemy, supplies can be secured from that
quarter......It is advisable to carry on *an
irregular warfare with light cavalry* [*jang-i-
kazzaqáná*] against the Shah, and not encounter
him in pitched battles after the manner of kings
and emperors [*jang-i-Sultani*]. When the
rainy season will arrive both sides will be unable
to move from their places, and at last the Shah,
who will be in a disadvantageous position [in
comparison with us], will of himself become
distressed and return to his own country. The
Afghans, thus disheartened, would submit to
your power" [*Imad*, 179-180]. He further
advised the Bhao that "one division of the army
should be sent towards the *east*, another towards
Lahor, so that by devastating those countries,
the supply of grain to the army of the Durrani
may be cut off.* We find Rajah Suraj Mal

---

* Abdul Karim Kashmiri, the author of the *Bayán-o-Waqa*,
corroborates the above statement, *viz.* Suraj Mal's advice "that
no pitched battle should be fought with the army of the
Durrani who has been joined by all the amirs of Hindustan."

and the Marathas in communication with the Sikhs of the Panjab, the most resolute enemies of the Abdali, and with Rajah Balwant Singh of Benares, who was a thorn in the sides of the Abdali's ally Shuja-ud-daulah, evidently with a view to prevent supplies being sent from Oudh and the Panjab to the Abdali's camp or to cause diversions in the rear and left flank of the invader.

All the chiefs of the Maratha army having praised his plan, declared with one voice that this was their opinion too. "We are ourselves predatory fighters [*kazzaq*] ; so this mode of fighting can bring no blame upon us. Our skill lies in flight, *i.e.*, evading blows. If the enemy cannot be conquered by stratagem, it is not wise to be entangled in a difficult situation and throw ourselves into destruction." But the arrogant Bhao looked upon this mode of fighting as unworthy of a prince like himself—the brother of the Peshwa, whose mere servants and agents had already achieved such brilliant exploits in Hindustan. He regarded this advice as the outcome of the senility of Holkar and other aged chiefs and the stupidity of the Jat upstart. All the chiefs thus dis-

---

He says that Suraj Mal advised the Bhao to leave his baggage at *Akbarabad*. [MS. p. 289].

appointed, and insulted went out, saying to themselves that some great reverse would bring this fiery and rash leader to his senses and make him more attentive to the opinions of his lieutenants (*Imad.* 180-181). Suraj Mal's enthusiasm for his Maratha allies somewhat cooled down and an injurious misunderstanding was avoided only by the tact of the other Maratha chiefs. They induced the Bhao to be more considerate to the Jat chief, whose adherence was represented to be of primary importance for the success of their enterprise.

Rajah Suraj Mal, accompanied by Ghazi-ud-din, joined the Bhao with 8,000 Jats. The allied army reached Delhi in July, 1760* and laid siege to it. Ghazi-ud-din threw himself into the task of capturing the city with his characteristic energy and resourcefulness. When the imperial capital fell, he had his revenge upon the Mughals [*i.e.,* Abdalis] and the Marathas their plunder. So much booty fell into their hands, that none remained poor among them (Sardesai, *Panipat,* p. 162). Ghazi-ud-din brought out of the imperial seraglio a

* The *Tarikh-i-Muzaffari* (MS. p. 180), gives the date of the Bhao's arrival as 9th Zihijja, 1173 A. H. = Wednesday, 23rd July, according to the *Waqa-i-Shah Alam Sani*, 10th Zihijja (p. 178).

9

prince of the royal line, seated him on the
throne, restored order in the city, and for the
first few days discharged the duties of the wazir,
which office was believed by all to have naturally reverted to him. But the Bhao suddenly
signified his unwillingness to recognise Ghazi-
ud-din as wazir. He conferred the title of
Raje Bahadur upon Naro Shankar, appointed
him commandant of the fort, and governor of
the capital, and formally invested him with the
office of wazir. Rajah Suraj Mal's word was
thus violated; he strongly represented to the
Bhao that the new appointment was unjust and
injudicious, and prayed for the reinstatement of
Ghazi-ud-din. Holkar and Sindhia supported
the Rajah's representation. But nothing could
shake the haughty obstinacy of the Bhao.
These disappointed chiefs remarked with grave
concern : "Our prestige in Hindustan is gone.
What will it lead to?" Suraj Mal came to his
mentor, the priest-politician Rupram Katari,
and told him that the Bhao had utterly dis-
regarded their joint and earnest representation
to restore the office of wazir to Ghazi-ud-din :
"It is no good staying here; some mishap may
come. It is prudent to try by every means to
draw our heads out of it." But Sindhia and
Holkar were encamped close by, there was no

way of escape. His mind became disturbed by anxiety.

The folly and perversity of the Bhao did not end there. The gilded silver ceiling of the *Diwan-i-am*, beautifully inlaid with jewels, attracted the greedy eye of the rude Southerner. At heart he deliberated "Here is this ceiling; I shall strip it off and melt it to pay the daily wages of my troops. And *in its place I shall make one of wood!* Having first decided he called Sindhia, Holkar and Suraj Mal to hear their advice about it. Nothing does so much credit to the heart of Rajah Suraj Mal as the following passionate appeal to the Bhao to spare this last relic of imperial grandeur. He said "Bhao Sahib! this room of the Emperor's throne is a place of dignity and veneration. Even Nadir Shah and Ahmad Shah Durrani, who had laid their grasp upon many a precious thing of the imperial palace, spared this ceiling. The Emperor and the amirs are now in your hands. We shall not see this [disfiguring of the place] with our own eyes. It can bring us no credit but only the odium of disloyalty.* To this humble prayer of mine about it to-day,

---

* Suraj Mal, though a habitual rebel from necessity, always considered himself, like other virtually independent rulers of his time, a subject of the Mughal Emperor.

you should kindly pay due consideration. If
you are short of funds, you have only to order
me. I am ready to pay you five lakhs of
Rupees [for sparing the ceiling]." The Bhao
paid no heed to these words, thinking that he
would get more by melting the ceiling. This
heartless act of vandalism was committed under
his orders, the ceiling was taken down and
weighed; but to his great disappointment the
bullion was found only worth three lakhs of
Rupees. Rajah Suraj Mal could restrain himself no longer; he went to the Bhao and burst-
ing with honest indignation said, "Bhao
Sahib! you have destroyed [the sanctity of]
the throne while I am present here, and thereby
brought odium upon me [as well]. Whenever
I make any request on any affair, you disregard
and reject it. We at heart profess to be Hindus.
Do you attach this much importance to the
Jamuna's water which you touched [as a
solemn proof of your alliance with me]?"

In October 1760, the Bhao having decided
to march against the Nawab of Kunjpura (a
place 78 miles north of Delhi, commanding a
ford on the Jamuna), summoned his chiefs,
Holkar, Sindhia, Suraj Mal and others, to
consult them. Suraj Mal took this opportunity
to vent his embittered feelings and with great

bluntness said to the Bhao: "You have taken off the silver ceiling against our wishes. Replace it to its former position......Give back to Ghazi-ud-din the office of the wazir, which of right belongs to him. Sindhia, Holkar and I myself are all embarrassed on this account, and our honour and good name have been affected by it. From this time, be kind enough to give greater consideration to our little requests. In that case you may consider me and all my resources at your disposal. I shall continue to help and supply you with provisions as before. You should not leave Delhi. Mature your plans from this place......It is not advisable to be now entangled in the affair of Kunjpura." These wholesome but unpalatable words of advice fell like a sprinkling of clarified butter [ghee] into the smouldering fire. "What!" replied the Bhao in haughty disdain, "have I come from the South relying on *your* strength? I will do what I like. You may stay here or go back to your own place. After overthrowing the Ghilcha [the Abdali], I shall come to a reckoning with you." Hearing these harsh words, Sindhia and Holkar in dismay sat motionless and dumbfounded.

Suraj Mal, greatly disgusted and mortified, left the assembly and returned to his place, curs-

ing his own folly in coming to the Maratha camp.
He was virtually a prisoner and his position was
one of great danger. Sindhia and Holkar had
pledged their word of honour for his safety, and
upon their fidelity depended his only chance
of escape. These two chiefs, now greatly
concerned, met secretly and thus deliberated:
"We have brought the Jat here by pledging our
word of honour to him; the design of the Bhao
is very bad. Balwant Rao and the Bhao have
secretly planned to arrest Suraj Mal Jat, imprison
him and plunder his camp. Suraj Mal must
be anyhow sent away in safety, so that the
blame of faithlessness may not be laid on us.
Let the master [the Bhao] do what he can
[to punish us] on this account." Having
deliberated thus, they sent for Rupram Katari,
the vakil of the Jats, and advised him thus:
"Do flee from this place to-night by any means.
The encampment of the Bhao Sahib lies at a
distance ; without letting him know it, slip out
in silence. The pledge of honour between you
and us is thus redeemed; say not a single word
to us after this"; saying these words the two
chiefs pulled their own ears in repentance and
made a silent vow not to compromise their
honour and involve themselves in such difficult

situations again for the benefit of such a haughty and faithless master.

Rupram Katari came back to the Jat camp and explained the whole situation to his master. Rajah Suraj Mal found himself between Scylla and Charybdis, the Bhao on one side and the Durrani on the other. He said to Rupram, "If by fortune we manage to escape to-night, we incur the enmity of the Bhao. Should he succeed by chance in beating the Durrani, my ruin is inevitable. If he is in earnest, I shall find no refuge and none will be able to save me. Should I stay here, in fear of this future danger, I become a prisoner. Both courses are beset with difficulties. What is to be done now?" Rupram replied, "You know the proverb— Escaping one bad astral conjunction in one's horoscope means a further lease of twelve years of life. Both the Bhao and the Durrani are equally strong and equally implacable enemies. Who knows which of them would come out successful? Till then, in our own place we shall sit silent, holding our breath. Whatever is destined ahead for us by God must be good. Why do you trouble yourself now by the thought of the future [which is uncertain]? Let what may come come afterwards; but to-night we must flee." Rupram's cool head and clear vision chalked out the right path for Suraj Mal, whose indecision might otherwise have brought down disaster on his head at this critical point.

When three hours of the night had passed away, the Jats silently struck their tents, packed their baggage, and marched off, with the connivance of Sindhia and Holkar, in the direction of Ballamgarh, the nearest Jat stronghold, 22 miles to the south of Delhi. Malhar Rao, whose policy was to run with the hare and hunt with the hounds, sent his Diwan Gangoba Tatiya to the Bhao, after Suraj Mal had covered four *kos*, to inform him that Suraj Mal without telling anything to anybody, had gone away; and that their forces had been sent in pursuit, and that the Bhao should send his own army to join them in the chase. Suraj Mal safely reached Ballamgarh; the Maratha troops who went in pursuit came back after plundering some bazars. The Bhao bit his lip in anger, and exclaimed in public, "God willing, if the Durrani is defeated, of what greater weight [the affair of] the Jat can be?"*

---

* These interesting and accurate details are taken from *Bhao Sahib chi Bakhar* (in Marathi, pp. 114-121) of which the above sketch is a free translation. The learned Maratha historian Mr. Sardesai gives four causes of the defection of the Jats : (i) the families of the Marathas were not sent to Gwalior; (ii) the wazirship was not given to Mir Shihab-ud-din

Panipat and its sequel.

The defeat of the Marathas at Panipat was not an accident but a foregone conclusion. They had been beaten by the Shah in the field of diplomacy, several months before their over-throw in the trial of arms at Panipat. Not to speak of winning the "non-Afghan Muslim

---

[i.e. Ghazi-ud-din Imad-ul-mulk] ; (iii) the removal of the silver ceiling of the darbar room; and (iv) the management of Delhi was not given to them. [*Panipat Prakaran*, p. 166]. The first point is undisputably true. The second is mentioned expli-citly in the Maratha chronicles only, but not in the Persian histories, which however make certain statements leading to confirm this, as we shall see next. As regards the third, the author of the *Siyar* says : "What had so much shocked the Jat prince was this :—They [the Marathas] stripped the imperial Hall of Audience of its wainscoting which was of silver, elegantly enamelled, and had sent it to the mint; and without any respect for things held sacred by all mankind, they had laid their sacrilegious hands upon the gold and silver vessels consecrated to the use of the monument of the sacred foot-prints, and of the mausoleum of saint Nizam-ud-din; nor did they spare Muhammad Shah's mausoleum, which they stripped of its incensory, candelabras, lamps and other utensils, all of solid gold, ... all of which were torn away and sent to the mint." [*Siyar* iii. 385-386]. *For the last point, bearing against Suraj Mal, Mr. Sardesai gives no authority*, and he silently passes over the treacherous design of the Bhao, which is attributed to him by the Persian historians as well as by the *Marathi bakhars*. The author of *Imad-us-Saadat* (Pers. text, p. 181) says that the Bhao demanded *two krores of Rupees* from Suraj Mal, and kept him under suspicious watch and that the Jat Rajah owed his deliverance to Malhar Rao.

nobles" as instructed by the Peshwa, the Bhao
had made an enemy of the only powerful Hindu
Rajah who had come to serve him loyally and
placed all his resources at the disposal of the
Marathas. The value of Suraj Mal's adherence
had hitherto been hardly appreciated by the
Bhao; but *one day's hostility* of the Jat brought
him to his senses. "Rajah Suraj Mal, accompanied by Ghazi-ud-din Imad-ul-mulk, marched
away to Tughlaqabad; grain became very dear
[at Delhi], and next day the Marathas went
to make a compromise with and pacify Imad-
ul-mulk and Suraj Mal Jat"* [*Waqa,* 178].
A large tract of the country about Delhi had
been so completely ruined by constant ravages,
that the Durrani became dependent on the
country of the Ruhelas for his supplies and
the Maratha army drew theirs from Suraj Mal's
kingdom. The foolishness and treachery of
the Bhao now dried up this inexhaustible source.
So it is no wonder that the Marathas had to
fight on an empty stomach at Panipat.

Rajah Suraj Mal's position was so conspicuous and his attitude so important that even
his neutrality was considered by both the

---

* The date is somewhat confused and indefinite. It was
between Safar 14, and Rabi I. 15, 1174 H. (*i.e.* Sept. 25—Oct.
25, 1760.)

parties as worth securing. He could not be
persuaded to join the Marathas again. He
thanked his star and the wisdom of his priest
Rupram for his recent escape. The vigilant
Abdali at once seized this opportunity to make
an attempt to win over Suraj Mal. He knew
that it was more easy for him to beat the Maratha
army than to capture the Jat strongholds, and
that his enemies could not be decisively crushed
till they had been deprived of such an impregnable base of operations as the country of Suraj
Mal. He had, without success, tried several
times before to detach the Jat Rajah from the
Marathas. He now opened fresh negotiations
with the Jat, through Nawab Shuja-ud-daulah.
"Rajah Devi Dutt, Ali Beg [of Georgia], and
others came, on behalf of Shuja-ud-daulah to
the Jat for negotiating the terms of a compromise. The Jat agreed to it, wore the khilat
sent by Shuja-ud-daulah and the Shah, and
exchanged oaths." The practical result of this
treaty was to ensure only the neutrality of Suraj
Mal, but not his active assistance on the Afghan
side. In spite of the harsh treatment of the
Bhao, the sympathy of Suraj Mal continued to
be with the Marathas. He entered into this
alliance with the Abdali only to provide against
an emergency, and because complete isolation

was too dangerous for any State in the then prevailing political condition of India.

Suraj Mal entertains Maratha refugees from Panipat.

After the fearful wreck of the magnificent Maratha army at Panipat (14 Jany., 1761), the survivors fled southwards. In their hour of misfortune, the very peasants stripped them of their arms, property and clothes. Naked and destitute the Maratha soldiers entered the country of the Jats who welcomed them to their hospitable doors and provided medicine, clothes and food for their relief. If Suraj Mal had not forgotten the wrongs done to him by the Marathas, and befriended them in their hour of adversity, very few of them would have crossed the Narmada to tell the woeful tale of Panipat to the Peshwa. And this he did at the imminent risk of incurring the enmity of the Abdali staking his life and fortune at the impulse of a pious and noble sentiment which would have done honour to the stoutest heart of Rajputana in her heroic days. All Muslim writers* extol the generosity of Suraj Mal; the Maratha writers also acknowledge this : "At

---

* *Imad*, p. 203; *Bayan-o-Waqa*, MS. p. 293.

Mathura they entered the territory of the Jats. Suraj Mal, impelled by the Hindu religious sentiment, sent out his troops to protect them, and relieved their distress in every way by distributing food and clothes to them. At Bharatpur was the Jat queen, who showed much charity to the fugitives. Thirty to forty thousand men were fed here for eight days; the Brahmans being given milk, *peda*, and other sweetmeats. For eight days all were entertained in great comfort. A proclamation was made to the citizens that quarters and food were to be given to the fugitives in the manner most convenient to each. None was to be put to trouble. In this way the Jat spent altogether ten lakhs of Rupees. Many men were thus saved. Shamsher Bahadur* came wounded to the fort of Kuhmir; Suraj Mal tended him with the utmost care; but he died in grief for the Bhao" [Sardesai, *Panipat Prakaran*, 205]. After relieving their distress, and pacifying their hearts, Suraj Mal gave one Rupee in cash, a piece of cloth, and one *seer* of grain to every ordinary man [common soldier and camp-

---

* He was the son of the Peshwa Baji Rao I. by a Muslim concubine and professed the Muhammadan faith. The author of *Imad-us-Saadat* says that Suraj Mal built a *masjid* and a house over his grave. (Pers. text, p. 203).

followers], and sent them to Gwalior" [*Bayan*, MS. 293].

Did Suraj Mal plunder Naro Shankar ?

Francklin, presumably on the authority of Munna Lal, gives a completely wrong version of this affair which amounts to calumny : "*It is said*, that he [Naro Shankar, the Maratha governor] was stopped in the way by order of Suraj Mal Jat, stripped of all his ill-gotten wealth and left to pursue his journey, in equal distress and terror, to Akbarabad" [*Shah-Aulum*, 23]. This hearsay is opposite the truth, as we learn from the letter of a Maratha fugitive who was with Naro Shankar : "Naro Shankar and Balaji Palandé, with two to four thousand troops had fled beforehand from Delhi. On the way they met Malhar Rao Holkar who had about eight or ten thousand troops with him. We are now staying with Holkar at Gwalior. At Bharatpur Suraj Mal took the greatest care of our safety and comfort. We stopped there for fifteen to twenty days. He paid us great respect and attention, and said with folded hands 'I am one of your own household, your servant; this kingdom is yours' and such other words. Alas ! there are so few like him. He sent his chiefs to escort us to Gwalior"

[Sardesai, *Panipat*, p. 193]. In another letter, Nana Fadnavis remarked: "The Peshwa's heart was greatly consoled by Suraj Mal's conduct" [*ibid*]. Nothing more is required than a mention of these facts to wipe off this unjust stain upon the memory of the great Jat ruler. To believe Francklin in the face of this unanimous Maratha assertion to the contrary, is to act in defiance of the laws of historic evidence.

After the victory of Panipat Ahmad Shah, having entered Delhi in triumph, contemplated an expedition against Suraj Mal who had given refuge to the Marathas. The Jat Rajah sent Nagar Mal to turn away the wrath of the Abdali (*Waqa*, 184), and hold out offers of submission. Suraj Mal who knew well that the war-worn Afghans would be reluctant to pass another summer in India, was not prepared to sacrifice much for peace. The negotiations were protracted from March to May, 1761. But during all this while, with cynical indifference to the presence of the Conqueror of Panipat at Delhi, he was engaged in capturing Agra, the second capital of the empire, from the Musalmans. After a siege of 20 days the conquest was achieved. Suraj Mal carried off 50 lakhs in the pillage of the city. [Wendel, Fr. MS., 46-47]. Only five days before the Shah's departure from

Delhi, "news arrived that the troops of Suraj Mal had forced the qiladar of Akbarabad to evacuate the fort, and entered it" (11 Shawwal, 1174 = 16th May, 1761; *Waqa*, 185). As a solace to the Shah, he paid one lakh of Rupees in cash and executed a new bond for five lakhs to be paid *afterwards, i.e.,* never. The claim to the five lakhs promised by Suraj Mal in 1757 was tacitly dropped. The rainy season was coming in, and the Sikhs had risen in his rear; the Shah was only too glad to get this much from the stubborn Jat. On the 16th Shawwal (21st May, 1761) he started from the garden of Shalimar* (outside Delhi) for his country, leaving Suraj Mal to pursue with impunity his more ambitious designs of aggression.

---

* This Shalimar stood near Badli (9 miles n. w. Delhi on E. I. Ry.).

CHAPTER VIII.

REIGN OF SURAJ MAL

Suraj Mal's conquest of Hariana.

The battle of Panipat was followed by a comparative calm—a quiet of exhaustion; Northern India at least ceased for some time to be the battle-field of the Afghan and the Maratha. The rapidly rising Sikh common-wealth served as a break-water to the Abdali invasion, while in the south Haidar Ali and the Nizam kept the Marathas busy. An inter-regnum, if not anarchy, prevailed in the empire. At Delhi Najib-ud-daulah watched over an empty throne and a widowed capital. The Emperor Shah Alam II was an exile in his own dominion, a protege and pensioner of Shuja-ud-daulah. The ruler of Oudh had his eye upon the subah of Bihar and was busy in intrigues with Mir Qasim, the Nawab of Bengal who was preparing for a manly struggle to throw off the English yoke. The victorious Muslim coalition broke up owing to the irrecon-cilable enmity between Shuja-ud-daulah and the Ruhela chiefs. Panipat had only shattered the

10

extravagant dream of the Maratha but brought
no permanent peace to Islam. The moment the
Maratha was overthrown, the Jat came in and
challenged her victorious champion who, weary
and exhausted, shrank from the contest and
retired beyond the Indus. The stubborn Jat
courage revived confidence in the prostrated
Hindu mind, and Islam was again thrown on
the defensive.

Suraj Mal wanted to seize these few
moments of his enemies' respite for carrying out
his two-fold object which he had long in view;
first to interpose a solid block of a Jat confederacy between the Abdali and the Ruhelas,
extending from the Ravi to the Jamuna;
secondly to expel Najib-ud-daulah from Delhi,
restore his protege the ex-wazir Ghazi-ud-din to
his former position and power, and through
him control the policy of the empire. But he
decided not to attack Delhi first but simply cover
it during his contemplated campaign. The
tract of Hariana dominated by powerful Muslim
jagirdars presented a dangerous gap between
the Sikh commonwealth and his own principality. Barred in the south and west by the
Rajput predominance and in the east* by the

---

* Suraj Mal's territory in the east touched the possessions
of the Ruhelas. The districts of Koel (Aligarh), Jaleswar and

Ruhela power, he sought the expansion of his dominion in this tract and the districts around Delhi, mainly inhabited by the Jats.

This was a move in the right direction for more reasons than one. The Jats of the Jamuna were being drawn as if by racial instinct towards the Jats of the Five Rivers. The two branches of one mighty stream which had bifurcated at Sindh in the dim days of hoary antiquity, now turned to meet again moved by the impulse of common blood as well as common political and religious interests. The Jat ruler was alive to the danger which was sure to arise from the consolidation of the Ruhela ascendancy at Delhi and the consequent growth of another Rohilkhand on his northern frontier (Mewat), driving a mortal wedge between it and the Sikh territory. The possession of this tract would, above all, enable both the Jat and the Sikh to make a firm stand with their backs upon one another, and fight confidently against the Ruhela and

---

Etah formed part of his kingdom. "On this side of the Jamuna from the gates of Delhi to the Chambal, there was no other government than his own, and towards the Ganges the condition was almost the same. After the reduction of Agra fort, he had not more to do for the extension of his dominion on the south. He then turned his thoughts to west of Delhi. He had also destined that country [Hariana] to be made a kingdom for his son Jawahir Singh" (Wendel, 45, 48).

the Abdali. Suraj Mal sent his eldest son Jawahir to conquer Hariana while another army was sent under his youngest son Nahar Singh to establish his authority in the Doab, and watch the movement of the Eastern Ruhela chiefs. Jawahir directed his attack upon Farrukhnagar, held by a powerful Baloch chief, Musavi Khan. But he having failed to capture it, Suraj Mal himself came with all his forces and big artillery and laid siege to it. Two months passed away and Musavi Khán being hard pressed, consented to surrender it "if Suraj Mal would take an oath on the Ganges water not to hinder his departure."* But the Jat on this occasion made the same unscrupulous use of the sanctity of the Ganges as that of the Qurán by some Muslim rulers.

The Baloch chief was made a prisoner and sent to Bharatpur. Sin prospered for a while only to make the retribution more terrible and shocking. Rewari, Garhi, Harsaru and Rohtak

---

* Wendel 49, the *Waqa* (p. 198) make entries which tell us that Najib Khan was coming to relieve Musavi Khan. But on the 19th Jamada I, 1177 A. H. (Nov. 25, 1763 A.D.), news reached him at Safdar Jang that "Suraj Mal Jat, having deceitfully [*áj-ráh-i-dagha*] imprisoned Musavi Khán Baloch, had captured Farrukhnagar by forcing the garrison to evacuate it." This seems to suggest that Musavi Khán was seized *before* the capture of the fort—perhaps during negotiation.

had already fallen into the hands of Suraj Mal.*
He now turned his arms against Bahadurgarh,
about 12 kos to the west of Delhi, the stronghold of another powerful Baloch chief Bahadur
Khán. In his distress, the Baloch chief
appealed for help to Najib-ud-daulah, who,
however judged it inexpedient to provoke a war
with Suraj Mal, before the arrival of the Abdali.

Death of Suraj Mal.

But a breach between Suraj Mal and Najib-
ud-daulah was unavoidable. About this time
another division of the Jat army under the
command of Nahar Singh, (the youngest son
of Suraj Mal), Balaram and other renowned
commanders, was carrying on war in the Doab,
wresting many remarkable places from the
officials of the Mughal Government. Suraj Mal,
knowing his chances of success greater, was

---

* All these places remained possessions of his house till
they were recovered for the Emperor Shah Alam II, by Mirza
Najaf Khan; after defeating Rajah Nawal Singh Jat. Their
positions, Rohtak, lat. 28°-55′, long. 76°-35′; Rewari, 28°-10′,
76°-40′; *Garhi Harsaru* 28°-35′, 76°-55′, about 8 miles east of
Farrukhnagar. It is said that in an assault upon Garhi Harsaru,
Suraj Mal's elephant, urged against the huge wooden gate
of the fort turned back exhausted and unsuccessful. Sardar
Sitaram, the Jat Ajax, seeing this, rushed forward with an
axe and hewed down the gate with great intrepidity. This
is one of his numerous feats of strength remembered by his
descendants, still living in the ruined castle of his, Kotman.

eager to come at once to a reckoning with Najib-
ud-daulah, while it was the policy of the latter
to postpone the trial of issue till the Abdali
would be in a position to come to his aid.   The
Ruhela chief dissembled and employed supple-
ness; but the shrewd Jat would not let this
opportunity slip away, and determined to strike
a decisive blow at his enemy at the moment of
his weakness. , "The Jat prince, finding from
this cautious behaviour of Najib-ud-daulah that
he was afraid of a war, became the more daring
and he demanded the *faujdari* of the Gird or
Circuit (the governorship of the districts around
the capital). [*Siyar*, iv. 30].

Najib-ud-daulah knew what it meant; it
was was like a demand for the surrender of the
outer approaches of a stronghold to the enemy.
With Suraj Mal* in possession of the Belt round
the capital, Delhi would become only a spacious
prison for him and the descendants of Timur.

The Afghan chief unwilling to see matters
come to a rupture sent Yaqub Ali Khán,

---

* Abdul Karim Kashmiri, author of the *Bayan-o-Waqá*,
says: "After seizing the persons of Musavi Khán and other
Baloch chiefs and sending them to Deeg, he sent words to
Najib-ud-daulah, telling him that he should leave the capital
and cede to him the Mian Doab. Although Najib Khán
compelled by necessity, offered to cede Sikandra and other
parganas, Suraj Mal was not satisfied." [*Bayan*, MS., 302.]

(brother of Shah Wali Khán, wazir of Ahmad Shah Abdali) as envoy "to endeavour by mild words to bring matters to a pacification, so as to smother the seeds of tumult and war." He took with him as a present two pieces of beautiful Multan chintz, painted in yellow and pink. If we are to believe the author of the *Siyar*, the present proved more acceptable than the message of peace.* Yaqub Ali went to the Jat for negotiation on the 14th Jamada II. but returned unsuccessful after an absence of four days (17th Jamada II, 1177 A.H. = 23rd Dec., 1763 A.D; *Waqa*, p. 199).

Driven to hostilities by the unjust demands of the Jat, Najib-ud-daulah, with an army of ten to twelve thousand horse and foot, and accompanied by his two sons Afzal Khán, Zabita Khán, and also by some other Ruhela leaders of note, such as Mahmud Khán Bangash (*Siyar*, iv. 31), crossed the Jamuna [19th

---

* According to the *Siyar*, Yaqub Ali was abruptly dismissed on the very day of his arrival, "with words that if he came for a pacification only he had better not come at all [*Siyar*, iv. 31]. There is no truth in it as is proved by the more definite and authentic entry in the *Waqá*. However there is no doubt that Suraj Mal's demand was extravagant and his attitude towards Najib-ud-daulah was haughty and unyielding. Father Wendel briefly remarks "But Suraj Mal demanded war" ....(Orme MS., 49.)

Jamada II = 24th Dec., 1763] to give battle to
the "proud uncircumcised." Suraj Mal leaving his son Jawahir at Farrukhnagar to look
after the recently conquered territories, had,
several days before, crossed the Jamuna. Both
armies now took up positions on the banks of
the Hindan (a small tributary of the Jamuna),
about seven kos, east of Delhi. The Jat army
entrenched themselves and planted their guns
on the other [eastern] bank of the Hindan. In
the earlier part of the day several petty engagements took place in which the Jats had the
better of the encounter. Towards the closing
hours of the day, Suraj Mal crossed the Hindan
with six thousand troops and attacked the
Muslim lines. An action took place in which
about 1,000 men were slain on both sides. In
the heat of action Suraj Mal Jat with thirty
horsemen only fell upon the centre of the
Mughals and Baloches and was slain" (Sunday,
19th Jamada II, 1777 A.H. = Dec. 25, 1763
A.D. *Waqa*, p. 199). So admirable was the
discipline of the Jat army, that though the news
of Suraj Mal's death spread through the ranks,
not a single soldier was shaken. They stood
on their ground as if nothing had happened,
while the Musalman army broke and fled to
their camp. Afterwards the Jat army left the

field with the mastery of victors [*Siyar*, iv. 32]. This was too great an event to be believed by the enemy. "His corpse did not come in to their hands. The news of his death was not verified at that time. Najib Khán remained standing on his ground throughout the night for the safety of his army. At midnight the Jats retreated from the opposite bank of the Hindan. Not a trace of the Jat army was to be found, and then only was the news of the death of Suraj Mal believed.* Najib Khán returned to the capital." [*Bayan*, MS. p. 303.]

Rajah Suraj Mal, "the eye and the shining taper of the Jat tribe—the most redoubtable prince in Hindustan for the last 15 years"— thus disappeared from the stage of life leaving his work half-done. His was a towering personality and a transcedental genius to which homage has been paid by every eighteenth century historian. "He was," says Father Wendel, "in one word, wise, politic, valiant and grand, above his birth and to the point of being admired and feared by foreigners" [Fr. MS. 51.]

---

* Najib Khán's caution is perhaps justified by the saying in the country-side "Don't believe a Jat to be dead till his thirteenth day [*Shārdhdha* ceremony] is over!"

APPENDIX

DETAILS OF THE DEATH OF SURAJ MAL

Documents and tradition by no means agree as to the manner of Suraj Mal's death. Father Wendel, writing within five years of the date of this incident, says, "One day Suraj Mal getting news that a large body of the enemy was coming to pounce upon Nahar Singh (his son and destined successor), who was in that expedition, marched in haste with a few thousand horsemen, to succour him. Unfortunately, in passing through a ditch (*nullah*) which the river Hindan had left there, he was surprised on both sides by a party of Ruhela infantry—who had been placed in ambush there. By a furious discharge of their muskets ...on the Jats still in disorder, they brought down Suraj Mal with all his retinue who lay there on the plain either slain or wounded" (French MS., 50). Suraj Mal died on Sunday 25th Dec. 1763 A.D. and the event was recorded in the *Waqa* only two days after its occurrence, *i.e.*, Tuesday. Besides those quoted in the text it contains the following details: "Sayyid Muhammad Khán Baloch cut off the *head* and a hand from the body of the Jat, and brought and *kept them with himself for two days*. After that these were taken to the presence of Nawab Najib-ud-daulah. Then only could he believe that Suraj Mal was dead." [*Ibid*]. The *Siyar* narrates the event as follows : "He was galloping up and down, to examine the field of battle, and to make his choice, after which he stopped awhile to make his considerations. Whilst he was thus standing, there passed by him some of Afzal Khán's troops who having been beaten by Mansāram Jat—who commanded Suraj Mal's vanguard, were flying by troops one after another. The few people that were with Suraj Mal, represented the impropriety of his remaining so near the enemy with only a few friends about his person; and Kalimullah, with Mirza Saif-ullah respectfully insisted on his returning. He paid no attention to what they said and seemed intent only on considering the enemy's motions. They both renewed their instances and he gave no answer; but sending for another horse, he mounted and stood in the same place. Whilst he was mounting, it happened that Sayyid Muhammad Khán Baloch, better known under the name of Seydo, was just flying close by him with about 40 or 50 troopers; when one of these turning about recollected Suraj Mal's features, and advancing to Seydo, he cried out that "the Thakur Sahib [Suraj Mal] was standing there ......Seydo hearing these words turned about and fell upon Suraj Mal; and one of his men singling the Jat prince smote him with his sabre, and cut off one of his arms, which bye the bye was maimed and actually entangled. Whilst the arm was falling off, two other men rushed together upon him and dispatched him, as well as Mirza Saifullah and Rajah Amar Singh and two or three more. The few remaining fled towards their own people. But one of Seydo's troopers taking up the severed arm, fixed it on the spear of a standard and carried it to Najib-ud-daulah. The latter could not believe it to be Suraj Mal's and continued doubting it for *two whole days* together. But it was past doubt in the Jat army, which had retreated with still a formidable countenance. The second [?] day Najib-ud-daulah, having received a visit from Yaqub Khán, showed him the arm, and the latter at once affirmed it to be Suraj Mal's not only from the maimed appearance but also from the sleeve which was on it, and which happened to be that very calico of Multan which Suraj Mal had put on in his presence. After this the death was ascertained and it became public" [p. 32]. The tradition as recorded by Col. Tod (*Rajasthàn*, 1223), and improved upon by Growse that Suraj Mal was ambushed by a party of Najib Khán's troops, *while hunting defiantly in the royal preserve near Shahdara,* is better suited to a heroic ballad of the Middle Ages, like *Chevy Chase* than true history.

It is proper to examine critically the above statements for getting an approximation to truth. Nothing can be more contemporary than the entry in the *Waqá,* yet some of its details cannot bear common sense criticism. Sayyid Muhammad Baloch, who must have known the value of his trophy *i.e.,* the head and hand of Suraj Mal, cannot be believed to have kept them uselessly *with himself for two days.* He did not cut off the head which could have at once settled all doubt; but only one hand, which was identified perhaps two days after by Yaqub Ali Khán.

Did Suraj Mal fall into an ambush as Father Wendel says? It is quite likely that the surprise of the reconnoitring party under Suraj Mal by Najib Khán's retreating troopers was taken as an ambuscade. But the versions of the Father and the author of the *Siyar* do not tally with that of the *Bayan* and the *Waqá-i-*

Shah Alam Sani. The *Bayan* says that Suraj
Mal led six thousand troops to the attack; and
according to the *Waqá* 1,000 men died on both
sides and Suraj Mal met his death in a rash
charge upon the enemy's centre.   This is much
more credible than the version of the *Siyar*, and
therefore cannot be justly rejected.   The narrative in the text appears to be the nearest
approach to truth.

CHAPTER IX.

LEGACY OF SURAJ MAL

Rajah Suraj Mal and his family.

Rajah Suraj Mal was about 55 years old
at the time of his death. He had virtually
exercised the sole management of the affairs of
the State for over twenty years before and after
the death of Badan Singh. By his four wives,
he left five* sons :—Jawahir Singh, Ratan
Singh, Nawal Singh, Ranjit Singh and Nahar
Singh. The first two were born of a lady,
popularly reputed to have been a Rajputni,
possibly of *Gaurua* caste, the third was the son
of a Malin (gardener class) mother, the last two
were born of the women of his own tribe. †

---

* Wendel says four; but it is a common fact of history
supported by the authority of Persian histories that Ranjit
Singh, who succeeded his brother Rajah Nawal Singh, was
also a son of Suraj Mal. This makes the number five. The
narrative of Wendel, though extremely valuable as a contemporary history, is vitiated by some inaccuracies about well-
known facts.

† Col. Tod says that Jawahir and Ratan Singh were born
of a wife of *Koormi caste* (an agricultural tribe inferior to the
Jats). But Father Wendel, who lived at the Court of Jawahir
Singh, and knew him intimately asserts that they were born
of a wife of the Goré caste (French MS., 51). Elsewhere he

But the mother of none of these enjoyed the
particular affection of the old Rajah, who loved
most dearly his masculine and barren wife, the
famous queen Rani Kishori, popularly called
Hansia. Jawahir was fortunate enough to be
adopted by this lady, whose influence and
affection shielded the rebellious youth from the
worst effects of the wrath of his father. He
and his brother rose to high rank, as mansab-
dars of the Mughal Court. But Ratan Singh,
addicted to pleasures in early youth, grew up a
voluptuary without any ambition for power or
martial fame. Nawal Singh and Ranjit Singh
were youths of mediocre abilities, and were little
heard of during their father's lifetime. Nahar
Singh, the youngest, whom Suraj Mal thought
of leaving as his successor and whom the Jat
chief had already begun to initiate in the arts of

---

adds, "There are men who claim that the Gorees are a little
more noble than the Jats, and that they are a *species of decayed
Rajputs*, either fallen into decadence or mixed, but always
one degree higher than the Jats as regards their extraction"
(*ibid*, p. 74). This exactly tallies with the notice of the
Gaurua caste, whom Sir H. M. Elliot calls "an inferior clan
of Rajputs" (*Memoirs of the Races*, i. 115). The author of
Imad-us-Saadat maintains that Jawahir's mother was a
Rajputni (Pers. text p. 56). "It has been asserted that the
Gaurua of the Mathura and Gurgaon districts is only a *Rajput*
who practises karewa (marrying elder brother's widow). [*Gaz.*
N. W. P. Old series, vol. viii, part I, p. 73.]

government, was a boy of dull and narrow outlook and of weak intellect. Nahar [the Lion]
resembled a lamb in character and presented a
sad contrast to his eldest brother. He was a
typical "good boy", obedient to his father's
will, respectful to his superiors, devout and
religious, with great reverence for the Brahmans,
unostentatious and docile, fit for anything but
ruling men and administering a State in stormy
times. Jawahir feared neither God nor man,
and would defy both in the pursuit of ambition
and revenge. Possessed of great military
talents and administrative capacity, subtle, active
and audacious he was a born ruler of men; yet
Suraj Mal rightly divined that this son of his
would bring ruin upon the Jats.

   The relation between Suraj Mal and
Jawahir could never be cordial, as between a
self-made miserly millionaire and his young,
foppish son who looks upon his father as no
better than a peevish and overbearing steward,
and makes a grievance of the salutary checks
laid upon his own extravagance. Theirs were
two different types of mentality incapable of
understanding each other. Suraj Mal, in spite
of the change of his former condition and the
immense wealth he had piled up, had not at
all given up the primitive simplicity of his race

11

in what concerned his own mode of living.
He, however, made a decent provision,—very
liberal according to his standard—which, he
thought, ought to suffice for the maintenance of
his son in dignity and affluence.   But young
Jawahir was extravagant and would always
press for a larger allowance from his father.
He soon created a circle of his own, and had
a Court and train, of which the expenses
amounted far above what Suraj Mal had given
him.   Though brought up in a rude provincial
town amidst peasant population, his equipage,
his fashion, his diversions all suggested an
Amir of the Empire and the courtly airs of
Delhi which he had not failed to observe well.
Suraj Mal was greatly displeased, and in many
ways tried to make his son understand the
extreme aversion that he felt for his conduct.
These remonstrances the more frequent and
pressing they were, the more they soured the
spirit of Jawahir. Already at a young age,
Jawahir had commenced to nourish very high
hopes and to indulge in outbursts of a fiery and
enterprising spirit. Suraj Mal employed the
military talents of his son in many expedi-
tions, where he acquired great fame.   He made
his son commandant of Deeg, hoping that
that would satisfy him. But contrary results

followed. A party opposed to Balaram, Mohan
Ram and other influential chiefs of his father's
Court, soon gathered round him there, and he
persuaded himself that Balaram's group were
turning his father's mind against him. Suraj
Mal rebuked his son, for allowing himself to be
guided by evil advisers, whom it was necessary
for his own good to dismiss. But these
paternal remonstrances were treated with usual
indifference. What was worse Jawahir prepared
for an armed revolt.

Jawahir Singh resolved to set himself as
an independent ruler at Deeg and defend it to
the last against his father. With the assistance
of his desperate associates, he took possession
of the city and did, in truth all acts of war.
Suraj Mal, having tried in vain to make him
return to his duty, had no other expedient than
to go and besiege his son in person. In order
to come most quickly to a conclusion with his
son, he threatened to apply extreme rigour to
the wives and children of those that followed
his party. Jawahir put up a stiff resistance.
Not content with defending Deeg against the
efforts of his father, he resolved to try issue on
the plain. He came out and attacked his
father's troops; a fierce struggle ensued under
the walls of the fort. After a while, the

rebels were forced to turn their backs; but not their Maloch-like leader. Jawahir who rushed into the thickest of the fray, and fought with ardour and courage befitting a nobler cause, was brought to the ground at last covered with wounds—a sword-cut, a lance thrust and a musket shot. Suraj Mal, who would rather see Deeg lost than his own son dead,—hastened out of breath to snatch him away from the hands of those who in spite of all the prohibitions and cries of the father, hurried to give him the death blow. His life was saved; but owing to the three wounds, his right arm became weak and he limped in after-life [Wendel, 34-36.]*

A dark cloud hang upon the mind of Suraj Mal; the prospect of another civil war and family dissensions after his death made the closing years of his life extremely unhappy. He

* In all fairness to Jawahir Singh, it is proper to add the following remarks of Father Wendel: "Although it is not other than very true that Jawahir Singh had been dragged into this wicked affair partly by his own spirit, and partly by the counsels of the persons he had about himself—nevertheless it is certain that mostly, the *aloofness of Suraj Mal* towards him and a *certain indigence* to which on certain occasions the son found himself reduced with all his comrades by the miserliness of his father, or the wickedness of those who, according to his [Suraj Mal's] orders, supplied the money for the maintenance expenses of Jawahir Singh, obliged him to take that measure of last violence." *This rebellion took place in 1755 before the invasion of Ahmad Shah Durrani.*

saw with alarm the rise of a strong party, headed
by his most powerful chiefs, Balaram, Mohan
Ram and others, who were bent upon opposing
with arms, if necessary, the succession of
Jawahir.   He knew the character of his people
which his son did not and cared not to understand.   Jawahir gave himself the airs of an
aristocrat and never failed to bring home to the
mind of his nearest kinsmen and relatives, his
own superiority and right to rule them by reason
of his birth.   Nothing was more offensive to
the Jat, who, like the Afghan would not fear to
tell any pretender to his face, "What art thou
that I am not?   What shalt thou be that I shall
not?"   Besides, the character of the prince was
least calculated to create confidence in others.
He was harsh, cruel, vindictive, and dissimula-
ting to a degree.   The pen of a sympathetic
observer could depict him as no better than as
a second Mihir-kula, a man who " has up to
the present time caused it to be seen that he is
never more satisfied than when he has occasion
to make war against some one, *i.e.*, to render
others unhappy, and cause to flow before his
eyes a river of human blood" [Wendel, MS.,
34].   He never forgave any injury or insult,
and never failed to retaliate.   All the old chiefs
became apprehensive of the safety of their

offices, wealth and lives under his regime. To have crushed these powerful associates of his cabinet and battle-field, in order to smooth Jawahir's path to the throne would have been, for Suraj Mal, the undoing of his life's work. So he decided to deprive such a son of his birth-right, rather than see the Jat power perish, although he esteemed silently Jawahir's reso-lution and bravery, and judged him to be *solely worthy* of succeeding him.

But it was too much to expect that Jawahir would sit idle, and tamely submit to this in-justice and be disinherited. So, Suraj Mal proposed to create for him another kingdom outside the hereditary dominion of his house which he meant to leave to his more tractable son Nahar Singh. This suggested the scheme of the conquest of Hariana and the formation of a buffer State where the exuberant energy and military genius of Jawahir would find ample occupation in holding his appanage against the Ruhelas and the Abdali. It was undoubtedly a wise policy, and the site chosen for the con-templated kingdom was excellent. Hariana, which was and still is ethnologically a Jat country, accepted Suraj Mal's rule with alacrity and welcomed it as a release from the unbridled tyranny of a Muslim military aristocracy.

At the time of Suraj Mal's death the possessions of the Jats consisted of the districts of Agra, Dholpur, Mainpuri, Hathras, Aligarh, Etah*, Meerut, Rohtak, Farrukhnagar, Mewat, Rewari, Gurgaon and Mathura, apart from the original principality of Bharatpur. "The right bank of the Ganges forms its [of the Jat kingdom] eastern boundary, the Chambal the southern, the subah of Agra included in the territory of the Rajah of Jaipur the western, and the subah of Delhi the northern; its length is about 100 kos, east to west and 70 kos, north to south. [*Le Nabob Rene Madec*, sec. 45]. As regards the finance of the State, Father Wendel says, "opinions differ on the subject of the treasure and property which he [Suraj Mal] left to his successor. Some estimate it as 9 (nine) krores, others less. I have inquired into his annual revenue and expenditure from men who managed them; all I could learn as more credible is that all his expenses were not above 65 lakhs a year nor below 60, and he had at least during the last 5 or 6 years of his reign, not less

---

* Etah :—Agra Division, bounded on the north by the river Ganges, on the south by Mainpuri district, on the east by Badaon district and the west by Jalesar pargana of the Agra district, lies between long. 78°-29′ and 79°-19′, and latitude between 27° and 28°.

than 175 lakhs of revenue annually. He added 5 or 6 krores of silver to his ancestor's treasure ....To-day [after the accession of Jawahir Singh] up to 10 krores are 'in the treasury of the Jats.........Much is buried—not known where. Suraj Mal fruitlessly dug at Deeg a large tract of land to recover part of the hoard of Badan Singh. This has given that city a tank and the citizens have thus got water to their advantage! Notwithstanding the common opinion regarding the treasure* of the Jats, I always believe that there is not so much money in their hands" [Wendel, 51, 52.] Years have not at all affected—but rather magnified—the popular belief, about the fabulous wealth of the house of Bharatpur. The secret vaults of its treasury are still supposed to contain many rarities and choice plunder of Delhi and Agra, which few can hope to see.

---

* *Imad-us-Saadat* is the only Persian chronicle which gives, though incidentally, a hint about the wealth of Suraj Mal. Rao Radha Kishan (informant of the author Ghulam Ali), who had been for a long time a trusted adherent of Suraj Mal says that, Suraj Mal made to him a prophecy about the issue of the Third Battle of Panipat and in the course of the talk said :—"I who possess *territories, yielding one krore and a half,* and have in *my treasury five or six krores of rupees,*" have been made to part company with him [the Bhao] for nothing (*Imad,* Pers. text. 72). This is substantially a correct estimate.

"Besides the treasure, Suraj Mal left to his successor nearly 5,000 horses, 60 elephants, 15,000 cavalry in his pay, more than 25,000 infantry (besides those in fortresses), more than 300 pieces of cannon and munition in proportion" [*ibid,* p. 55.] The author of the *Siyar* says "He [Suraj Mal] had in his stable twelve thousand horses, mounted by so many picked men, amongst whom he had himself introduced an exercise of firing at a mark on horseback, and then wheeling round in order to load under shelter, and these men had by continual and daily practice become so expeditious and so dangerous marksmen, and withal so expert in their evolutions, that there were no troops in India that could pretend to face them in the field. Nor was it thought possible to wage war against such a Prince with any prospect of advantage." [*Siyar,* iv. 28]. Suraj Mal as we learn from the *Memoire of Jean Law,* the French free-lance captain, was also on the look-out for Europeans for training his infantry regiments in European discipline, so much admired by all his contemporaries. The party of M. Law* was attacked

---

* See *Memoire of Jean Law* (pp. 312-313), edited by Alfred Martineau. The *Kalini river* of the text is evidently the *Kalindi* river, a tributary of the Ganges, flowing through the *tahsil* of *Atrauli* (16 miles to the north-east of Aligarh on the Ramghat Road).

by 10,000 cavalry under Rao Durjan Singh (a relative of Suraj Mal and commandant of a small province of Atrauli in the Doab), on 23rd March, 1758, while he was encamped on the eastern bank of the Kalini river.   His intention was to capture the Europeans and send them prisoners to Suraj Mal, who had been long desiring to have such people in his service.   Fortunately, however they escaped and the desire of the Jat Rajah remained unfulfilled.

CHAPTER X.

MAHARAJAH SAWAI JAWAHIR SINGH BHARATENDRA (1764-1768)

Jawahir's accession to the throne.

After the death of Suraj Mal, the baronial party, headed by Balaram, brother of Rani Hansia proceeded to place Nahar Singh on the *gadi* of Bharatpur, as desired by the late Rajah. But one bold and well-judged stroke of Jawahir's policy brought about a dramatic change of the situation. He sent a messenger from Farrukhnagar with a stern warning to his brother and the nobles, reproaching them with cowardice and unworthy scramble for gain. This was no season, so they were told, to think of giving a successor to the illustrious dead but to exert themselves to propitiate his departed soul, crying for his slayer's blood. He would not claim at present, he said, his own birth-right, but would go with the small force that remained with him against the enemy, and afterwards see who deserved most to succeed his father. This threat disconcerted the chiefs and so dismayed Nahar Singh by nature timid and cowardly, that he fled the following night. With his family and partisans, he retreated to Dholpur (which had been given to him as an appanage during Suraj Mal's lifetime) to wait for a more favourable time to recover his legacy. Balaram gave up all hopes of resisting Jawahir's claim to the throne and thought it prudent to submit. Jawahir Singh returned to Deeg, and was installed there as master and sovereign of the Jat territory.

Weakness of Jawahir's position.

But his position was as yet one of peril and uncertainty. The submission of the old chieftains was nothing more than a tardy recognition of his title. They retired to their own estates unwilling to participate in the work of the new government. Balaram, the leading chief, general of the cavalry and governor of Bharatpur (where the State treasure was deposited), shut up the gates of the fort in the face of Rajah Jawahir Singh, and would not reveal to him the secret sites of Suraj Mal's treasure in other places. Nahar Singh was at Dholpur ready to lend himself to any intrigue for his brother's overthrow, and Bahadur Singh (son of Suraj Mal's brother, Pratap Singh), who held the fief of Wair, refused to acknowledge the authority of the new Rajah and was making preparations for asserting his own independence. Nothing but a military success, grand enough to capture the imagination of the people, was likely to check the disruptive forces in the State, and consolidate the rule of Rajah Jawahir Singh.

He dissembled for the moment and behaved as if he had forgotten and forgiven the faults of his father's nobles in consideration of their helping him to the throne. Sentiment and interest alike demanded that a retaliatory expedition should be undertaken to avenge the death of Suraj Mal on Najib-ud-daulah. The ex-wazir Ghazi-ud-din, who had been living at Bharatpur as a pensioner of the Jats since 1760, also fanned the flame of Jawahir's wrath in the hope of regaining his exalted office and bringing about another revolution at Delhi. But none of the Jat chiefs approved of this design, and the proposition was generally rejected. Jawahir Singh set little value on the armed help of his chiefs, if he could only get money. In spite of his turbulence and ingratitude, Rani Hansia loved Jawahir, her adopted son, with all the tenderness and warmth of an indulgent mother. She could not but respond to the passionate appeal of Jawahir and furnished him, without the knowledge of her brother Balaram, with large sums for the expenses of the expedition.

The War of Revenge.

Towards the end of October,* 1764, a
formidable Hindu army, second only to that
which Maharashtra had sent forth in 1760 to
assert her dominion in Hindustan—appeared
before the gates of Delhi, to demand satisfaction
for Suraj Mal's blood, and to undo the effects
of the Muslim victory at Panipat. Jawahir
Singh brought against Najib-ud-daulah 60
thousand troops and 100 pieces of cannon of
his own, 25 thousand Marathas under Malhar
Rao Holkar, and some 15 thousand Sikhs—both
as hired allies, to ensure a rapid success. Doubtful of the issue but determined to fight it out to
the last, the brave Ruhela chief had prudently
removed beforehand his family and treasure to
the strong fort of Sakkartal† in Saharanpur, and
throwing entrenchments around the city of Delhi
stood ready for a long siege. He summoned
other Ruhela chiefs to his aid and sent urgent
entreaties to the Abdali, informing him of the
perilous situation. Delhi was closely invested;
the Marathas were posted to the north of the
city, and the Sikhs to the north-west, while

---

* Pers. Record i. 352. This news was brought from Delhi
to Calcutta in 16 days, on Nov. 11, 1764.

† Also called Sakkartal, situated in the confluence of the
Solani river and the Ganges, at its highest navigable point.

Jawahir planted part of his army on the eastern
bank of the river and the rest before the Delhi
and Ajmir gates. The fiery Jat, impatient of
delay, sent a challange to Najib Khán, to come
out like a man and fight in the open instead of
hiding himself in a corner. He chivalrously
withdrew his army five or six *kos* off the city
in the direction of Faridabad (about 16 miles,
south of Delhi), to allow the Afghans to come
out unmolested. Lashed to fury Najib-ud-
daulah sallied out and gave battle to the Jats
(15th Nov., 1764), who, however proved
stronger and drove the Afghans back into the
city, each side lost about a thousand in killed
and wounded. Jawahir Singh, accompanied
by Holkar and other chiefs, crossed the Jamuna
and plundered Shahdara, and planted batteries
on that side (17th November). The day after
the loot of Shahdara, the troops of Najib Khán
owing to the heavy cannonading of the enemy
left the sandy plain [*reti*] below the fort and
went inside; shells began to fall into the city*
(19th November). Three months passed away
in distress and hardship. All attempts of the
Afgháns to cut their way through proved futile.

---

* The battle, loot and bombardment took place within the
first 26 days of Jamada I, 1178, on Thursday, Saturday and
Monday (*Waqá*, 198-199).

On the 12th of Shaban, 1178 A.H. (4th Feb., 1765), Najib fought another battle with the Sikhs and the Jats on the ridge near Nakhás [cattle-market] and Sabzi-mandi [the well-known fruit and vegetable market of Delhi]. The action began with a heavy musketry fire; a large number of men were killed and wounded, and again the Afghans had to retire discomfitted (*Waqa*, 204). No choice was now left but starvation or surrender; shops were closed and the utmost exhortation of the Government failed to pacify the people. The very next day, the inhabitants of the Old and the New city rushed into the Jat camp, begging for a supply of corn to save them from starvation. This was a virtual surrender of the city—the defenders retired within the citadel.* There was no prospect of relief coming from any quarter whatsoever; the Sikhs were ravaging Saharanpur and other possessions of Najib-ud-daulah and there was little chance of the Abdali coming.†

---

* Pers. correspondence i. 372; the date 9th Jan., 1765 is evidently wrong there.

† The Abdali crossed the Indus in Oct., 1765, about 7 months after the conclusion of peace between Najib Khán and Jawahir Singh. So the report of his coming could in no way terrify the Játs and influence the negotiations between two parties.

Treachery of Malhar Rao.

When complete success seemed almost within his grasp, Rajah Jawahir Singh was baffled by his faithless ally, Malhar Rao, "who spoiled the affair" as Father Wendel says, "by showing greater slackness and open partiality for Najib Khán. He proposed peace at a time when the Ruhelas could not have delayed any longer in offering unconditional surrender, and at last obliged Jawahir Singh to consent to it" [French MS., 59]. Najib Khán opened negotiations for peace; "Sujan Misra, Rajah Chait Ram, and the nephew of Rupram,* (the family priest of the Bharatpur Raj) went to Malhar Rao to talk of peace and returned (14th Shaban; 6 Feb., 1765). About two *gharis* before sunset, Nawab Zabita Khán started, and going up the Jamuna, brought with him Gangadhar Tatiya and Rupram to Najib-ud-daulah" [*Waqa*, 201]. The two parties evidently came to an

---

* Rupram figured prominently also in the reign of Suraj Mal. The Marathi chronicles mention him several times with his title Katari. He "having acquired great reputation as a Pandit in the earlier part of the last [the eighteenth] century, became *Purohit* to Bharatpur, Sindhia, and Holkar, and was enriched by those princes with the most lavish donations the whole of which he appears to have expended on the embellishment of Barsáná and other sacred places within the limits of Braj his native country" [Growse's *Mathurá*, 178.]

12

agreement but it is not known on what terms.
On the 17th Shaban (Feb. 9), Najib-ud-daulah
went to pay a visit to Malhar Rao in his camp;
and thence [after the interview with Holkar]
they proceeded to the camp of the Jats, and
towards sunset returned to the city bringing
with them large quantities of grain loaded upon
pack horses." [*Waqa*, 201]. On the 20th
of Shaban, (12th Feb.), Rajah Jawahir Singh
marched away to Oklàh, 5 miles south of
Delhi. [*Waqa*, 202]. Malhar Rao had the
reward of his treachery to his ally. On
the 21st of Shában (13th Feb.) he paid a
visit to Najib-ud-daulah who presented him
with an elephant, two horses, and nine plates
of jewels and bestowed one hundred and twenty-
nine robes of honour to his companions [*ibid*,
202]. On the 22nd of Shában (14th Feb.),
Jawahír Singh received a visit from Zabita Khán
who had brought with him an elephant and a
robe of honour on behalf of the Heir-apparent,
Jawan Bakht" (*ibid*). Here the affair ended.
That he was not pleased with the compromise
which was in a sense forced upon him by the
untrustworthy Maratha chief is evident from the
fact that he departed earlier from the capital
without returning the visit of Najib-ud-daulah
as courtesy required. He went away to Deeg,

bearing a grudge against Malhar Rao who, the Jat knew, had him spend without much benefit 160 lakhs of Rupees. "He had no other gain from this expedition" as Father Wendel says "than to have under his command the chiefs and the army and to make himself more respected by his people."* (French MS., 59).

Jawahir Singh crushes the refractory chiefs.

After his return from the expedition against Delhi (March, 1765), Rajah Jawahir Singh thought it high time to make himself master of his own household first, and to crush the enemies within, before he should indulge in the vision of foreign conquest. He suspected, not without reason, a secret connection between Malhar Rao and his discontented chiefs who had reluctantly accompanied him to Delhi, out of fear and shame. Two old chiefs, Balaram, commander of the cavalry, and Mohan Ram, general of the artillery had almost monopolised all power in the State: the treasure and army

---

* The above account has been mainly reconstructed from the account of Father Wendel and the *Waqa*. Harcharan, the author of *Chahar-Gulzar-i-Shujai*, says that at the very beginning Najib Khān made proposals of a compromise which was rejected by Jawahir Singh remembering the enmity arising out of his father's blood. He then approached Malhar Rao and through his mediation peace was effected. Najib Khān visited Jawahir Singh in his camp and offered apologies to him.

of Suraj Mal were in their hands and their relatives occupied all the important public offices. Besides the memory of old grievances, and their intrigue to set him aside from succession, the idea of getting enriched at one stroke by killing these *golden geese* entered his mind. The notorious German captain Somru, having quitted the banners of Shuja-ud-daulah, sought service and safety in the Court of Bharatpur (April, 1765). Here was a man after Jawahir's heart, a capable soldier without a conscience, who would unhesitatingly carry out with skill and thoroughness any dark design of a good paymaster. The reputed wealth of Bharatpur attracted many veteran mercenaries discharged from the service of bankrupt princes. Having recruited a powerful corps of foreigners who could be trusted more than the Jats, Rajah Jawahir Singh proceeded to chastise the inimical nobles (*circa* July, 1765).

"Fortified with these helps, he believed himself strong and secure enough to demand with much firmness, satisfaction from those of his kinsmen whom for a long time past he had desired to seize. It was probably with this design that he came to Agra where having summoned those whom he wished to seize, and commanded his foreign troops to guard well the

roads, he caused to be arrested Balaram with
the others in different places, and *on the same
day* all persons appertaining [attached?] to
them were seized. Balaram and one other chief
with him, full of hate and spite at what had
happened to themselves, and probably to prevent a greater ignominy, cut their own throats
with their swords shortly after, the one face to
face with the other. The others were conveyed
under strong guard as prisoners to Bharatpur
where afterwards they ransomed themselves
with the money which was demanded of them
on the account of Suraj Mal whose affair they
had had in their hands.........Certain [of the
chiefs] let themselves be rather killed than give
up money, although they had the reputation of
having much wealth and were already convicted
of malversation in the administration............
Not to speak of Balaram and his riches, Mohan
Ram alone was estimated to possess nearly 80
lakhs in cash, without reckoning the property
and other wealth that he was master of.........
He let them cut his head off after many tortures
and cruelties rather than deliver the least part of
that which he in truth, owed, and which he
could not fail to have very well guarded" (Fr.
MS., 61-62). Thus Jawahir Singh revenged
himself upon the old nobles of his father. This

bloody affair proved a great mistake and a sorry failure as a means of recovering Suraj Mal's treasure. "He was very ill-advised, all spoiled by haste and harshness. A slow and pleasant method of extraction would have been more fruitful. All that Jawahir Singh could seize was not more than 15 or 20 lakhs" [ibid]. This was a political blunder too, which ultimately brought about the downfall of the house of Bharatpur. "This conduct of Jawahir Singh at the beginning of his reign sent", says Father Wendel, "consternation among his relatives and dismayed entirely the Jats in general, at the same time that it soured their spirits and removed totally their attachment to his person. And although for many reasons of State he was almost obliged to act in that fashion, it was, however, very hasty and unreasonable" [ibid, 62].

Next came the turn of Jawahir's rebellious cousin, Bahadur Singh who held the field of Wair,* "a man" as Father Wendel says, "so courteous for a Jat and of a spirit above most of his race." He had served his uncle Suraj Mal very faithfully and was rewarded with

---

* Wair is within the territory of Bharatpur, lying about 12 miles north-west of Biana, situated in lat. 27° and long. 77°-15/.

several additions to his appanage. He was wealthy and powerful, possessed a good and numerous artillery, and had in his pay a considerable army. After the death of Suraj Mal, Bahadur Singh believed that he had at least as much right to the dominion of the Jats as Suraj Mal or Jawahir Singh, and showed, by his activity and conduct that he desired to govern Wair as a *master* and not at the pleasure of another. "And in spite of the fact that Jawahir Singh had indicated to him his displeasure, he did not cease, but commenced to fortify more and more the place which was well fortified, increase the garrison, munitions and provisions, and put himself in a state to defend it against whomsoever would contest it. Jawahir Singh marched in the midst of the rainy season [August, 1765] against *Vaer* [Wair] and invested it on all sides. Bahadur Singh defended himself valiantly for three months; the besiegers underwent great hardship, because that year the rain fell in a deluge. Partly by false peace proposals, and partly by the treachery of some chiefs within, the fort was carried by assault and Bahadur Singh seized and carried off prisoner to Bharatpur (November, 1765) whence he was released at last with Musavi Khán [of Farrukhnagar], at the birth

of a grandson [of Suraj Mal]*. But two Rajputs (who were known to have instigated
Bahadur Singh in that war against Jawahir
Singh and had afterwards forbidden him to
admit proposals for a compromise, which he
was about to make),—were by order of Jawahir
Singh, in a manner that has not yet been seen
or practised among the Jats,—as a warning to
others, impaled on the road to Bharatpur, and
there remained a long time as an awful spectacle
to the passers-by''. [Wendel, French MS.,†
63-64]. This expedition cost Jawahir Singh
more than 30 lakhs, rather a heavy drain on the
State treasury. But it was not to be the last.

---

* The grandson, referred to in the text, is Kheri Singh,
born to Jawahir's younger brother Ratan Singh. Rajah Jawahir
Singh being without issue and also without the hope of having
any one, adopted this child. It was on this occasion that these
political prisoners were set free. The exact date of the birth
of Kheri Singh is nowhere mentioned. This can, however, be
inferred from an entry in the *Waqa*, dated 23rd Ziqada, 1179
(May 3, 1766), on which date, Afzal Khán, son of Najib, had
an interview with Nawab Musavi Khán [*Waqá*, 208], presumably after his release. So the child was born and the
prisoners were set free probably in the month of April, 1766.

† The original MS. contains a long account of the siege
and sack of *Wair*, considerably abridged here to suit the
narrative.

CHAPTER XI.

REIGN OF RAJAH JAWAHIR SINGH

Overthrow of Nahar Singh.

While Jawahir Singh was engaged in the siege of Wair (July—November of rains 1765), Nahar Singh (the youngest son of Suraj Mal) was making preparations at Dholpur to strike a blow for the *gadi* of Bharatpur. It was quite apparent that his turn would come next, should Jawahir succeed in crushing Bahadur Singh. About this time Malhar Rao Holkar was on the other bank of the Chambal, carrying on hostilities against another Jat principality, Gohad.* Nahar Singh commenced a correspondence with the Holkar in order to buy Maratha support and with the latter's aid to raise himself to the Raj. Jawahir Singh and Malhar Rao had an old score to settle ever since the Delhi expedition of 1764. The cunning Maratha had made a fool of the Jat by taking his money and at the same time

---

* Gohad is situated to the north-east of Gwalior. This principality was bounded on the west by the Gwalior territories, on the east by the Kali Sindu river, on the north by the Jamuna and on the south by the hills of Sirmur [?] See Renell's atlas.

baffling his object. But he had soon to repent
his trickery when Jawahir, who was anything
but a saint himself, bluntly refused to pay the
unpaid half of the stipulated sum of twenty-
two lakhs, alleging breach of faith on the
part of the Holkar. Malhar Rao seized this
opportunity of making his claim good, and
eagerly accepted the proposal of Nahar Singh,
whom, as usual the Holkar made his *dharma
putra* [God-son], because Nahar Singh was
rich enough to pay a good price for this paternal
affectation.

Malhar Rao sent his troops across the
Chambal and garrisoned the fort of Dholpur
along with the men of Nahar Singh. Jawahir
Singh summoned his brethren of the Panjab,
the Sikhs, to his aid, and arrived quickly on
the bank of the Chambal to carry war into
the enemy country (December, 1765). One
division of the Maratha army which had
penetrated into the Jat country was surrounded
and captured. Dholpur was next besieged and
when it fell into the hands of Jawahir Singh,
many Maratha chiefs who had taken shelter
there during the retreat, became prisoners of
war. Flushed with this success, Jawahir
wanted to pursue Malhar Rao and clear Malwa
of the Marathas. But the Sikhs refused to

keep the field any longer as summer had already set in and they had suffered a good deal from the intolerable heat and scarcity of water. "Nahar Singh who had already retired to the army of Malhar lost his estates......and was afterwards abandoned by the Marathas to whom he wished to deliver the country......He took refuge at Chopor, the citadal of a petty Rajput Rajah on the further side of Kerauli, where he at last ended his life in despair by swallowing poison. His family retired to the protection of the Rajah of Jaipur, where they *are at present* [*i.e.*, 1768], having carried the most part of their riches and probably the knowledge [of the whereabouts] of the great part of the treasure of Suraj Mal, of whom Nahar Singh, the destined successor, had been the confidant"* [Wendel, Fr. MS., 65].

Jawahir fights Raghunath Rao, 1767.

The unrealised dream of Suraj Mal, namely to build up a great Jat confederacy

---

* The *Imad-us-Saadat*, is the only Persian chronicle (Pers. text, p. 56) which notices the death of "the good natured" Nahar Singh by self-administered poison. On the 10th December, 1766, the news came from Jaipur that "Nahar Singh *is dead of his disorder*. This news has been received with utmost concern by Maharajah Jawahir Singh. All the cavalry officers who were in the army of Nahar Singh immediately

extending from the Chambal to the Ravi domi-
nating the whole of Northern India appeared to
become well-nigh an accomplished fact by
the establishment of more intimate relations
between Jawahir Singh and the Sikhs, the
recent victory of their united forces over the
Marathas under Holkar, and the successful
resistance of the Sikh commonwealth against
the Abdali. Success opened new vistas of
aggression to Jawahir who thought of widening
the confederacy further so as to include the Jats
of Northern Malwa, and raise a stronger barrier
to Maratha invasion. The brave Rana Chattar
Sal of Gohad had been carrying on for years a
heroic struggle against the Marathas. The
obstinate courage and undaunted spirit of the
race shone no less brilliantly in Malwa than in
the Panjab or Bharatpur. But they were losing
ground every day, being only a handful, however brave, compared with the locust hordes of
the South. Should the Marathas succeed in
overthrowing the Rana of Gohad, their full
strength, Jawahir knew too well, would be
pitted against him. "Proud of success over
Malhar, Jawahir Singh resolved to give *himself*

---

returned to Jawahir Singh to consult what was most advisable
on the occasion" [Pers. Cor. ii. 6]. The death took place
evidently on the 6th or 7th of Dec., 1766.

{of his own accord?] help to the Rana [Chattar Sal] Jat, his ally, and thus finish the Marathas beyond the Chambal and outside his own country" [Wendel French MS. 65].

The Peshwa Madhu Rao viewed with alarm the growth of this formidable coalition and sent Raghunath Rao in the autumn of 1766, to retrieve the prestige of the Maratha armies in Hindustan. His army, together with those under the Holkar exceeded 60,000 horsemen, and had a choice artillery of more than 100 pieces. Raghunath began with the siege of Gohad, and made certain haughty demands upon Jawahir Singh, who was about this time suffering from a dangerous malady. As soon as he recovered, he "marched anew with the design to attack the Marathas, if they would not give up, of themselves the claims which they thought to have against him. But treason lurked in his own camp, which frustrated his object. Raghunath Rao seduced two of his principal chiefs, Anup Gir Goswain and Umrao Gir Goswain, (the leaders of the Nagas), from their allegiance to the Jat Rajah. The traitors promised to make Jawahir Singh a prisoner in his camp and hand him over to the Marathas, and they were to get, as a reward, certain territories in the direction of Kalpi. The spies

of Jawahir Singh gave their master timely
warning of this plot. At midnight Jawahir
Singh got his troops ready and suddenly fell
upon the camp of the Goswains. The traitors
escaped with difficulty, but a considerable
number of their followers were taken prisoners
and their camp thoroughly pillaged. About
1400 horses, 60 elephants, 100 pieces of cannon, and other valuable booty, fell into the
hands of Jawahir Singh. The dependents of
the household of these two Goswains who were
at Agra, Deeg and Kuhmir were brought to
one place and kept under watch. [Chahar
Gulzar-i-Shujai MS.]*. About this time (Feb.,
1767) Ahmad Shah Abdali made some progress
in the Panjab and threatened to advance upon
Delhi. Raghunath Rao and Jawahir Singh,
who were equally interested in keeping the
Abdali out of Hindustan, made up their quarrel
in the face of this common danger. They met
in friendship and adjusted their claims; the
terms of the treaty were as follows:

---

* Harcharan Das, author of the Chahar, makes some
confusion about the date which he puts as 1179 A.H., the
correct date being 1180, A.H. He estimates the gain of
Jawahir as more than two krores, which, however, Wendel
with perhaps greater accuracy puts as 30 lakhs. Nevertheless
the account of Harcharan is substantially correct, and is corro-
borated by the version of Wendel. (French MS., 66.)

1.   The Maratha prisoners at Bharatpur, are to be released.

2.   Jawahir Singh should execute a new agreement to pay up the balance of 15 lakhs of Rupees, due to Malhar Rao, after the conditions of the original agreement had been fulfilled [by the Marathas].

3.   Raghunath Rao cedes to Jawahir Singh a small tract of the Rajput country, lying contiguous to the territory of the Rajah on a yearly quit rent of 5 lakhs of Rupees [Pers. Cor. ii. 4-7].

The treaty was a make-shift arrangement, neither party meaning to respect it if its violation would bring greater advantages. The fear of the Abdali wore away towards the middle of the year (1767) when the Sikhs considerably regained their ground. Jawahir Singh projected a campaign in the rainy season. "The country of the Rajah of Atter* and Bhant had been formerly tributary to the Marathas........

---

* Atter is situated north-east of Gwalior and due north of Gohad. Bhant is difficult to identify. It is perhaps the same place as Binde of Renell's atlas, lying close to Atter and to the south-east of it. The territory of the abovementioned Rajah was perhaps the tract between the Chambal and the Kali Sindu rivers near their confluences with the Jamuna. These two places lie on the west and east of long. 79° and on lat. 26°-30ʹ.

Jawahir Singh, seeing the Maratha parties so
weak, imagined that he had there as much right
as they, and took it into his head, without any
other reason, to make the conquest.........This
enterprise also led him much further than he
had proposed to himself. Going with superior
forces to that side, he seized in the rainy season
(July-Sept. 1767) all the dominions of the
Marathas and other petty zamindars as far as
Kalpi. If he had as much skill in preserving
the recently conquered country, as he had
success in seizing them, he could have been
praised for his enterprise and would have been
entirely glorious : but it is just this in which he
failed more, namely in wisdom and moderation" [French MS., 66].

Rajah Jawahir Singh and the English.

A revolution of the greatest magnitude
had in the meanwhile taken place in Bengal,
and a new and foreign power, the English, now
emerged as the most potent factor in the politics
of Northern India. They paid at Gheria and
Udaynala, the necessary price in blood for the
kingdom of Bengal, which had been handed
over to them by her treacherous sons at Plassey
(1757). A high spirited and able prince who
tried to do his duty fell a victim to the

commercial greed of the English East India Company. Mir Qasim fled from his lost kingdom to Oudh. His new protector, the Nawab wazir Shuja-ud-daulah, appeared in the field to dispute the fair-prize with the victors. On the ,morrow of the battle of Buxar, the English merchant Company appeared with a monarch's sceptre before the astonished peoples and princes of India. The wazir of the empire bowed before it and received back his lost territories with an assurance of protection from his generous enemies. The homeless Emperor recognized the rising power and set up a melancholy Court at their fort of Allahabad, with the fond hope of shining in borrowed light.

But the new masters of Bengal could not repose in peace so long as Mir Qasim was at large plotting against them, from his refuge among the Ruhelas. He had sent *vakils* to Ahmad Shah Durrani imploring his aid against the English. To this was added the urgent entreaties of Najib-ud-daulah who was being crushed between the two millstones, the Jat and the Sikh, by their concerted pressure. The Bengal Government had every reason to fear an Abdali invasion on a grand scale against them, resulting in another Panipat on the border of their territory. The Ruhelas were bound both

13

by interests and racial sympathy to the Abdali.
Shuja-ud-daulah could hardly be relied upon
because the ruler of Oudh was to profit most
by the extinction of the English Power in
Bengal. Less reliable were the Marathas who
found in the territorial ambition of the European
merchants, the greatest obstacle to their national
aspirations both in the north and the south.
The Bengal Government did not fail to notice
that there was only one Power in Hindustan
with a well-organized government and a powerful army, namely the Jats of Bharatpur, who
were likely to prove their surest allies; because
situated as both powers were, one had nothing
to gain by destruction of the other, on the other
hand both were equally interested in keeping
back the Durranis and the Marathas. Rajah
Jawahir Singh could be of great service to the
British in more than one way. First, he could
keep the Abdali busy in the Panjab by backing
the Sikhs. Secondly, should the invader
threaten to march against the English, he could
create a diversion in his rear or possibly draw
off the invader to the siege of the Jat forts,
giving time to the English to organize resistance.
Thirdly, he could place the Emperor Shah
Alam on the throne of Delhi and maintain him
there with English help: a friendly Emperor

on the throne of the Mughal capital and a powerful ally in possession of the surrounding tracts would mean the domination of the whole empire by the British. If the Emperor would leave the English protection and turn hostile to them, Rajah Jawahir Singh could equally check his anti-British designs. Such were the great possibilities of an alliance between the Jat and the English.

But the first approaches of alliance made by the English Government were not received with much eagerness by the Jat. The Governor of Bengal wrote a letter to Rajah Jawahir Singh (19 Aug., 1765), requesting him to dismiss the notorious Somru who had taken shelter and service with him; on his fulfilling that condition, the prospect of a defensive alliance was held out to him (Pers. Cor. i. 427). Rajah Jawahir Singh had no hostile design against the English in affording refuge to Somru, who was entertained simply because the Rajah had the need of a European captain to organize an infantry brigade for him. He did not like the mandatory tone of the Governor's letter; and as there was no enemy at his doors, he chose to take no serious notice of it. Clive foresaw the necessity of creating against the Abdali and the Maratha, a confederacy admitting the Jats and

the Ruhelas also to the advantages of a defensive alliance with the English. He advocated
this scheme in the congress at Chapra, but the
majority was opposed to him on the ground of
heavy responsibilities it was likely to impose on
the Government of Bengal. At the beginning
of the year 1767, the Durrani king invaded the
Panjab with a firm resolution to root out the
Sikhs, and then to reinstate Mir Qasim to the
throne of Bengal. He inflicted several defeats
upon the Sikhs, penetrated as far as the Sutlej,
and threatened to advance upon Delhi. The
progress of his arms created a stir among all
the native powers and none were more alarmed
than the Bengal Government. The emergency
which Clive had foreseen now arose. His
successor Mr. Verelst asked the wazir, who
had some influence with the Jats, once his
father's allies, to open negotiations* with them
afresh.

At this time Rajah Jawahir Singh with the
Abdali on one flank and Raghunath Rao on
the other, was himself equally anxious for an
alliance with the English. He now entered

---

* The correspondence which passed between the Bengal
Government and the wazir, reveals how eagerly the English
sought to win over Rajah Jawahir Singh. (Letters Nos. 201,
234, 255; Pers. Cor. ii. pp. 56, 69, 77).

with alacrity into the scheme of a combined resistance to the Abdali.

Impressed by the fidelity of the English to their engagements, Jawahir wished to cement the proposed defensive union with them by a regular offensive and defensive alliance. He had made approaches through Muhammad Rezá Khán and sent a letter to him by the hand of one Srikrishan, a dependent of his, requesting the Khán "to use his influence with the gentlemen of Calcutta to seal a vow of friendship and alliance with the writer [Jawahir Singh], so that he may be able to make war successfully with the Shah and obtain success, ——[bringing about] the tranquillity of the people of God and the settlement of the affairs of Hindustan......... [the writer] asked to be considered now as invariably attached [to the English] and determined to preserve with them a union in which there will never be the least failure.........Should it be thought advisable, the writer will place His Majesty Shah Alam on the throne of Delhi and proclaim *Ghazi-ud-din Khán wazir*, [the writer] makes *one proposal beforehand*, namely, that *the fort of Ranthambhar should be placed in the writer's hands*" (*ibid*, p. 87, letter No. 296, dated April 12, 1767). The Governor of Bengal wrote in reply directing the Khán that "Rajah Jawahir Singh may be informed that if he is really sincere in his desire to enter into an alliance with the English, he should send a trustworthy *vakil* to Benares, where the writer [the Governor] is going, and where the subject can be thoroughly discussed" (*ibid*, p. 91; letter No. 315, dated 20th April, 1767). Accordingly Jawahir Singh appointed one Don Pedro De Silva as his *vakil* (*ibid*, p. 129). The wazir informed the Governor that he "does not place dependence on the Rohillas or repose any credit in them; but Jawahir Singh can be relied upon to some extent. [Writer] imagines that he [Jawahir] will gladly embrace 'our' alliance.............If Jawahir Singh is inclined to enter into an alliance and compact, and give his firm and unshaken promise to take up the sword for the service of the English Company, and if the writer, and the English engage to give him assistance should the Shah invade his territories, in what terms could an answer be returned to him? Hopes that the Governor will ponder over this question and inform the writer of his sentiments in order that he may act agreeably thereto" [*ibid*, p. 99, letter No. 346, dated April 25, 1767]. Jawahir had kept the Shah in good humour by professing loyalty and

obedience to him. His *vakil* waited upon the
Shah on the 17th of February 1767, and a
special envoy, Karimullah, son of Rajah Jawahir
Singh's head munshi Yahya Khan went soon
afterwards with presents of various sorts to the
Shah's camp (Pers. Cor. ii. 26, 32). There cannot be any better proof of the sincerity and
honesty of the Jat Rajah than the fact that after
the date (12th April) of his opening negotiations for an alliance with the English, he kept
no correspondence with the Shah which might
be construed as a proof of bad faith towards
them.

Assured of the English help against the
Abdali Jawahir did not hesitate to provoke the
hostility of the Marathas. Immediately after
the conclusion of this alliance, he began to
occupy some places taking advantage of the
temporary retirement of the Marathas. The
Governor in a letter to the wazir expresses his
anxiety at the conduct of his new ally and asks
him "to keep the eye of observation on the
movements of those restless people [the
Marathas], while Jawahir Singh enforces his
pretensions to those districts which once acknowledged the authority of the Marathas" [*ibid*,
p. 145].

About this time a war broke out in

the Deccan between the English Government,
and Haidar Ali, who was joined by the Nizam
of Haidarabad, of late an ally of the English.
The Marathas also, seeing the Madras Government very hotly pressed by their enemies, contemplated hostility against the English. Rajah
Januji Bhonsla made certain irritating demands
upon the Governor of Bengal, who very
courageously resented them and wrote to the
envoy of Januji to tell his master that "it will
not be difficult to convince him [Januji] that
the English are not less formidable enemies than
sincere friends." (Ibid, p. 152, letter No. 583,
dated Sept. 27, 1767). As the Abdali had
retired to his country, virtually defeated by the
Sikhs, the Marathas were thinking of reconquer-
ing Hindustan. It was rumoured that Rajah
Januji and Raghunath Rao had united their
forces for invading Hindustan. The Peshwa
Madhu Rao also felt the pulse of the wazir
through his vakil who wrote a letter : "It is
rumoured here that the Europeans are not on
good terms with the wazir and give him innumerable troubles. If so......the wazir will......
favour him with letters for Sri Mant [Raghu
Nath Rao]* and Madhu Rao, the writer's

---

* Somewhat confusing because Sri Mant in the Maratha
correspondence is generally applied to the Peshwa himself.

gracious master. [The 'vakil] tells him [the wazir] to send a deed under his seal making over the subah of Bengal to the Marathas, that they may collect revenue there" (ibid, p. 181 ; letter No. 667, Nov. 1767). The wazir forwarded the letter to the Governor and wrote in reply to the Maratha vakil that there was the most perfect friendship subsisting between the English and his Government. Apprehensive of a serious Maratha invasion of Hindustan the defensive union which had been formed against the Abdali was now set in motion by the English Government against the Marathas. The Jats had already begun hostilities and the wazir was firm in his attachment to the English. The Marathas became discouraged by their state of isolation in Hindustan and consequently gave up their aggressive designs. Rajah Jawahir had received letters from the Governor for readjusting their old alliance to meet the new exigency and build up a more solid confederacy to preserve the peace of Hindustan against all enemies, including the Marathas. The Rajah signified his regard for the friendship of the English and sent Padre Don Pedro to Calcutta "to communicate to the Governor the secrets of his heart" (ibid, p. 171 ; letter No. 642, Oct. 31, 1767).

Jawahir's Pilgrimage to Pushkar
[Nov.-Dec. 1767].

Rajah Jawahir Singh had reached the very summit of his power and glory by a series of brilliant victories. Proud of his army and wealth, he thought he could with impunity, insult and oppress his weaker neighbours who appeared like so many pigmies to his delusive vision. Angry Providence soon hurled him down from the pinnacle of fortune and humbled his pride. "Delivered from all the troubles which the Marathas could give him, and also in a certain degree above them, feared by the Ruhelas, and respected, beyond what he could claim, elsewhere, master of a vast country flourishing and tranquil, he knew not," says Father Wendel, "how to taste long the advantages of his good fortune or rather he himself sought to interrupt it and wished to invert by his own hands the high fortune, which up to the present had not ceased to follow him; in spite of the efforts which often he had made himself to banish it." [French MS., 67.]

Jawahir owed his misfortune to the unhappy issue of a quarrel which he himself most wantonly provoked with Maharajah Madho Singh of Jaipur. As close neighbours the rulers

of Bharatpur and Jaipur had causes enough for
bad blood.   The latter could not be expected to
watch with satisfaction the growth of the new-
born Jat Power, a permanent menace to his
State.   It was nevertheless true that the Bharatpur principality could not in its infancy have
lived and prospered without the patronage of
Maharajah Sawai Jai Singh, and this was grate-
fully acknowledged by Jawahir's father and
grand-father who always showed—more out of
goodness than fear—proper respect and homage
to the ruling house of Jaipur, as to a superior
and patron.   But the accession of Madho Singh,
—against whom Suraj Mal had fought on behalf
of Maharajah Iswari Singh—disturbed this cordial relation; the haughtiness of the new ruler
offended the Jat chief, who ceased to attend the
darbar of Jaipur on the day of the Dashera.   As
human nature goes, patrons become enemies
when their patronage is no longer required; so
this coldness developed into bitter enmity when
Jawahir succeeded his father, and haughtiness
was pitted against haughtiness.   Rajah Jawahir
Singh believed too seriously in his reputed
Yádava descent to feel, like his ancestors, any
diffidence, due to consciousness of a less exalted
birth, in claiming equality with the Rajput ruling
houses of the Solar and Lunar races.   Once, it

is said, some advisers of the Rajah, told him
that he ought to show deference to the Maharajah of Jaipur, at least in consideration of his
descent from Ráma, who bridged the ocean.
"Well," replied Jawahir, "if his ancester threw
a bridge across the ocean my ancestor [Shri
Krishna] held up Govardhan hill for seven days
on his little finger !"   His father and grand-
father were content to be addressed as Braj-Raj
[King of Braj, *i.e.*, the Mathura district] as a
compliment to their sovereignty over that tract.
But Jawahir, as if to pique the ruler of Jaipur,
assumed the lofty title of Maharajah Sawai
Jawahir Singh Bharatendra [Lord Paramount of
India, Fr. MS., 71] and, vying in splendour
and magnificence made his Court outshine that
of his neighbour.   "In short", as Ghulam Ali,
the author of *Shah Alam Nama* says, "Jawahir
raised his head to the stature of Maharajah
Madho Singh" (Pers. MS., p. 3).   The ruler of
Jaipur who had not the power to resent it, bore
the humiliation in silence.   But his aggressive
adversary at last compelled him to take up arms
for preserving the honour of his house and the
sanctity of the soil of Amber.

No incident of the history of the eighteenth
century is so green in the memory of the
country-side, and nothing is so much distorted

by national prejudices as the armed pilgrimage
of Jawahir Singh to Pushkar through Jaipur
territory—the fierce battle of Mawdá [Maonda],
and his inglorious retreat. The Jat attributes
the disaster to the intrigue of the Rao Rajah
Pratap Singh, the founder of the Alwar State—
who having quarrelled with his suzerain, Madho
Singh of Jaipur, fled for protection to Suraj Mal,
and afterwards incited Jawahir Singh against his
overlord. He is said to have treacherously
deserted Jawahir and directed the Jaipur army
to attack the Jats when entangled in a difficult
pass. The Rajput version on the other hand is
that Jawahir Singh demanded the surrender of
the wife of Nahar Singh, which the Maharajah
of Jaipur declined, because the lady feared ill-
treatment at the hands of Jawahir. She afterwards swallowed poison,* lest a calamity should
befall her protector on her account. The brave
Naruka chief whose patriotism prevailed over
his sense of gratitude for the hospitality of the
Jat, came over to the army of Jaipur and fought
for upholding the honour of his country. No
more authentic account of it can be found than
that in the unbiassed narrative of Father

---

* Appendix, p. 111, *Life of Maharajah Sawai Iswari Singh,*
(in Hindi) by Thakur Narendra Singh Varma, Vaidic Press,
Ajmir.

Wendel, who penned it within twelve months
of its occurrence.

"The Jats.........had for many years past
some quarrels [with the Rajah of Jaipur] regarding a small tract of country* not far from Deeg,
where there was always subject for misunderstanding, as ordinarily happens on the frontier
between different territories. It went at last to
the extent of having troublesome consequence
by an open rupture which appeared inevitable.
This affair, however, had been, or seemed about
to be settled by compromise. Jawahir Singh,
proud of his forces† and riches and puffed up
by his fortune, did not cease to treat haughtily
the Rajputs and their Rajah, and also with a
certain insolence which was neither seasonable
nor decent for him......He at this time took the
fancy to go and make a pilgrimage to the
Pushkar lake in Marwar territory, close to

---

* This refers to Kama (long. 77°-20′ lat. 27°-40′), situated
about 15 miles north-west of Deeg. Kama was for a long
time a bone of contention between the two States. Rajah
Ranjit Singh Jat got it from Mahadji Sindhia, and since then
has been in possession of the Bharatpur Rajahs.

† Jawahir Singh had a large and well-disciplined army
led by able European captains. Somru had been in his
employ since 1765 and M. Rene Madec, the renowned French
general, joined his service in the month of June or July of the
year 1767. [Le Nabob Rene Madec, p. 43]. The restless
mind of the Rajah hit upon this adventure as an opportunity
to test the mettle of his army upon the Kachhwas.

Ajmir, and to have also an interview with the
Rathor Rajah of that country, with whom he
commenced a sort of limited friendship.........
Having then with this design assembled all his
forces, more to make a show than from necessity, in spite of the dissuasions of others, he
began the journey of more than 70 *kos* outside
his own country with a numerous* army, as if
he was going to fight against all the Rajputs and
conquer their territories" [French MS., p. 67].

With banners unfurled and drums beating,
the Jat proudly set his foot upon the soil of
Amber and marched triumphantly towards the
holy lake, doing great damage to the Rajput
territory. A momentary stupor had seized the
Kachhwa, but the heir of Mān Singh and Mirzā
Rajah Jai Singh could not long bear the defiant
flourishes of the enemy, (challenging him to a
trial of strength). The whole of Amber,
peasants and lords, rose to their feet to strike
a blow for her honour. Maharajah Madho
Singh, whose fiery Sisodia blood had been
cooled down by old age and misfortune, was
roused to a sense of his honour by his feudal
chiefs : They said to him in indignation and

---

* Harcharan, author of the *Chahar-Gulzar-i-Shujai* gives
an exaggerated estimate of Jawahir's army : "Sixty thousand
horse, one lakh of footmen, and two hundred guns."

sorrow, "Will you suffer to be thus insulted by
a man whose father and grand-father were the
tenants of your house and who stood with folded
hands before your ancestors?" "By no
means" replied the Rajah "so long as the seed
of Kachhwas remains on earth." The *levy en
masse* of Amber was ordered. Dalil Singh and
other Rajput chiefs with twenty thousand horsemen and an equal number of infantry occupied
the road by which Jawahir was expected to
return.

Rajah Jawahir Singh had reached the holy
lake and after finishing his ablutions there, he
halted for some days and sealed a vow of friendship by the exchange of turbans with Rajah
Bijay Singh Rathor, who met him there. The
Rajputs were watching his return march; but
his army being a large and powerful one, they
did not offer him a pitched battle. Jawahir
Singh avoided the direct route, and tried to make
his way through Tornawati, a hilly country,
thirty miles north of Jaipur. Rao Rajah Pratap
Singh who had been for several years a refugee
at Bharatpur, now deserted Jawahir Singh, and
joined the forces of Jaipur. He counselled an
attack upon the Jat army while it was threading
its way through a defile and the famous battle
of *Maonda* was fought on *the 14th Dec. 1767*.

This battle has been the theme of many a stirring ballad; each side claiming the victory and extolling the heroism of their respective chiefs. The memory of this ancient feud still causes some heart-burning to both peoples. M. Madec who had accompanied Rajah Jawahir Singh to Pushkar, and fought for him on that occasion, has left the following account of this event. "The latter [Rajah of Jaipur], piqued by the insult, followed the Jats, with his army, on their return. He had 16,000 cavalry. Near Jaipur the Jats had to traverse a defile. They made their baggage go ahead, in such a way as to cover them. They hoped to escape the pursuit of their enemies, but were overtaken and attacked at a disadvantage. The Jats routed them by a counter-march. The artillery and infantry of the assailants were too slow. The Jats took advantage of it to enter the defile, preceded by their baggages at a distance of three leagues. The Rajah of Jainagar engaged in pursuing them in the gorge, and overtook them in the middle. The Jats then made a half-turn to offer battle.

They engaged towards noon. The enemy cavalry put at the very first, that of the Jats to the rout. The latter saved themselves by

14

falling back upon their baggage, crying out that all was lost; the peasants then plundered a great part of the baggage. But the party of Madec and that of the German Sombre, who laboured in that affair with all the bravery and prudence of a great soldier, restored the battle and defeated the Rajah of Jainagar. Nearly 10,000 men fell in the two armies together, among them nearly all the generals of the enemy's army. The victors, deprived of their baggage, of which they could not find even the fragments, were themselves put to great hardship. They had to abandon a part of their artillery* on

---

* Wendel thus describes the plight of the vanquished: "The fortune of the Jats remains shaken and the result has been entirely fatal to them. They have returned home despoiled, stupefied and overthrown, and Jawahir Singh, having left there all his train of artillery (70 pieces of different calibres), tents and baggage" [French MS., 68]. Suraj Mal, the bard of Bundi, commemorates this episode thus :

" तावत छव भर तीप कीस लुद्दे कच्छवाहन ।
भरतनेर गयी जइ मारवाय बिपाइन ॥
जिसे कुरम औौष नाग अइन बिबि नाहव ।
समत वेड्डनु संग आय पकरीह्दि कवाहर ॥
संख्जत भुजङ्ग सस्सिमान सक १८२४ हमतक यरु जग हुर ।
अयनेर विजय अइन मजन भर बिदित आब्रज भुव " ॥

The Kachhwas captured the Umbrella of Royalty, guns and treasure. The Jat, after having his soldiers slaughtered, fled to Bharatpur. As the king of beasts looks upon the elephant [as his prey] so did the Kurma [Kachhwa] warriors look upon the Jats. Had not Somru been in the company

account of the state of the road" (*Le Nabob Rene Madec*, pp. 49, 50).

On that fateful day Jawahir Singh fought with his accustomed vigour and tenacity, and maintained his ground till the darkness of evening brought him respite. Dalil Singh, the brave commander-in-chief of the Jaipur army fell in the fight with three generations of his descendants and none but boys of ten remained to represent the baronial houses of Jaipur. The aggressor, however, was overthrown and once more it was proved that God is not always with the heaviest battalion as tyrants believe.

Jawahir's struggle with his numerous enemies.

Maharajah Jawahir Singh now presented a sorry figure, shorn of his power and splendour, derided by enemies, and deserted by friends. "Now is the moment," was the exultant cry that his enemies raised from every quarter. At the first report of his defeat, the country beyond the Chambal rose against him, and it was lost as suddenly as it had been gained. Maharajah Madho Singh entered the Jat territories with

---

Jawahir would have been captured...................The battle took place in the year 1824 [of the *Vikrama era*]. This victory of [the ruler of] Jaipur, and the defeat of the Jats became known to the furthest limit of the land of *Braj*.

60,000 soldiers and took ample vengeance by
ravaging them. Nawab Musavi Khan Baloch of
Farrukhnagar (who had been released a year
before from his confinement at Bharatpur), and
the Ruhelas were ready to co-operate with the
Rajputs. His unprincipled allies, the Sikhs
began desolating his two outlying provinces
(Wendel, 69; *Le Nabob Rene Madec*, 50).
The Emperor Shah Alam II. was invited by
Maharajah Madho Singh either to come in
person, or if that was not possible, to send
some English commander with a battalion of
European troops to reinforce him. "Now is
the opportunity" he wrote, "which Your
Majesty should seize.........your old and hereditary servant and the other Rajahs in his confederacy are ready in allegiance with their
levies......The royal seat of Akbarabad will
fall to Your Majesty." [Pers. Cor. ii. 224].
The Emperor sent,—though he disavowed it
afterwards—"a royal mandate to Rajah Madho
Singh to advance and take possession of the
fort of Agra, after effecting a junction with
Musavi Khan's forces who was to proceed from
Delhi [*ibid*, 234].

Every one counselled Jawahir to make a
compromise with the Rajputs; but the Jat

preferred breaking to bending and to abide by
the chances of a war than to sue for terms from
his victorious enemy. He decided to carry on
war by buying over the Sikhs. He paid them
7 lakhs of Rupees to keep them away from
plundering his territory, and opened negotiation with them to enlist into his service 20,000
of them. The lethargy caused by the late
defeat was shaken off, and warlike preparations
commenced in earnest. M. Madec got an
increase of Rs. 5,000 to his monthly allowance
for increasing his corps. [*Le Nabob Rene
Madec*, p. 50].

Meanwhile a plot was being hatched by
Nawab Shuja-ud-daulah to crush Jawahir's
power. The wazir suggested to the Emperor
a comprehensive and plausible plan, which, if
acted upon, would have brought about the
extinction of the Jat Power. He asked the
Emperor first to dissuade the Sikh sardars from
assisting Jawahir Singh by the offer of the same
amount of subsidy on behalf of Madho Singh
and the grant of royal favours; secondly to send
a prince of the royal line with *farmáns* to the
Ruhela chiefs to unite them under him and
conquer that part of Jawahir Singh's territories
that lay on the left of the Jamuna and bordered
on the Ruhela possessions;—the conquered

territories were to be left in the Ruhela hands
in order to ensure their loyalty. The wazir
most enthusiastically offered his services to
carry out his plan against Jawahir Singh:
"Whenever His Majesty thinks fit to call upon
the writer [Shuja-ud-daulah] *he will perform*
what he has represented." [Pers. Cor. ii.
234, 235, letter No. 835, dated March 2, 1768].
In short Jawahir's enemies were drawing a net
around him, which appeared too strong for him
to break through. At this critical moment the
attitude of the Bengal Government became the
decisive factor. Leaving active hostility out of
account, if the English had even secretly
countenanced this scheme, the Emperor, Shuja-
ud-daulah, Najib Khan and all the Ruhelas
would have been in full march against Jawahir
Singh whom even the Sikhs could not have
saved. But the Bengal Government, with an
integrity and firmness rare in the politics of the
eighteenth century, stood true to their alliance
with Jawahir, and vigorously checkmated all the
hostile designs of his enemies. The Emperor
and Shuja-ud-daulah dared not move without
the consent of the Governor of Bengal. When
Madho Singh found no response to his appeal
from any quarter and saw the Sikhs coming to
the assistance of Jawahir Singh, he made peace

with the Jats and retired to his own country before the arrival of the dreaded cavalry of the Panjab.

Death of Jawahir Singh.

Reverses failed to teach any moderation to Jawahir Singh. Strife was the very breath of his nostrils and without it life seemed to have had no charm for him. "The war having been ended on this side [against Madho Singh], it broke out on another. The Jat Rajah sent Madec to besiege a fort where another Rajput clan was entrenched. In a month and a half Madec succeeded in climbing one of the bastions, but the assault failed on account of his being abandoned by the Indian troops who were frightened by the terrible fire of the defenders. He clung to the foot of the breach for making a second attack. The garrison in fear capitulated. [Le Nabob Rene Madec, 50].

Never did the fierce will and the untiring energy of Rajah Jawahir Singh shine forth more brilliantly than during the 6 or 7 months following his reverse in Rajputana. With great rapidity he mastered a desperate situation and brought it back to normality. The late reverse appeared to have done little injury to

him, and he was up again on his legs. His
arms were recovering their wonted lustre and
his territories their erstwhile prosperity. He
threw himself heart and soul into re-organizing
his army, and particularly increasing the
European corps and the field artillery. His
authority was re-established everywhere in his
dominion and his name respected and feared
abroad. His neighbours trembled at the prospect of a more tremendous outburst of his
wrath ; fortunately for them the swift hand of
destiny silenced this unspent volcano.

The story of Jawahir's violent death (July,
1768) runs as follows: "It is said that
Jawahir Singh formed a friendship with a
soldier whom he admitted to very great intimacy
and showed him regard and honour exceeding
proper limits and raised him from a low to a
high rank. The degree of this man's com-
panionship made him superior [in status] to
other courtiers. By chance, some improper
acts were done by him, and Jawahir Singh
forbade the soldier to come to his private
audience and bedroom, disgraced and humbled
him, and made him contemptible in his own
eyes and in those of the public. This man,
being roused to a sense of honour, sought for
some means of killing Jawahir Singh. One

-day Jawahir Singh with a small party rode out for hunting. This soldier, at that time, took horse and arrived with sword and shield, and at a place where Jawahir Singh was standing carelessly with a few men, he struck him down with his sword crying out "This is the punishment for the disgrace and insult you did to me." This event happened in the month of Safar, 1182 H. (June-July 1768).*

Popular traditions, as recorded by Growse (*Mathura*, 25), attributes the murder of Jawahir to the instigation of his enemy, Maharajah Madho Singh of Jaipur. The sudden death of Jawahir Singh within 8 months of his quarrel with the Rajah of Jaipur who undoubtedly benefited by this event, possibly gave colour to this unjust calumny which has no foundation in truth, or documentary proof. As regards the murder of Jawahir Singh the author of the *Siyar*† says: "He gave a chobdar named

---

* *Chahar Gulzar* MS.‡ this date, though not very definite, is undoubtedly correct. From a letter of the Emperor to the Governor of Bengal, dated 27th August, 1768, we learn that Jawahir died before that date (Pers. Cor. ii. 299).

Don Pedro De Silva formally announces the death of Jawahir Singh and the accession of his successor Ratan Singh, to the Government of Bengal on 7th Sept., 1768 (*ibid*, p. 304).

† The translator of the *Siyar* puts it thus: "He put one Haidar, a chobdar of his own at the head of his affairs and army; a measure that lost him the heart of his troops, and

Sada, predominant authority over the whole body of his *sardars,* and thus made them all extremely oppressed,—they instigated one to slay Jawahir Singh. A short time after his occupying the throne of his father he was killed treacherously.'' [Pers. text, *Siyár,* iv. 34]. M. Madec, who was in the service of Jawahir Singh at the time of his death, does not accuse anybody : stating simply that the Rajah was murdered by an unknown man, who beheaded him with one stroke of his sword [*Le Nabob Rene Madec,* 50].

Character and policy of Rajah Jawahir Singh.

Rajah Jawahir Singh lacked neither the soldierly qualities nor the administrative capacity of his father. Apparently engrossed with the exciting game of war, he was never remiss

---

shocked his commanders to such a degree that one of them resolved to fall upon him and put him to death. This man having a favourable moment, killed him upon his very *Mesned* ! !'' (Eng. trans. iv. 34). Sàda is perhaps the more correct reading, because Abdul Karim Kashmiri, author of the *Bayan-o-Waqa,* says that ''Jawahir Singh was slain by an oppressed *Brahman''* (MS. p. 302). However it is likely that Mustapha, the translator, who used only one manuscript, quite naturally preferred the reading, Haidar, to Sada, a rather obscure name. But he cannot be excused for his want of fidelity to the original text which is little likely to have varied so greatly. Those who put implicit faith in translations should take a warning from this.

in his attention to the details of the civil administration, or indifferent to the promotion of the arts of peace. His Court was splendid and magnificent, the best market in Hindustan for the valour of a soldier, skill of an architect,* and the flattering harp of a native bard. He paid his troops more regularly and more handsomely than his father, and there was no occasion when he did not generously recompense good services. "His finances were in the best order and his people the least imposed on in the country and he had political views" which appeared very wise to his European military chief [*Le Nabob Rene Madec*, 51]. He left behind him not a set of turbulent and rebellious military chiefs, but a numerous and well-disciplined army, commanded by loyal officers, who faithfully obeyed even a contemptuous voluptuary like Ratan Singh, his successor. His clemency spared his younger brothers, though he knew them to be so many thorns in the path of his adopted minor son. At times, he could rise to the height of generosity and forgive his worst enemies, as we find in the release of Bahadur Singh and Nawab Musavi

---

*A detailed account of the buildings of Jawahir Singh along with those of Suraj Mal and other Jat Rajahs will be found in a subsequent section, *The Jat style of Architecture.*

Khán Baloch,—dangerous political prisoners—
on the occasion of his nephew's birth. Friends
remembered him as a knight-errant, bold,
magnificent and open-handed, and enemies as a
man, capricious and obstinate, a narrow bigot
and blood-thirsty tyrant—a comet in the political
sky of Hindustan.

Rajah Jawahir Singh, unlike his father,
had little control over his passions, no respect
for antiquity and tradition, no catholicity of
heart. At any rate, tradition, no doubt preju-
diced to a great extent, associates his name with
the despoilation of the relics of the Mughal
imperial grandeur. He is said to have seated
himself on the black marble throne of the
Emperor Jahangir,—a sacrilege which made the
proud seat of the Great Mughal, to burst in
pique as it were, leaving a crack which is still
to be seen! It was perhaps during the regime
of Jawahir Singh, the strongest and most vindictive among the Jat Rajahs that "The Great
Mosque of Agra was changed into a market:
the grain merchants had order to expose their
goods for sale there. The butchers' shops were
closed. They [the Jats] made very severe pro-
hibition of the slaughter of oxen, cows and
also of kids [?]...All public profession of the
Muhammadan religion was interdicted under

very harsh treatment. The *muazins* were ordered to cease their functions. One man gave the *azan* but the Government of Agra pulled his tongue out.''* Though it is but human to retaliate, it was certainly unworthy of the son of Suraj Mal who had honoured the bones of a Muslim refugee,—Shamsher Bahadur, by building a mosque over it at Deeg. [*Imad*, 203.]

Jawahir Singh too prematurely and too violently changed what was more or less a tribal confederacy into a centralized State, and rendered himself a despot with the help of mercenary troops. He crushed life out of the State and the people; the one ceased to grow of itself, and, the other, cowed by mercenaries and relegated to a secondary position, lost their vitality and spirit. Suraj Mal built up a

---

* *Le Nabob Rene Madec*, 47. M. Madec says : "I saw, some years ago, that unfortunate man, who begged alms, supplied with a letter from the *mullahs* of the Great Mosque of Agra, in which they attested that the faithful one, exercising the ministry with which he was charged, had been so cruelly treated by the idolators'' [*ibid*].

It is doubtful whether some deception was not practised upon the credulity of the stranger, which is, by means uncommon to this day. M. Madec does not specify the name of Jawahir Singh but says *"When the Jats became possessors of Agra."* The known character of Jawahir Singh warrants the above inference.

structure which reflected faithfully the political
instinct and tradition of his own people. But
to the eye of Jawahir Singh, it appeared anti-
quated, inelegant, lacking in sympathy and
compactness, unworthy of a *Prince*, though
comfortable for a Jat. As in society Jawahir
regulated his life according to the then up-to-
date fashion of a Prince or an Amir, discarding
the old simplicity of his father, so in politics
he breathed the atmosphere of imperialistic
Delhi. People to a certain extent imitated the
fashion of the Prince, and one could see [the
vices, maxims, etiquette] Delhi near Deeg,
Kuhmir and Bharatpur as some of our countrymen see to-day London in Bombay and
Calcutta. With the new society established in
these places, the customs, dress, buildings,
language and all in general, had changed,
among the Jats.*   Jawahir seemed to move with
the spirit of the time when he set about transforming a feudal confederacy into a centralized,
despotic Government of the Mughal type.
But as he was eager to make himself master
of his own household, so was every Jat, who

---

* Wendel, French MS., 40, 41. He adds : "It must be
confessed that at the same time [in spite of considerable polish]
one may always notice their naive rusticity in the midst of very
brilliant fortune with which they see themselves surrounded"
[*ibid*, 41].

resented autocracy and whose innerself remained the same, in spite of all his outward polish. Without making a tactful compromise, he removed every powerful opponent to his fierce will and thereby recklessly destroyed a considerable amount of national energy and efficiency. If the Jats were the ancient Yadavas, Kansa (the uncle of Shri Krishna, who usurped despotic authority over the Yadava confederacy with the help of mercenary fighters, and oppressed his kinsmen) was perhaps reborn among them in the person of Maharajah Sawai Jawahir Singh Bharatendra !

CHAPTER XII.

CIVIL WAR .

Rajah Ratan Singh Jat (1182 A.H., May 1768—April 1769).

The glory of the Jats departed with Rajah Jawahir Singh and confusion fell on their kingdom when his iron grip no longer held the tribe together. His younger brother Ratan Singh, an imbecile and profligate youth, succeeded him, and reigned, according to the author of *Imad-us-Saadat*, for ten months and thirteen days. The few months of his rule were uneventful and spent wholly in ignoble diversions. Four thousand dancing girls surrounded his person; with them he started, a few days after his accession, for Brindában [Madec, 51] to enjoy the rainy season there in gay revelry. All the scenes of the mythic past were acted once again by this reputed descendant of the Divine Lover of Braj, perhaps in a more magnificent manner. He never returned to his capital; his life tragically ended there at the hand of a Gosain named Rupánand.

M. Madec, the French Captain, was also

in the retinue of Rajah Ratan Singh during this
pilgrimage. He was impressed very much by
his magnificent *fêtes* on the Jamuna, and his
extravagant piety. He says, "The Rajah had
another weakness [besides his passion for
women]—namely that for magicians, enchan-
ters, and alchemists. He had taken away one
of these last [=alchemists] to the festivity at
Brindában. For a long time the alchemist
kept the Rajah deluded by pretending to have
made gold. Finally the Rajah pressed him
and threatened [to kill?] him in case he did
not show it to him. The deceiver promised to the
Rajah to make it in his presence, if he should
remain alone with him far from indiscreet
people. When the Rajah consented to it, the
magician drew out a dagger and opened the
belly of his master.* Before dying, the latter

---

* We learn from a letter, entered under the date, the
1st of August, 1769, sent by one Rajah Parsudh Ray: "Ratan
Singh Jat has been assassinated by the hand of an alchemist,
and has been succeeded by his son Kheri Singh, an infant of
a year and a half. Dan Sáhi has been appointed Regent."
[Pers. Cor. ii. 386.] This corroborates the notice in the
French Memoirs. Ratan Singh died perhaps in *April, 1769;*
because the wazir informed the Governor about his death
in a letter entered under the date 11th May, 1769 (Pers. Cor. ii.
357). The *Waqa* says: "On the 5th Zihijja 1182 A. H.,
[April 12, 1769], news reached that Rajah Ratan Singh Jat,
has been killed at his camp in Sri Brindában by Gosain
Rupánánd with the blow of "*Kátár.*" Sada Sukh and Khushhal

called the highest chief of the nation and
motioned to him his minor son" [Madec, 51]
Abdul Karim Kashmiri, the author of the
Bayán-o-Waqá, gives an almost identical description of this event, "Rajah Ratan Singh
went to him and pressed him hard saying, 'If
you do not prepare the sample [*lit*. first fruits]
of gold [*lit*. alchemy], I shall kill you'. The
darwesh declared 'The sample [*namunah*] is
ready; it will be shown towards the latter part
of the night'. Ratan Singh owing to his
curiosity and eagerness kept himself awake
throughout the whole night. The *Bairagi* sent
word that the Rajah should have privacy *i.e.*,
be alone, and that he was bringing the sample.
Ratan Singh ordering his attendants to go out
sent for the Bairagi. When he was found
alone, the Bairagi despatched him with one
blow of a dagger" [*Bayan* MS., p. 302.]
Harcharan's details about this affair are rather
confusing, but he gives the date of the incident
correctly, *viz.*, 1st *Zihijja, 1182 A.H.* [8th
April, 1769], which is borne out by a more
accurate authority, the *Waqa-i-Shah Alam II.*
(*Waqa*, 225).

Ray cut off the head of the Gosain" [*Waqá*, 225.] We thus
find the calculation of *10 months and eleven days* of the *Imád*
to be fairly accurate.

The regency and civil war.

After the sudden death of Rajah Ratan Singh at Brindában, a great assembly of the chiefs was convoked at Deeg, by Dán Sáhi, who had been entrusted with the person of the infant heir. The child, Kheri Singh, was seated on the *masnad* and Dán Sáhi assumed the regency, with their approval. But as soon as they were back to their provinces, they refused to submit to the regent, who had no more right to rule than any other person among them. This discontent was fanned by the intrigues of Nawal Singh and Ranjit Singh, half-brothers of the late Rajah. While M. Madec, who supported the regent Dán Sáhi, was absent from Deeg trying to reduce the provinces to submission, a revolution was carried into effect by these two brothers [Madec, Sec. 51], who overthrew his regency. But they quarrelled over the coveted office of regent. Nawal Singh being the elder had a better claim, but the younger preferred the decision of the sword. The turbulent nobles, keen about securing their own independence, formed factions and kindled the flames of civil war, [beginning of 1770, A.D.] Ranjit Singh, unable to contend against his brother, turned a

traitor to his house and purchased the assistance
of the Sikhs to crush him.

M. Madec took the side of the elder
brother and led an army against Ranjit Singh,
who had shut himself up in the fort of Kuhmir.
He laid siege to it when 70,000 Sikhs, invited
by Ranjit Singh, came to its succour [Madec,
52.] He raised the siege in order to go and
encounter the Sikhs. One morning Madec
went out with 500 men, 2 guns and one elephant
on which he was mounted, to reconnoitre the
enemy's position and incautiously pushed too
far ahead. He was hemmed in by the Sikhs
[*ibid* 52] and was only saved by the arrival of
Jat reinforcements. Nawal Singh inflicted a
defeat upon the Sikhs [Pers. Cor. iii. 43], but
fearing the advent of the Marathas bought them
[Sikhs] off by the payment of a large sum of
money. The Sikhs departed for their country,
leaving the traitor to his fate. (March, 1770.)

The Maratha interference in the civil war.

Within a decade from the third battle of
Panipat the Marathas recovered from the shock
of that great disaster. But they became none
the wiser by their late overthrow and drew no
lessons from it. Towards the end of 1769,
Visaji Pandit, Ramchander Ganesh, Tukoji

Holkar, Mahadji Sindhia and others crossed the
Narmada with a large army to reassert the
dominion of their nation in Hindustan. The
energy and enthusiasm of these chiefs like those
of their predecessors were more conspicuous in
harassing the helpless Rana of Gohad and in
tormenting the worn out and afflicted Rajput
rulers than in fighting their sturdier opponents.
Instead of playing the noble rôle of strong
peace-makers among the warring peoples and
princes of Hindustan, they chose to play the
part of mischief-mongers, fomenters of treason
and civil strife. While the sons of Suraj Mal
were fighting out with swords their claims to
the regency, the Marathas were watching the
struggle with satisfaction from Karauli, the seat
of their operations against the Rajah of Jaipur.
When Nawal Singh, the elder and more legitimate claimant to the regency, well nigh brought
the civil war to an end by defeating the unjust
pretensions of his younger brother Ranjit and
appeasing the Sikhs, the Marathas entered the
Jat country, began pillaging the neighbourhood
of Bharatpur and instigated Ranjit Singh to
re-open* the fratricidal war. (Middle of March,

---

* "The Marathas.....................*entered into correspondence
with Ranjit Singh.................*Consequently he met them at a
small distance from the fort of Kuhmir, his residence." Pers..
Cor. iii. p. 41.]

1770). They acted as if Maharashtra had sent them this time not to avenge the slaughter of her sons and the dishonour of her daughters led away into captivity from the field of Panipat, but to destroy those who risked their all to save and relieve the misery of her fleeing children. They sent an invitation to Najib-ud-daulah—who was the author of all their misfortune and shame—to come and join them in crushing the Jats once for all. The Ruhela chief, who had retired to his safe retreat at Najibabad for fear of Maharajah Jawahir Singh and his Sikh allies, eagerly seized this opportunity of extracting one thorn with another,. and with a powerful army reached as far as Sikandrabad in the Doab. The piety which Rani Kishori acquired by feeding the fugitive Maratha Brahmans with milk and sweets indeed brought a swift return.

The Marathas ravaged a considerable portion of the Jat territory and everywhere appointed officials in the name of Ranjit Singh. Unwilling to risk a pitched battle with the army of Nawal Singh, formidable on account of the presence of Somru and M. Madec, the Marathas concentrated their forces under the shelter of the fort of Kuhmir, 13 miles south of Deeg. Nawal Singh who was encamped at

a short distance from the town of Deeg, tried
in vain to bring the enemy to an engagement.
On the morning of the 9th Zihijja [April 5,
1770 A.D.], he "sent a challenge to the
Marathas to quit their position under the walls
of the fort and give him battle." At noon news
reached him that "Tukoji Holkar, and Jai Ram
were on their way to meet Najib-ud-daulah."
In the afternoon tents were ordered to be struck,
baggages were sent ahead to Govardhan (about
six *kos* east of Deeg), and Nawal Singh with
his army started in that direction. The resolution was too sudden; scarcely any *risalah* was
ready and many soldiers went to Deeg to
procure their necessaries.

Two high roads run almost parallel west
to east from Deeg and Kuhmir, gradually
diminishing the distance in between, till they
meet at Mathura. The army of Nawal Singh
was moving along the northern road, while the
Marathas who also began to march eastward
took the southern road. These two roads are
joined by a cross path running from Govardhan
to Sonkh, the distance being not more than 5
miles. Somewhere between these two places,
the hostile armies came within a distance of
two *kos* from each other. Till then Nawal
Singh had no idea of giving battle on that day;

but the proximity of the enemy tempted two of his chiefs to offer fight. One of these was Dan Sahi, brother-in-law of Nawal Singh and a dashing cavalry officer, very proud of his *risalah* of horse composed of Rajputs and Bhadauriyas; the other was Gosain Balanand the brave leader of the impetuous Naga *sannyasis*. But Somru and M. Madec objected to this proposal on the score of the lateness of the hour. Nawal Singh was carried away by the rash exhortation of Dan Sahi and ordered an attack. The Marathas formed themselves near the fort of Sonkh to meet the onset. A fierce battle ensued which went on even after nightfall. Dan Sahi led a gallant charge at the head of 2,000 choice horse; but before he could be effectually supported the Marathas with their artillery and rockets forced him to fall back with heavy loss. After a short artillery duel both the parties came to a close fight with swords. Ganga Prasad and Jud Raj led the division under the personal command of the regent. But Nawal Singh lost his head as well as heart in the heat of action. He alighted from his elephant, and mounting a horse retired behind the impenetrable lines of Somru's sepoys. Even there he trembled for his life; he threw away his insignia of royalty lest he should be recognised by the enemy, and fled into the fort [Govardhan?]. The issue of the fight was still hanging in the balance; several *sardars* of rank immediately afterwards went in search of their faint-hearted chief into the fort and urged him in vain to show himself in the field, telling him that the fortunes of the battle might still be retrieved by their steadiness and courage. But no assurance could stimulate his craven heart. The true Jat fought well, but the Maratha fought better in the darkness of the night. The squares of Somru and M. Madec very bravely stood repeated and determined charges of the enemy. Worn out and exhausted, and deserted by their timid master, the army of Nawal Singh at last broke and fled. "Never was a greater number of *sardárs* killed and wounded in any battle. As to the rank and file it [was] computed that 5,000 horse and foot were wounded and 2,000 killed. All the artillery was left on the field except two light pieces which Somru [had] brought off. The army was so completely broken that numbers returned after wandering about seven *kos*, from the battle-field. Had it not been for the intrepid behaviour of Madec and Somru in covering the retreat, not a single man would have escaped the

sword of the Marathas" [Pers. Cor. iii. 52-
53.]* Nawal Singh stood a siege, barricading
the gates of Deeg. The Marathas who had also
lost a considerable number of men contented
themselves with watching him from beyond the
range of the fort guns.

A formidable coalition was now set on foot
to crush the Ját power altogether. Najib-ud-
daulah joined the Marathas, and with their aid
began to conquer the possessions of the Játs in
the Doab. Ghazi-ud-din Khán† hurried from
his retreat at Farrukhabad and united with the
Marathas. Repeated petitions were sent to
Shah Alam II to repair to his capital; but he

---

* Madec's division was almost annihilated. He alone lost
1400 men, and had not more than the wounded and the guard
of the camp left at Deeg. [Madec. sec. : 56.] This shows
that the number of the killed must have been greater than
that reported by the English news-writers. The *Waqa-i-Shah
Alam Sani* has an entry under the date 13th Zihijja, 1183, A. H.
"News reached...............that on the *8th*, a great battle was
fought between Nawal Singh and the Marathas.....................
Nawal Singh at first fled to garhi of *Aring* [? 5 miles *east* of
Govardhan, eight miles north-east of Sonkh, in a *contrary
direction*] afterwards to Deeg." [*Waqa*, 224]. Thus, we
notice one day's difference between the dates given by the
Waqa and the Pers. Cor. Harcharan gives an accurate and
fairly detailed account of the civil war between the two Ját
brothers. The author of the *Bayan-o-Waqa*, only notices it
briefly (p. 305).

† Ghazi-ud-din had fled from Bharatpur disgusted with the
conduct of Jawahir Singh. (Wendel).

was restrained by the opposition of Warren Hastings. Thus the Jats for the second time escaped utter annihilation from a combination of their relentless enemies through the silent and faithful services of their English allies. The Marathas made Mathura their head-quarters and began, in concert with the Ruhelas, a systematic conquest of the Jat country in the month of *Muharram 1184 A.H.* (May, 1770, A.D.) Najib-ud-daulah captured *Shikohabad Saádabad** and other parganas belonging to the Játs [*Waqa*, p. 229]. Next he proceeded to Koel [Aligarh] and took possession of the Ját territories there in the name of the Emperor. [*ibid*, p. 230.] Nawal Singh was saved from almost certain destruction by the disunion and jealousy which sprang up among his enemies after their first success. The Marathas themselves were divided into two parties, led respectively by Tukoji Holkar and Ramchander Ganesh on one side, and Visaji Pandit and Mahadji Sindhia on the other. Tukoji was in favour of an alliance with Najib-ud-daulah, but Sindhia and others distrusted him. The appearance

---

* Shikohabad is a pargana in the Mainpuri district on E. I. Ry. (lat. 27°.10′, long. 78°.40′). Saádabad is a tahsil of the Mathura, 28 miles east south-east of Mathura (lat. 27°.30′ long. 78°.5′).

of Ghazi-ud-din in the Maratha camp and
Sindhia's support of him created a distrust in
the minds of the Emperor and Najib-ud-daulah.
Nawal Singh took advantage of this situation
to send his *vakils* to the Ruhela chief, to negotiate a secret and separate peace with him. In
the first week of Jamada I, 1184 A.H. (last
week of August, 1770 A.D.), Najib secretly
made up his quarrel with the Jats [*Waqá*, 232].
More fortunate for Nawal Singh was the inter-
ception of a letter from Najib-ud-daulah to Hafiz
Rahamat Khán Ruhela, which contained some
reflections on the Marathas. Consequently a
coolness sprang up between Najib-ud-daulah and
Ramchander Ganesh. The Marathas under the
cloak of friendship prevented him from leaving
their camp, and sent for the vakil of Nawal
Singh Jat to talk of a compromise. A treaty of
peace was concluded [17th Jamada I, 1184
A.H.* *September, 8, 1770*], on the following
terms: (i) Nawal Singh should pay 65 lakhs
of Rupees in all, *exclusive* of the revenues

---

* The *Waqa-i-Shah Alam II* says : "News reached that
on the 17th Jamada I, 1184. A. H. [September 8, 1770]
Najib-ud-daulah holding *darbárs* day and night settled the affairs
of the Jats with the Maratha chiefs, gave *khilats* to the Maratha
chiefs, and took leave of them, leaving Nawab Zabita Khan
in their camp." [*Waqa*, 232.]

accruing from the provinces conquered by Najib and the Marathas, (ii) out of these 65 lakhs, he should pay down 10 lakhs in twenty days, 15 lakhs in two months, Rs. 7,50,000 in the month of Phagan, and the remaining half in three years; (iii) he should pay an annual *nazaránd* of 11 lákhs to the Marathas (iv) a jagir of 20 lakhs should be settled upon Ranjit Singh [Pers. Cor. iii. 97-98].

———

CHAPTER XIII.

REGENCY OF NAWAL SINGH

Difficulties of Nawal Singh.

A mutilated State, a factious nobility, a demoralised army, a depleted treasury and an anticipated revenue were the legacy of the civil war to Nawal Singh who now became the *de facto* Rajah of Bharatpur, though nominally a Regent for his infant nephew Kheri Singh. Prospects abroad were equally gloomy for him. The interregnum at Delhi had come to an end. The exiled Emperor Shah Alam II re-entered the imperial city in Nov. 1771. Though the Emperor was weak, incapable and vacillating, the empire showed signs of recovery under the able administration of Mirza Najaf Khán, the last of the great foreigners who graced the Court of the Timurids. With the re-establishment of the legitimate authority of the Mughal Emperor, the Jat Rajah stood revealed as the arch-rebel and usurper. The dispossessed Muslim jagirdars of the Doab and Hariana, the shaikzadas of Mewat—whom Suraj Mal had expelled from their estates, looked up to the Emperor to restore their rights to them. Mirza Najaf Khán was preparing a formidable army to subdue the Jats. The Marathas, upon whom Bharatpur had a moral claim for friendship and help, proved no less inimical than her worst enemies. Though Nawal Singh was at peace with the party of Mahadji Sindhia, the other party led by Tukoji Holkár made no secret of their intention to attack Jat territories after subduing Zabita Khán, against whom they were then carrying on war. The Maratha leaders, being virtually independent of the control of the Peshwa, had no unanimity among themselves and followed no common policy. Nawal Singh could, therefore, hardly count upon the help of the Marathas against the Mughals. Misfortunes came thick upon him; the first of the series was the desertion of his faithful French captain M. Madec.

M. Madec leaves the Jat service (1772).

M. Madec, the French free-lance captain, had since 1766 been serving the Bharatpur Raj with rare fidelity and devotion. He had shown steady courage and skill in every action, though it was often his misfortune to be always beaten and to suffer most for the indiscretion and cowardice of others. His corps had been almost annihilated, his horses, camels, arms and artillery captured by the Marathas in the last

battle near Govardhan (April, 1770). Rajah
Nawal Singh had the fairness to compensate the
brave captain for his losses. M. Madec set
himself to work with all possible quickness in
re-organizing his corps. He bought back his
fusils from the Marathas who knew not how to
handle them. He cast 12 pieces of cannon and
one mortar at Agra, and exercised the raw
recruits during the rainy season and winter
(July, 1770—Feb. 1771). At spring his corps
was completely reformed and during the peace
that followed he repaired his fortune too. He
now thought of returning to France but was prevailed upon to stay by the French governor of
Pondicherry, who represented to him that his
departure from India at that critical moment
would injure the cause of France. Throughout
the year 1771 the enemies of England were
watching with intense interest the progress of
the Maratha arms in Hindustan and the diplomatic tussle between Warren Hastings and
Mahadji Sindhia for securing the control of the
shadow of the Great Mughals.

At the beginning of the year 1772 M.
Madec was sent by Nawal Singh to raise contri-
butions from the districts in the Doab. He
returned eminently successful and was generously rewarded for his services. Soon after

this he was employed in the reduction of two fortified places where two of the near relations of the Regent had rebelled against his authority.* It took 15 days to reduce one fort, and one month and a half to capture another. The defenders gained only safety of life and *were conducted outside the frontiers*. But the besiegers lost one thousand men. Rajah Nawal Singh paid dearly for his ill-advised clemency. These traitors, as we shall notice hereafter, joined Mirza Najaf Khan, and rendered valuable services to him in enslaving their own kinsmen.

About this time Rajah Nawal Singh was virtually at war both with the Emperor and the Marathas. Najaf Quli Khan, lieutenant of Mirza Najaf Khan, was carrying on the conquest of the Jat possessions in Hariana and Niaz Beg Khan in the Doab. The Marathas† made no

---

* M. Madec does not give us the names of these places. He says : "The Regent had confided the defence of two cities to two of his relatives who proud of the confidence had turned rebels and declared themselves masters." [*Le Nabob Rene Madec*, sec. 76.]. One of these places was perhaps Ballamgarh which was, as we know from other sources, was taken away by Nawal Singh from the grandsons of Ballu Jat, its founder (*Delhi Gaz.*, p. 213).

† Khair-ud-din says : "In their [Marathas] heart sprang up the design of exterminating [*fiqar dar ándakhtan buniyad-i-haiyat*] Zabita Khán and Nawal Singh." (*Ibratnama*, MS., p. 214).

16

secret of their intention to attack Nawal Singh
after the subjugation of Zabita Khan. Fortunately for Nawal Singh, some differences had of
late arisen between the Marathas and the
Emperor through the intrigue of his faithless
minister Hisam-ud-din who became jealous of
the ascendancy of Mirza Najaf Khan in the
Court. The Jat chief took this opportunity to
sound the Emperor's views for a common defensive alliance against the Marathas, as he had
despaired of any permanent alliance with them
on fair and honourable terms. He sent M.
Madec as his envoy to Delhi (beginning of
October, 1772) to bring about a peaceful settlement of the territorial dispute and negotiate for
the Emperor's help in the emergency of a
Maratha invasion of the Jat territories. But
M. Madec became a changed man altogether by
breathing the atmosphere of the imperial Court,
which was now turned into a centre of anti-
English activity. He had been receiving
repeated letters from M. Chevalier, governor of
Pondicherry, who urged him to join the service
of the Emperor Shah Alam II. A war was now
expected between England and France in
Europe, and in anticipation, the heated brains
of the Frenchmen in India struck out many a
brilliant though futile plan of driving the

English into the Bay of Bengal. M. Duzarde was visiting every native Court in Hindustan to persuade the Indian princes to assemble under the standard of the Great Mughal, which was to move towards Bengal at an opportune moment. Though M. Madec had no complaints against the Jats who had been his regular and liberal paymaster, he resolved upon leaving their service in obedience to the call of his country. On the 1st Shabán, 1186 H. (28th October, 1772; *Waqa* MS., p. 236), he was granted an interview by the Emperor who gave him a *khilat* of seven pieces, an aigrette, and a sword. Madec immediately returned to Deeg with the design of removing secretly his family, property and troops. This, however, proved no easy affair. The following story of his escape, told by Madec himself, is interesting as well as instructive, showing the helplessness of the Indian armies of the old school before European discipline.

"I returned to Deeg without receiving orders from the Regent. This movement made them [the Jats] suspect me of having some understanding with the Emperor, and they began to watch me carefully. On the day of my arrival, I encamped outside the city, beyond the range of the fort-guns. The same evening I departed with 50 horsemen and the same number of infantry, and the conveyances necessary

for the transport of my family and property which
were at Barpur [Bharatpur]. I arrived at the city
six hours from the morning and spent that day in
preparing for the transport of my baggage to Deeg.
I sent messengers to Agra, and to all my gardens
and villages ordering my soldiers, who were guarding them, to come and join me ; but they could not
arrive on that day. The Regent,......having learnt
that I had departed for Bharatpur with a detachment of troops, inferred rightly that I went there
to bring away my family and property. He immediately ordered all troops within his reach to oppose
my enterprise ; he also sent orders for the villagers
on the road from Bharatpur to Deeg, that they should
take up arms and arrest me. It could not be done
so secretly as not to become known to me. I knew
all the dangers to which I was going to be exposed
with my family and the difficulties I was to have
in rejoining my corps with so few soldiers as I had
with me. There was no time to be lost. I hastened
the arrangement of my affairs, and four hours from
evening (about 10 P.M.), all being ready I set out
on my journey with my family and all that I possessed in the world.

At 8 hours from the evening (2 P.M.), having
travelled four leagues, I met a force of the Rajah.
The chief who commanded it asked to speak to me
on behalf of the Regent. I made him approach, he
told me that he was sent to request me to go to
the Regent. I replied that I was going to rejoin my
camp, and that it was very late. At the same time
I ordered my baggage to march and seize the path

in advance. I remained to talk with the chief.
After about one hour I thought it was time to join
my baggage. I quitted the troops of the Rajah.
The chief summoned me to follow him to talk with
the Regent. Seeing that I was not going to obey
him, he began firing upon my detachment. I caused
all lights to be put out immediately, and returned
his fire. The peasants of the neighbourhood, who
had been commanded, on hearing the sound of
muskets assembled. Other troops arriving, I found
myself engaged in a most serious affair against one
entire part of the forces of the Rajah. Having with
myself not even one hundred combatants, my
greatest anxiety was on the side of my camp, I felt
sure that if it was attacked, on account of my not
being present there terror would seize them and they
would be routed by the Regent. These thoughts
made me hasten my march in order to join them
before day-break. To effect this, I was obliged to
abandon to the Rajah's troops 3 pieces of cannon
which I was removing from Bharatpur, and also many
carts loaded with my property. The troops of the
Rajah constantly fought me up to the entrance to
my camp, where I arrived three hours after day-
break. The pursuers then quitted me, and my
arrival reassured the frightened spirits. I caused the
drum to be beaten at once and departed for Kama.
.........And at the first movement which I made to
take the road, I had the whole army of the Rajah
pursuing me, and all the peasants of the neighbourhood, who are more dangerous on these occasions
than regular troops. That army, including the

inhabitants, was not less than 100,000 men. I formed
a battalion in hollow square in which I put my baggage, and I marched in that manner constantly fighting. The cavalry of the Rajah made marvellous
efforts to break my battalion in order to carry off
my family. But my continual fire of musketry
rendered their efforts fruitless. They made all sorts
of movements to prevent me from passing a large
marsh which I had to cross. I halted in order to
make two pieces of my artillery file to that side of
the marsh in order to help the passage of my baggage. At that moment the troops of the Rajah redoubled their efforts and I received a bullet wound
in my arm. I caused to be discharged a terrible fire
which made my enemies to turn aside. As soon my
baggage had passed I crossed the marsh. On the
other side I was in the territory of the Rajah of
Jainagar [Jaipur]. The army of the Jat Rajah
remained a long time to watch me and they retired
in the evening after seeing me encamp under the
walls of Kama. I lost in that affair more than 200
men in killed and wounded, and some camels. I
saved the rest of the baggage which had escaped in
the first attack." [*Le Nabob Rene Madec,* 84-87.]

It was certainly a remarkable feat of courage
and skill. In less than 36 hours, M. Madec
had to make a march of 55 miles by the least
computation (Deeg to Bharatpur, 21 miles
doubled, *plus* 13 miles between Kama and
Deeg), and cut his way with a large convoy
through the huge host of the enemy. After

having rested eight days at Kama, M. Madec
reached Delhi in the first week of November,
1772.

*Nawal Singh's alliance with the Marathas and
Zabita Khan against the Emperor.*

By the end of September, 1772, the
Marathas had reduced Zabita Khan to the same
plight in which his father Najib-ud-daulah had
twice been thrown at Delhi,—besieged there
once by Raghunath Rao (1757), and the second
time by the allied armies of the Jats, Marathas
and Sikhs (1764). But they had in their camp
Tukoji Holkar the adopted son, to take care of
Malhar's *dharma-putras* among whom the father
of Zabita Khan was the most illustrious. The
Ruhela chief made a successful appeal to Tukoji
Holkar, who procured from the other Maratha
leaders very favourable terms for his submission. (*Ibratnama* MS., 214). They not only gave
back all his territories, but also promised to force
the hand of the Emperor to restore to him the
conquests of the imperial commanders in the
Ruhela country if Zabita Khan would join them
in an attack upon Delhi.

Having finished the affair of the Ruhelas,
the Maratha leaders entered the Jat country
immediately after the desertion of M. Madec

with his corps. Nawal Singh's army was driven
under the shelter of his forts. He held out not
with any confidence in his ultimate success but
only to secure better terms of submission. The
Emperor did not raise a finger to help him except
by writing a letter to the Marathas to desist from
pillaging the Jat country! Meanwhile, Mirza
Najaf Khan redoubled his efforts in recruiting
and equiping the imperial army, which made
the Marathas more reasonable in their demands
upon the Jats. Nawal Singh could wait, but the
Marathas could not; so they readily accepted
whatever sum of money they could presently get
from him, and started for Delhi to attend to the
business of another client of theirs, Hisam-ud-
din Khan. They held out the same inducement
to Nawal Singh for an offensive alliance against
the Emperor as that offered to Zabita Khan,
viz., restitution to him of all his territories seized
by the imperial officers. Nawal Singh could
not fail to see that the Emperor was more interested in crushing the Jat power than in free-
ing himself from the Maratha control. As he
was equally interested in the destruction of the
army of Najaf Khan, he threw in his lot with
the Marathas. Towards the end of November
1772, the allied army of Marathas, Jats and
Ruhelas, numbering more than one lakh [?] of

troops appeared before Delhi. Against this huge host, Mirza Najaf Khan could hardly bring into the field 38,000 horse and 8,000 infantry.

On the 28th of December (1772) a pitched battle was fought under the walls of Delhi for about 9 hours. The Marathas and their allies displayed determined valour and compelled Mirza Najaf Khan to take shelter behind the lines of M. Madec. While the battle was surging to and fro, the traitor Hisam-ud-din with two regiments of sepoys, 30 guns and His Majesty's own *risalah* of Horse, stood idle near the *haveli* of Ghazi-ud-din, watching intently its varying fortunes. As soon as the Marathas threatened to move in his direction, the Khan fled more in joy than in fright into the city. His troops joined hands with the Marathas in plundering the camp of M. Madec (*Le Nabob Rene Madec*, sec. 96).

The Maratha army with Zabita Khan and his Ruhela horse, the Jats and the artillery of Somru, surrounded the city like a complete circle. Hisam-ud-din cleverly represented to the imbecile monarch that Mirza Najaf Khan was the sole cause of all these troubles and quarrel with the Marathas. That faithful general as well as all his Irani and Turani comrades-in-arms were dismissed from service and ordered to leave the city. The Hindustani party rejoiced over the fall of their rivals; the Marathas got 9 lakhs from the royal treasury and 9 lakhs from the private purse of Hisam-ud-din, who further offered one lakh more separately to Tukoji Holkar, if the latter succeeded in removing the Mirza from Delhi. The Marathas took Najaf Khan with all his troops into their pay and marched away with him (March, 1773) to invade the territories of Nawab Shuja-ud-daulah and Hafiz Rahamat Khan (*Ibratnama* MS., 219-221). The Jats had the satisfaction of plundering the Mughal territories and regaining many of their lost possessions. Nawal Singh got a short respite to recoup his strength and had reason to feel as much satisfaction and relief as Hisam-ud-din himself at the temporary eclipse of Najaf Khan's fortune.

Mirza Najaf Khan's first campaign against the Jats.

Mirza Najaf Khan, who had fallen under the momentary displeasure of the Emperor, and been banished from the Court through the intrigue of Hisam-ud-din, returned to Delhi three months after (end of May, 1773), with his reputation and power greatly increased by serving as a *condottiere* general in the Maratha service in their campaign against the Nawab of Oudh and Hafiz Rahamat Khan. About this time Abdul Ahad Khan, a disaffected subordinate and an apt pupil of Hisam-ud-din in the art of intrigue, joined hands with Najaf Khan for the overthrow of his master. Matched in cunning and excelled in warlike fame by these two redoubtable adversaries, poor Hisam-ud-din lost his hold upon the Emperor's mind and with it his place and fortune. The Emperor cast him away with as little compunction as a man feels in making fuel of a broken stick. Abdul Ahad Khan became *naib-wazir* in his place and was given the title of Majd-ud-daulah. Mirza Najaf Khan was created Second Bakhshi and exhalted to the rank of *Amir-ul-umra* (June 5, 1773).* Rajah Nawal Singh, alarmed at the re-appearance of the Mirza at Delhi, opened negotiations with the Sikhs to secure

---

* Mirza Najaf Khán returned to Delhi at the beginning of Rabi I. 1187 H. Hisam-ud-din was removed from the office of *naib*-wazir in the first week of that month. On the 14th Rabi I. (June 5, 1773) Najaf Khán was created Second Bakhshi, and on that very day Hisam-ud-din was arrested who remained in captivity in the house of Najaf Khán for about five years. His property, worth nine lakhs in cash and goods, was confiscated; one-third of this amount was given to Najaf Khán as a token of the Emperor's favour; the remainder went to the imperial treasury (*Waqa*, 270-273).

their help against the Mughals. He planned
a campaign against the imperial territories to
be fought simultaneously in three important
theatres : one division of his army was to act in
the region to the west of Delhi from a base at
Farrukhnagar*, another division was to ravage
the Doab from Aligarh, while the main army
under him was to threaten Delhi from Ballamgarh. The Sikhs were expected to reinforce
and act in concert with the Jat army in Hariana
and in the Doab. Mirza Najaf Khan pitched
his camp at Badarpur(?),† 14 miles south of
Delhi, blocking the great road leading to Delhi
from Ballamgarh. About six miles to the west
of the Mughal encampment, there was a small
Jat fort called Maidangarhi, built in the time of
Suraj Mal and still held by a Jat garrison. One
day the Jats out of sheer bravado drove away

---

* Farrukhnagar (lat. 28°-35′; long. 75°-10′) is situated on
the Rajputana-Malwa Railway about 10 miles from Garhi
Harsaru junction,

† The *Waqa* names the place of Najaf Khán's encampment as Badarpur or Baranpur which cannot be identified in
the map. Khair-ud-din calls it Barahpulah (*i.e.,* the bridge of
twelve arches near Humayun's tomb); but he is not very
accurate. Badarpur is mentioned as one of the stages on the
Agra-Delhi road in the *Chahar Gulshan* [Prof. J. N. Sarkar's
India of Aurangzib, XCVII]. We take it to be the same
place as Madanpur, which lies two miles to the east of
Tughlaqabad.

some cattle and horses of the Mughals. Mirza Najaf Khan at once ordered an assault upon the *garhi*, which was captured after several hours of tough fighting. "This victory proved" as Khair-ud-din says "the title page of Mirza Najaf Khan's record of victories and the first rung in the ladder of his fortune" [*Ibratnama*, MS., p. 212]. We may, with as much truth call it the ominous presage of an era of misfortune for the house of Bharatpur.*

Hostilities were thus precipitated before the rainy season was hardly over. It was only the beginning of September and the Sikhs were

---

* Maidangarhi (*Ibratnama*, MS., p. 212) is situated 2 miles to the south of Tughlaqabad and 6 miles south-west of Madanpur. Khair-ud-din's narrative, though well written, is inaccurate and sometimes deceptive. He says that the capture of Maidangarhi and the defeat of Dán Sahi and Chandu Gujar near Dankaur took place *before the siege of Delhi* by Tukoji Holkár [December, 1772—March 1773.]. This is simply absurd, being opposed to every other authority Persian and English. His story of the opening of fire by the Jat garrison upon the cavalcade of Najaf Khan while proceeding from Delhi on a pilgrimage to Qutb-ud-din's shrine, appears to be baseless. We hold, on the authority of the *Chahar Gulzar-i-Shujai*, that the hostilities were precipitated by the carrying off of cattle by the Jats. I have to reject in many places the details of this campaign of Mirza Najaf Khán against Nawal Singh published in my paper in the *Proceedings* of the Fifth meeting of Indian Historical Records Commission, because it was based mainly on the narrative of Khair-ud-din.

wholly unprepared to take the field in such an
early season. But Nawal Singh's blind fury
could brook no delay in retaliating for this
defeat. He sent under the command of his
brother-in-law Dan Sahi, a strong division to
reinforce Durjan Singh Gujar and Chandu
[Chandan] Gujar, his own governors at Atrauli
and Rāɪngarh (modern Aligarh). Dan Sahi
and other Jat and Gujar chiefs mustered about
20,000 men under their command and began to
ravage the Doab. They plundered Sikandrabad* and other parganas as far as Ghaziabad,†
and were literally carrying out the command of
Nawal Singh to "hang every Mughal official
who would resist his authority" [Ibratnama
MS., p. 212]. In the western theatre another
Jat army under Shankar Jat from its base at
Farrukhnagar, overran the greater portion of
the open country around it, and laid siege to
Garhi Harsaru. The situation became so
desperate for the imperialists that the Emperor
wrote to the Governor of Bengal a letter‡ asking

---

* Sikandrabad lat. 28°-25ʹ, long. 77°-45ʹ.

† Ghaziabád (on E. I. Ry.) about 20 miles east of Delhi.

‡ It runs as follows : "The Jats have rebelled round the
capital, and have sent their army to Sikandrabad. Having
committed depradations and outrages upon the inhabitants
they have advanced to oppose the royal army and reached
close to it. They *have also invited the Sikhs* to join them.

.for his help. Mirza Najaf Khan refused to
move from his encampment at Madanpur. He
despatched several Turani and Baloch chiefs
such as Niyaz Beg Khan, Taj Muhammad Khan
Baloch and others with five thousand horse
against Dan Sahi. They were reinforced by
the Emperor with one regiment of Lal Paltan
and several pieces of artillery under the
command of Ramu Kamadan [commandant].*
At the approach of the Mughal army Dan Sahi
fell back upon Sikandrabad; but the Mughal
commanders, having made a forced march of
10 or 12 kos, surprised him at night when he
was encamped carelessly near that place. The
Jats retreated to Dankaur, 25 miles south-west
and in its neighbourhood offered battle to the
enemy on 15th September, 1773. Chandu
Gujar, who was the commander-in-chief of the
Jat army, led the Van and attacked the sepoy
regiments and the artillery of the Mughals.

.........Desires the Governor to send immediately an English
army under the command of brave officers." This is entered
under the date September 22, 1773, Calcutta. [Pers. Cor :
MS.]

* Waqa, p. 282; Ibratnama, p. 212, says "two regiments
of sepoys"; Chahar mentions Lal Paltan; Ramu Kamadan's
name is mentioned in the Shah Alam-nama (MS., p. 34) of
Ghulam Ali.

With an intrepidity which astonished even the
veteran Mughal cavaliers, the valiant Gujar
chief charged the enemy's artillery at full
gallop, animating his brave followers. But the
volleys of musketry and artillery fearfully shattered the attacking column; only a small body
of troopers headed by their wounded leader
succeeded in penetrating the lines of the sepoys
and fell there pierced by bayonets after performing prodigies of valour. The battle raged
furiously for two or three hours; it was an awul
struggle of native valour of man against science
and discipline. Undaunted by the fate of
Chandu Gujar, the son of Rao Durjan Singh
Gujar (Governor of Atrauli) led his *risalah* of
five hundred horse to the attack and lost two
hundred men. Two Jat leaders of cavalry,
each at the head of three hundred men, next
delivered determined charges with equally
disastrous results; these bands also were slain
to a man. Dan Sahi, the second in command
on that day, was severely wounded and forced
to take shelter in a small mud-fort (where he
died two days after). The remnants of the Jat
army broke and fled across the Jamuna.
Besides heavy losses in the field, the river
exacted a further toll of two hundred lives.

during the passage.*   Greater disasters awaited
the arms of Nawal Singh in other quarters.

The Battle of Barsana.

The Mughal victory at Dankaur (15th
September, 1773) removed the serious menace
caused by the Jat offensive in that quarter.
About a fortnight after it news arrived that the
Jats were making attacks upon Garhi Harsaru
from their stronghold at Farrukhnagar. Mirza
Najaf Khan at once sent a strong force under
the able command of his lieutenant Najaf Quli
to relieve that place, and put an end to the
dominion of the Jats in that quarter. In order
to fill this gap in the main army, opposed to

---

* The fullest account of this battle is known from the
extract of a paper of news dated 12th October, 1773 [Pers.
Cor. MS.]

The news of the Mughal victory reached Delhi on the
29th of Jamada II., 1187 H; allowing two days for the transmis-
sion of the message, the battle was perhaps fought on the
27th [15th September, 1773; Waqa MS., p. 273]. Khair-ud-
din says that this battle was fought after the capture of
Maidangarhi which is quite correct; but both these incidents
took place after and not before the siege of Delhi by Tukoji
and Nawal Singh (i.e., before March, 1773). He calls Chandu
Gujar "Bahadur be-badal" [unequalled in bravery], and says
that he was killed within the ranks of the sepoys pierced by
their bayonets [Ibratnama, MS., 214]. Pers. Cor. MS. says
that his head was cut off by Taj Muhammad Khán Baloch.
Harcharan gives pretty accurate details of this battle; the
date Jamada II, 1187 H. given by him is correct.

17

Nawal Singh, he recalled his troops from the Doab. Nawal Singh who was encamped at *Fatehpur Sikri* [Baloch]* 5 miles south of Ballamgarh became disheartened by the news of the disastrous defeat of his army in the Doab, and throwing a strong garrison at Ballamgarh retreated to Palwal and thence to Hodal, about 53 miles south of Delhi. Mirza Najaf Khan followed the track of the Jat army and came up with it at the village of Bainchari, 3½ miles north of Hodal (middle of October, 1773). Hira Singh and Ajit Singh,† the dispossessed heirs of Ballamgarh, had come to offer their

---

* The MS. of *Chahar Gulzar* as well as a letter written to the Governor of Bengal by Mirza Najaf Khan [Pers. Cor.] mentions Fatehpur Sikri as the place of Nawal Singh's encampment. One *Sikri* is mentioned as a stage between Pirthala and Ballamgarh (3 miles north of the former and 5 miles south of the latter) on the Agra-Delhi road. [Prof. J. N. Sarkar's *India of Aurangzib*, xcvii]. No such place is to be found in the modern atlas. A glance at the map would show that Fatehpur Baloch is the place meant. This is situated at exactly the same distances from those places. It lies in lat. 28°-20′; long. 77°-25′. Curiously enough Harcharan confuses this Fatehpur Sikri with the famous residence of Akbar near Agra. He mentions the next stage of Najaf Khan's halt as Dholpur to be consistent in his error. *Dholpur* may however be a copyist's error for *Hodal* which is the place really meant.

† Ajit Singh was the son of Rao Kishandas and Hira Singh son of Bishandas. Ballamgarh was taken away from their fathers by Nawal Singh. Ballamgarh was taken after a long siege in

services to Mirza Najaf Khan. He appointed
Ajit Singh, commandant and governor of
Ballamgarh, and left him with a small detachment to besiege that fort. Hira Singh accompanied the Mughal general to play the usual
role of a traitor to his country and his people.
Both armies encamped at a distance of four
miles from each other; several days passed in
skirmishes in which the Muslim troopers had
generally the better. One day by sheer accident the Jat camp was surprised. Jamadar Ali
Quli Khan captured some men from the
neighbourhood of the enemy's camp and
learned from them that at that time Nawal
Singh was eating his meal and that his soldiers
were quite busy in cooking theirs. A party at
once rode out from Najaf Khan's camp. "A
cloud of dust was seen approaching from the
west. Some soldiers [in the Jat camp] cried
out that the troops of Najaf Khan were coming.
The Jats became panic-struck and fled in all
directions. Nawal Singh, quite at his wit's end
stood dumb for a while, and then mounting an

---

the third week of April, 1774 [Safar, 1188 H; *Waqa* p. 277].
Najaf Khan gave the title of Rajah to both the cousins and
Hira Singh was honoured with the additional distinction
Salar Jang [*Delhi Gaz.* p. 213.]

elephant fled towards Kotman. (*Ibratnama*, MS. p. 233).

In the meanwhile Najaf Quli was making steady advance, keeping the hills of Mewat to his right and driving the Jats westward. In his first encounter with the Jat army, he captured four wheeled field-pieces [*rahkalah*] from them. Next he reached Bawal* (?) and the enemy was reported at a distance of 7 *kos*. On the 19th October, a letter of victory from Mirza Najaf Khan brought to the Emperor the happy news "Nawal Singh has fled and taken shelter in his *garhi* [*i.e.*, Kotman]; Shankar's army has been defeated [Nawal Singh's general at Farrukhnagar] and all his equipages of artillery [*ásbáb-i-topkháná*] captured by the [imperial] troops; Najaf Quli has gone in pursuit of the enemy" [*Waqa*, p. 270.] Najaf Quli cut off the retreat of this division of the Jat army to Mewat and drove it northwards into Farrukhnagar. He laid siege to this place, but was soon after recalled to Sahar by his chief. Nawab

---

* Our MS. of the *Waqá* writes Palwal, which is a place 30 miles due south of Delhi. It is absurd to suppose that Najaf Quli should go to Palwal on his way to Farrukhnagar (!) It is certainly a copyist's error for some other place name. Nearest approach to correct reading is perhaps *Bawal* a place 10 miles south of Rewari.

Musavi Khan Baloch, the ex-lord of Farrukh-nagar, succeeded him in command there.

After the flight of Nawal Singh Mirza Najaf Khan summoned at night (17th Oct.) a council of war for discussing the future plan of campaign. All his officers were unanimously of opinion that next morning they should start in pursuit of the fugitives and the camp should be removed from Bainchari to the deserted site of the Jat encampment. But Hira Singh Jat submitted to the Nawab that there was yet no certainty about the break-up of the army of Nawal Singh, who might prepare for battle with his rear resting upon the fort of Kotman;—men who had been enjoying the bounty of the house of Bharatpur would not so lightly desert the Rajah but would surely sacrifice their lives for him on the day of battle. He further pointed out that it would be injudicious to risk an engagement at this stage with such men so strongly posted, because the bulk of the army of the Amir-ul-umra was composed of raw levies of untried valour. "It is advisable" he said "to push rapidly towards Deeg, giving up the project of pursuing the enemy. If Nawal Singh comes out of Kotman, knowing this intention of yours, you can offer him battle [with advantage] ; if through God's grace he remains

inactive in his own place, the capture of Deeg,
left without a master, will be easily accomplished. Mirza Najaf Khan approved of this
proposal of Hira Singh and at once issued orders
for a march upon Deeg. Leaving Kotman at
a distance of 4 or 5 miles to the east, the Mughal
army moved along the old Delhi-Agra royal
road. They plundered Koshi,* Chhata,† and
other parganas on their way and reached Sáhár‡
(22nd October) to take the road to Deeg, *via*
Govardhan. Nawal Singh guessing the design
of Mirza Najaf Khán against his capital, left
Kotman with his army, and taking a shorter
route *via* Nandgaon§ arrived at Barsana‖ about
the same time. The march of the Muslim
army was thus arrested by the sudden appear-
ence of Nawal Singh on their right flank. The
surprise of Deeg was no longer feasible, because
the Jats were at least one march nearer their
objective. Najaf Khán encamped at Sáhár,

---

* Koshi, 7 miles south-east of Kotman.

† Chhata, 10 miles south-east of Koshi and about 11 miles
north of Sáhár.

‡ Sahar, 15 miles n. w. of Mathura and 7 miles west of
Barsana.

§ Nandgaon, 8 miles south-west of Koshi and 6 miles north
of Barsana.

‖ Barsana, 22 miles n. w. of Mathura and 12 miles due
north of Deeg.

but after a day or two moved his tents to Shah-
pur [?] half way between Sahar and Barsana,
leaving his heavy baggage and the camp-
followers behind. Skirmishes went on for
more than a week. Owing to the exhaustion
of supplies in the neighbourhood, hardship
began to be felt by the troops of the Nawab,
who was hard-pressed by his officers to attack
the enemy.

The key of the situation was in the hands
of Nawal Singh. He was encamped with his
rear protected by the fortified hill of Barsaná;
he could safely refuse to fight as long as he
wished, because the whole resources of the
surrounding tract were at his disposal. He
could kill his enemy by playing a waiting game
as indeed the officers of Mirza Najaf Khán
apprehended. But Fabian tactics were unsuited
to his excitable temperament and weak nerve.
On the morning of the 31st October [14th
Shábán, 1187 H.] Mirza Najaf Khán led out
his forces in the array of battle to try the temper
of the enemy. Nawal Singh, who had a strange
eagerness without ability for a fight, was easily
provoked and a general action began after five
gharis of the day had passed.

Nawal Singh divided his army in three
divisions and stationed them at a little distance

from each other. Somru with six battalions
of musketeers drilled in European fashion, and
three battalions carrying flint guns with fuses,
and bayonets fixed at the muzzle, commanded
by French officers, was stationed on the right
wing. Twelve thousand *Naga Bairágis* resem-
bling leopards and tigers [in courage], with
about ten thousand horse and foot under the
command of the Rajahs who had come to
Nawal Singh's assistance, formed the left wing.
The artillery, tied together with iron chains,
was placed in front; trustworthy commanders
were stationed in the rear as a reserve; and
Nawal Singh himself surrounded by a magnificent retinue stood in the centre. On the other
side, Mullah Rahim Dad Khan with his Ruhelas
was stationed against the *Naga Bairagis;* Reza
Beg Khan and Rahim Beg Khan with their own
cavalry and two battalions of His Majesty's
infantry were placed opposite Somru's division;
and Najaf Quli Khan and Afrasiyab Khan
stood in the centre facing the enemy's artillery
and Nawal Singh. Mirza Najaf Khan mounted
on a fleet horse spurred to and fro encouraging
his chiefs, while Masum Ali Khan was made
to take his seat upon the elephant of the Amir-
ul-umra, a dangerous distinction for which
the poor man paid with his life. A furious

and stubborn fight began. Nawal Singh's left was broken by the determined charge of the Ruhelas, animated by the example of their brave leader Rahim Dad; while Somru checked and afterwards put to flight the left wing of Najaf Khan. The Jats made a gallant dash at the Amir-ul-umra's elephant, and capturing it despatched Masum Ali with many blows of dagger, taking him to be Mirza Najaf Khan himself. The day seemed to be almost lost when Mirza Najaf Khan made his way to the centre and ordered Najaf Quli and Afrasiyab to charge the enemy's artillery with drawn sabres. Nawal Singh's centre gave way under the tremendous shock of Najaf Quli's charge : Nawal Singh himself fled on an elephant. The Muslim army fell upon the baggage in the rear and dispersed in search of booty. But Somru, entrenching his position, placed the cannon in front and kept together his sepoy battalions, quite ready to receive the enemy. Jud Raj, diwan of Nawal Singh, with 500 fresh horse-men was seen preparing for fight behind Somru's sepoys. Mirza Najaf Khan thundered and stormed in vain to bring together his scattered troops mad after looting. At last in frantic rage he flung himself upon Jud Raj's horse, followed only by forty troopers, and

after an obstinate contest broke their ranks and
put them to flight. Somru, considering it
fruitless to continue the fight, ordered a retreat
and marched away in good order. But one
Frenchman, a lieutenant of Somru, refused to
turn back and urged his men to fight. They
fired volleys with such rapidity and precision
as to deprive the Musalmans of their senses.
Najaf Khan himself charged them several times,
but their ranks stood firm and unshaken. At
last matchlockmen and guns were sent for by
the Khan to fire upon them. By the grace of
God, the very first shell struck the enemy's
powder-chest, the second, guided as if by the
hand of destiny hit the Frenchman on the head,
and the third fell in the very midst of their
ranks, carrying to them the message that it was
high time to depart. The sepoys slowly
marched off dragging their guns behind them.
With their departure life seemed to come back
to Najaf Khan, and smiles of joy appeared on
his face for the first time on that fateful day*

---

* Both the *Waqa-i-Shah Alam Sani* [MS. p. 271] and a
paper of news in Pers. Cor. MS., dated November 17th, 1773
give the same date *i.e.*, 14th Shábán 1187 H. The paper of
news gives the following details which differ to a certain
extent from those of the *Ibratnámá* "Najaf Quli and Taj
Muhammad on the right; Niyaz Beg Khan and Fath Ali Khan
Durrani on the left; the English battalion and the artillery

Nawal Singh had fled from Barsana towards Deeg. Abdul Ahad Khan and the Emperor heard the news of the great victory at Barsana with misgiving and apprehension. They sent letters to Nawal Singh encouraging him to fight the Amir-ul-umra. Some of these letters were captured by Najaf Khan's soldiers. Najaf Khan gave several days' rest to his army at Barsana. He sent Rahim Dad to besiege the fort of Kotman,* held by Sitaram,

---

were on the front............at about one o'clock in the afternoon an attack was made upon Nawal Singh's army with artillery which kept up a continuous fire till five o'clock. Nawal Singh fled; Somru and Balanand and few others continued the fray. A hot battle followed and in the end Balanand and several others were mortally wounded......About 200 of the enemy [Jats] were killed. Somru lost most of his men; about 2,000 Mughals were killed and 300 wounded."

* Kotman (in the Mathura district) is also known as Kotban. It lies on the Delhi-Agra Trunk Road a furlong or two beyond the boundary line of the Gurgaon district. I have visited this ruined fort in course of my historical tour. Only the *mahal* (harem), and Kachhári (Court-room) which is now the *Choupad* or village Common-hall, stand intact. These lie within the brick-built inner fort of which only the big gate, about 50 yards away from the Káchhári still remains. There is also a large *pucca* tank outside the gate. The descendants of Sitaram still live there as humble peasants. I met some of them; I was told that the fort had an outer wall of mud 18 cubits high and 16 cubits broad, with a ditch around. One Giribar Prasad, a tall, fair and blue-eyed peasant nearing 50 told me the story he had heard from his grandfather, how the Jats were surprised by the troops of Najaf Khan when they were preparing *roti*, how they came to Kotman and next went

the father-in-law of Nawal Singh. After
defending his fort for several days [18 days as
local tradition says] Sitaram one night escaped
with the garrison. About this time news spread
that the Nawab Wazir-ul-mulk [Shuja-ud-
daulah] was coming to the assistance of Nawal
Singh; in fact he had sent in advance a detachment for taking charge of the fort of Agra from
the Jat garrison. Najaf Khan hearing this gave
up his plan of subduing the Jat country around
Deeg, and, practically running a race for Agra
reached there just in time to prevent the junction
of the Jats with the troops of the Wazir-ul-mulk.

From the time of Abul Mansur Khan
Safdar Jang, the Oudh Nawabs had been the
allies of the Jats. Shuja-ud-daulah had no
mind to see Nawal Singh crushed, and, besides,
the ambition and ability of Mirza Najaf Khan
had made him uneasy. He reached only as far
as Etawah when the news of the victory at
Barsana and arrival of Najaf Khan at Agra was
heard. Finding his own design upon Agra
anticipated, he at once changed front and, with
consummate duplicity, sent a letter of congra-
tulation to Najaf Khan, assuring him that he

---

to Barsana, where they fought a battle for 18 days; in short
a tradition exactly coinciding with written history. Harcharan
says that Kotman was defended for nineteen days by the Jats.

had come to these parts only to assist the Amir-ul-umra! At the same time Major Polier—the commandant of the detachment sent ahead —was thus secretly instructed: "If the *qiladar* of Akbarabad consents to give up the fort according to previous agreement and understanding, then, throwing off the mask at once, you should try to get into the fort by every possible means. If you fail you are to act under the command of Najaf Khan and obey him as your superior." The citadel of Agra was besieged by Najaf Khan aided by Major Polier. The *qiladar* tried without success many tricks to bring in secretly the troops of Shuja-ud-daulah. After defending it bravely for some time he gave up the fort on the promise of the safety of life and property of the garrison. He came out and encamped at Naharganj; but apprehending treachery from the Muslims fled towards Bhadawar, leaving his baggage and treasure behind. Najaf Khan appointed Daud Beg Khan Karchi to the command of the Agra fort.*

---

* Najaf Khan entered the city of Agra on the 26th Ramzan, 1187 H. (Dec. 11, 1773). The fort fell in the month of Ziqada between 7th and 29th of that month *i.e.,* about the beginning of February, 1774 [Harcharan; *Waqa* p. 273]. He crossed the Jamuna on the 15th of Zihijja, 1187 H. (Feb. 27, 1774) to meet the Nawab Wazir-ul-mulk [*Waqa* p. 284]. He

With the capture of Agra from the Jats, the first campaign of Najaf Khan ended. Soon afterwards, he went to Etawah to pay a visit to the Wazir-ul-mulk. His attention was engrossed for a few months by Ruhela affairs and the Court intrigues of Abdul Ahad Khan.

———

was given valuable presents and made naib-wazir on behalf of Shuja-ud-daulah on the 22nd Zihijja (ibid, p. 285). Khair-ud-din wrongly calls the Jat commandant of Agra Dan Sahi, who had died about six months before. The news of his death two days after the battle of Dankaur reached Delhi on the 2nd Rajab 1187 H. (19th September, 1773). The Jat defender of the Agra fort was not Dan Sahi but *his brother* as we learn from the *Waqa* (p. 273).

CHAPTER XIV.

DECLINE OF THE HOUSE OF BHARATPUR

Nawal Singh provokes fresh hostilities with Mirza Najaf Khan.

May 1774 was the most unfortunate month in a year of Nawal Singh's misfortunes. Every week brought the news of some great disaster to him; Ballamgarh surrendered to Hira Singh Jat; Farrukhnagar opened her gates to Musavi Khan, and General Somru, hitherto the greatest terror to the enemies of the Jats, deserted to the imperial Court. All these heavy strokes of an adverse fate came down upon him in swift succession within the first twenty days of this month.* Rajah Nawal Singh bore these losses with equanimity. Though he was destitute of the cool courage and strong nerve of a Jat, he had that optimism and that perseverance verging on obstinacy which characterise his tribe.

---

* According to the *Waqa* (MS. p. 277) Ballamgarh and Farrukhnagar were surrendered by the Jats between the dates 19th Safar and 8th Rabi I, 1188 H. Somru had an interview with the Emperor on the 9th Rabi I (20th May, 1774), received *khilát* and was appointed faujdar of Panipat and other parganas (*ibid*, p. 278).

Mirza Najaf Khan was well satisfied with the results of his late campaign against the Jats. He had no mind to risk his fame and fortune by besieging their impregnable forts which had baffled the energy, skill and resources of many a great conqueror.   He considered the task of the subjugation of the Jats as well nigh finished, and now turned his attention to the other rebels against the imperial authority.   He started from Delhi to co-operate with the Nawab of Oudh in his contemplated campaign against the Ruhelas.   But the battle of Miran Katra (April 17, 1774) had been won by Shuja-ud-daulah before he could arrive on the scene.   He proceeded to Bisauli where a general treaty* for the partition of the territories of the Afghans and of the Mian Doab was concluded with the wazir.   He returned to the capital by the end of June with the determination of taking the field against Zabita Khan to enforce the conditions of this treaty and punish him for his late

---

* Two conditions of this treaty were (1) the possessions of Najib-ud-daulah and Zabita Khan, lying to the west of the Jamuna, such as Panipat, Sonepat, Maham Gohana, Hansi, Hisar etc. should pass under the authority of Najaf Khan on behalf of the Emperor. (2) Should Zabita Khan submit to His Majesty the Emperor, and swear friendliness to the Amir-ul-umra and promise not to deviate by a hair's breadth from his authority, the chakla of Saharanpur was to be left to the Ruhela chief. [Ibratnama, MS. pp. 260-261.]

acts of rebellion. But the strange perversity of Nawal Singh drove him to fresh acts of hostility with the Mirza who was compelled to march into the Jat country soon afterwards. The Jat chief imprudently sought a war with a stronger enemy at the moment of his own absolute political isolation. The Sikhs were unwilling to hazard much for a lost cause and Shuja-ud-daulah, who had proved a dubious ally, was now an active enemy and in league with Mirza Najaf Khan. The Marathas who would, in their own interests, have given him help against the Mughal general, were still preoccupied with their internal dissensions arising out of the murder of the Peshwa Narayan Rao. Nawal Singh acted like a gambler grown desperate by repeated failures and yet bent upon persisting in a losing game, allured by the hope of gaining all in the last throw.

During the absence of Mirza Najaf Khan, Rajah Nawal Singh made an attempt to recover his lost ground. He issued out of Deeg with his army and began to expel the *amils* of Mirza Najaf Khan from the country. Not content with this, he threatened to march upon Delhi. Mirza Najaf Khan decided to postpone the intended campaign against Zabita Khan till he had crushed the Jat Power once for all. While

18

the monsoon was still raging in its full fury, he
started on his second campaign against Nawal
Singh. The Jat army retreated before the
advance of the Mughals and hurriedly sought
the shelter of the fort of Sankar* [Sunukhar?]
when the Mirza arrived at Barsana in pursuit
of them. The Khan had no other alternative
than to besiege the enemy there, as any advance
upon Deeg leaving the field army of the Jats
unbeaten in his rear was extremely dangerous.
The heart of the Jat country now presented a
formidable chain of strong forts, Sunukhar,
Kama (the neutral territory belonging to Jaipur),
Deeg, Kuhmir, and Bharatpur.

The task of dislodging Nawal Singh from
his fortified retreat, protected in the rear and
flank by the neutral territory of Jaipur, proved
a task of exceptional difficulty to the Muslim

* The name of the place as written in a MS. of the
Ibratnama warrants the reading of Sankar, Singar or Sunkar.
There is one Singar (lat. 27°.25′; long. 77°.20′) in the Gurgaon
district and about 20 miles north of Kaman [Kama]. The
same authority tells us that the besieged Jat army at this place
could so easily draw their supplies from Kama that without
first reducing Kama, operations against the former place proved
futile. So this cannot be Singar, at such a great distance from
Kama. Sunukhar (lat. 27°.45′, long. 77°.18′), about 8 miles
north of Kama and 12 miles west of Barsana and situated in
a marshy tract answers the description best. About half a mile
south of Sunukhar there is a ruined fort called Sabalgarh.

army. No longer proud of his mercenaries, the regent became more considerate to the Jats. They, too, thus cornered by the enemy and compelled to fight for their very existence, began to show their wonted courage and stubbornness. They sallied out daily and fought skirmishes with the Muslim troopers, who could no longer claim success in every encounter. The siege dragged on for many days without making the least impression upon the besieged, who were fed by supplies sent secretly from the fort of Kama. The Rajput princes became equally alarmed at the revival of the imperial authority and did not fail to realise that as soon as the Jat resistance would fall to the ground the victorious Mughal would again carry war into the heart of Rajputana and demand tribute from them. The old animosity between the Bharatpur Raj and Jaipur had been buried in oblivion with the bones of the haughty Jawahir and the sensitive Madho Singh. The regency which controlled the affairs of the Jaipur State during the minority of Maharajah Prithvi Singh II. decided to help the Jats in their struggle with Najaf Khan. The amil of Kama under instructions from his Government continued to supply secretly provisions to the army of Nawal Singh. Mirza Najaf Khan could neither storm

the enemy's position defended by numerous
guns, nor could he by any means induce his
adversary to leave the shelter of the fort and
give a pitched battle for the decision of the long
drawn out issue.   The siege continued for four
months when Mirza Najaf Khan was called
away to the capital by some intrigues of Abdul
Ahad Khan.   He left Najaf Quli in supreme
command of the army, and after his return to
Delhi sent the notorious Somru* to reinforce
the besieging army at Sunukhar.

        Somru, who was well acquainted with the
situation of the place, represented to Najaf Quli
Khan that as long as grain and fodder would
continue to reach the Jat army from Kama it
was impossible to bring the siege of Sunukhar
to a successful close.   Najaf Quli wrote to the
amil of Kama not to give any assistance to the
Jats.   This remonstrance having proved ineffec-
tual, that impetuous soldier decided upon attack-

---

* According to Khair-ud-din, Somru deserted to the camp
of Najaf Khan during the siege of Sankar, *i.e., at the end of
the rainy season* of 1774.   He gives a dramatic touch to the
whole affair at the sacrifice of accuracy.   We have the unassailable testimony of the *Waqa* that on the 20th of May,
1774 [see *ante*] Somru was given leave to depart for his fief
Panipat.   It is more likely that Mirza Najaf Khan recalled him
from Panipat and sent him against the Jats to aid Najaf Quli
with his intimate knowledge of the Jat country and their
weaknesses.

ing Kama without reflecting upon the political
consequence of his action. He sent a portion
of his army to besiege that fort. Nawal Singh
having left a strong garrison at Sunukhar withdrew with his army to Deeg. The Kachhwas
now openly joined hands with the Jats to resist
the imperialists. Najaf Quli's guns made very
little impression upon the walls of the fort of
Kama, which are said to have been so broad
that two carts could drive side by side on their
top without the least danger. He held out the
promise of giving that fort to the brave Ruhela
chief Mullah Rahimdad if he would succeed
in capturing the place by a *coup*. One day
Rahimdad at the head of his dare-devils
stormed it by a rush, unmindful of the tremendous cost in the lives of his followers. But Najaf
Quli broke his word and appointed Somru to
the charge of Kama. Mullah Rahimdad,
vowing eternal enmity to both, marched away
with his 12,000 Ruhelas, horse and foot, to seek
service with Nawal Singh [*Ibratnama*, MS.
p. 266.]

Nawal Singh gave a warm welcome to the
Ruhela chief and his brave followers. He
assigned suitable pay for every man and gave
them large jagirs;—in short he showed them
every consideration except trusting them within

the gates of any of his forts.   Prospects became
more promising for the Jat at the beginning of
the year 1775.   Mirza Najaf Khan had not
only to fight with the sword the enemies of the
empire abroad, but he had also to hold his own
at the Court with the subtler weapons of diplomacy against the Emperor and His Majesty's
well-wishers like Abdul Ahad Khan.   Scarcely
had the Mirza. succeeded in disentangling himself from the meshes of the Court intrigue, when
he fell dangerously ill.   The news spread abroad
that he was dead, and this encouraged the Jaipur
darbar to make a vigorous effort for the recovery
of the pargana Kama.   Mirza Najaf Khan recovered from his illness, and on the 4th April,
1775 [Safar 2, 1189 H.] he took leave of the
Emperor to march against the Jats and Rajputs
(*Waqa*, 287).   When the news of the coming
of the Mirza became known, Rajah Nawal Singh
left Deeg with his army and came to Sunukhar
which was still holding out.   The forces of
Jaipur also joined him, and the allied army encamped under the shelter of the fort and
strongly entrenched their position.   Mullah
Rahimdad, now in the Jat service, was posted
with his Ruhelas outside the fortifications of
Sunukhar.   Several petty actions took place
in which the Afghans fought against their late

comrades with all the vehemence of injured pride. Mirza Najaf Khan tried without success to win them back to his side, promising Kama and in addition several other parganas to Rahimdad as jagir. But Nawal Singh and his shrewd counsellors could not repose in peace on account of their Pathan ally whom they suspected to be in collusion with the imperialists. They feared that Rahimdad was waiting for an opportunity to fall upon them at some unguarded moment. They now hit upon a clever device to avoid a breach with the Ruhela chief and yet relieve themselves of his distrusted presence in their camp. Rahimdad was asked to start on a plundering expedition against Hinduan and Biana; all property acquired there as booty was promised to him as a free gift, and the districts conquered as jagirs to his troops. Rahim, without suspecting the motive of the Jat, readily agreed to this and at once began his march against those places [*Ibratnama*, MS. p. 267.]

M. Madec, who held Hinduan and Biana as jagirs from the Emperor, became extremely agitated at the news of Rahimdad's departure in that direction. He left, without Najaf Khan's approval, his post at Barsana and reached the neighbourhood of Fatepur Sikri by rapid marches. At a little distance from this place

his troops, while in the act of fording a small
stream, were surprised by Rahimdad and
Ambaji Maratha.   The sepoys of M. Madec
formed their ranks with great rapidity, but they
missed the first volley owing to their cartridges
being spoiled by water. Before they could reload, the Ruhelas fell upon them with drawn
sabres and put some to death and others to
flight. The rout was complete: M. Madec did
not pause to breathe till he reached the fort of
Agra. Rahimdad created such an uproar in
that quarter that Najaf Khan was compelled to
send against him a large detachment of troops
under Muhammad Beg Khan Hamadani, who
was appointed governor of Agra.

Nawal Singh and his Rajput allies decided
to attack the army of Mirza Najaf Khan considerably weakened by the absence of two renowned chiefs like M.Madec and the Hamadani
with their divisions. They came out of their
entrenched position and offered battle to the
Muslim army on the 18th of May, 1775 (17th
Rabi 1, 1189 H.; *Waqa*, MS. p. 287). The
superior generalship of the Mirza more than
made up for the deficiency of the imperialists
in number. The Jats and Rajputs sustained a
defeat and fled to Deeg.

Death of Rajah Nawal Singh.

Rajah Nawal Singh paid dearly for his folly in rekindling the flames of war which did not subside even after consuming him to death. In spite of many disasters and defeats the Jat chief was as obdurate as ever. The victorious Mughal army was thundering before the gates of Deeg, demanding his submission or a fight to the end. But Nawal Singh coolly refused both. Fond hope whispered in his ear that he need not yet despair of success. Abdul Ahad Khan tried what diplomacy and intrigue could to baffle or divert the arms of Mirza Najaf Khan. He was instigating the Marathas* to crush timely the formidable power of the Mirza—the more dangerous to their national safety on account of his alliance with the English who supported the pretensions of Raghoba. In the Deccan the battle of Arras had been fought (18th May, 1775), the issue of which was not very encouraging to the patrons of the usurper. Nawal Singh was heartened by the prospect of a Maratha invasion of Hindustan after the rainy season which would surely compel the Mirza to retire from the Jat country. More hopeful

---

* See Mirza Najaf Khan's letter to the Governor of Bengal, entered under the date 24th January, 1775. (Pers. Cor. MS.)

was the news of an alliance of Zabita Khan with the Sikhs and their joint attack upon the imperial territories. The son of Najib-ud-daulah looked upon the office of Amir-ul-umra and all the territories around Delhi as a part of his heritage from which Mirza Najaf Khan and the Marathas had ousted him under the pretence of restoring the authority of the Emperor. He aspired to play the dictator at the imperial Court like his father; the Ruhela confederacy having disappeared he relied on the Sikhs who were to be pitted against the Marathas. The Sikhs plundered and burnt Paharganj (the western suburb of Delhi between Qadam Sharif and Raisina), and the Ruhela chief himself was ravaging the Doab. The situation was menacing enough to create grave anxiety in the mind of the Emperor, who wrote to Nawab Asaf-ud-daulah* for help against the rebels. Mirza Najaf Khan refused to move leaving a half-conquered enemy to insult his rear and resolved not to turn his back upon Deeg without capturing it. God spared the Jat chief the mortification of witnessing the inevitable doom of his country and people. Rajah Nawal Singh, who

---

* See *ibid*, letter of Asaf-ud-daulah to the Governor dated 31st May, 1775.

seemed to have vowed not to die on the battle-field, was happy enough to breathe his last on a sick-bed, two *gharis* after sunset on Thursday, 10th August,* 1775. He was sickly in constitution, cowardly in action and rash in speculation. He was obstinate on the wrong side of it and brave in everything except what concerned his personal safety. As a soldier and patriot he was of the type of Demosthenes who could deliver *Philippics* at the forum of Athens, without courage to bear the sight of Philip's phalanx on the field of Charonea. Though he had disappointed his officers and troops at critical moments by his nervous timidity, they never ceased to believe that he would behave better next time. "He did not possess much administrative ability and generalship."† Nevertheless, he was loved by his people for his amiable virtues and generosity, and his death was sincerely mourned by all of them.

Rahimdad's treachery and his expulsion from Deeg by Ranjit Singh Jat.

Mullah Rahimdad, after his successful raid in the Biana and Agra districts, had returned to

---

* 12th Jamada II, 1189 A.H; *Waqa* MS. p. 289.

† Ghulam Ali's *Shah Alam Nama* MS. p. 4.

Deeg at the beginning of the rainy season, and
pitched his camp under the shelter of the fort-
guns along with other commanders of the Jat
army.   He proved faithful to his paymasters
while nothing very covetable tempted his
fidelity.   On the very night of Nawal Singh's
death the Ruhela determined to try his luck by
a bold piece of treachery.   "Having come to
learn that the men inside the city had given
themselves up to mourning and were neglecting
the defence of the place, Rahimdad Khan considered this to be the most opportune moment,
and got four or five thousand of his Ruhela
soldiers ready for action.   At first he himself
with a few chosen companions went to the gate
of the city which lay opposite to his camp, and
secured entrance under the pretence of taking
a mere stroll.   He seized that gate, and with
the assistance of his veteran soldiers, made himself master of the whole city.   He posted
Ruhelas at every gate to keep watch over it,
and going to the door of Jawahir Singh's
[palace] got hold of the person of his infant son
Kheri Singh by deluding the ladies of his harem
with smooth words of deception.   He seated
Kheri Singh on the *masnad*, and got himself
appointed his Deputy"   [*Ibratnama*, MS.
p. 270.]   He established his authority over

every department of the State after expelling
from Deeg those officers of Nawal Singh who
showed hostility to him. Rahimdad took into
his pay and confidence a considerable number
of Jat soldiers and made preparations to give
battle to the Amir-ul-umra. His attitude was
a strange one; he determined to hold Deeg in
independent authority against the Emperor as
well as the sons of Rajah Suraj Mal. A counter-
revolution was being planned against him in the
fort of Kuhmir, where Ranjit Singh secretly
assembled all the loyal chiefs of his tribe and
intrigued with those in the city of Deeg for the
expulsion of the usurping mercenary leader.
One night he started for Deeg with a select body
of troops. He himself entered the fort with a
few companions and directed Awlia [Inglia ?]
Maratha, who had 2,000 horse with him, to
attack the encampment of the Ruhelas outside
the walls of Deeg. They executed their task
with skill and bravery, and falling unawares
upon the Ruhela camp threw it into utter confusion. Rahimdad on hearing this news hurriedly
went out to the rescue of his camp without
suspecting the trap laid for him by his clever
enemy. In his absence the whole city of Deeg
rose against his followers. Reassured by the

presence of the prince even those Jats whom Rahimdad had taken into his service joined their brethren in destroying the faithless Ruhelas. Fighting men who had hitherto remained in concealment among the townsfolk issued out simultaneously from every street and lane and within a short time cleared the city of the Afghans, killing many and capturing a considerable number of them. Rahimdad,* seeing that fortune would no longer befriend him in that country, marched away towards Delhi. Ranjit Singh was installed at Deeg as Rajah in the place of his infant nephew Kheri Singh, whose claim was set aside in view of the great danger to the Jat nation.

---

* Khair-ud-din says that Rahimdad after his expulsion from Deeg again rejected the offer of Mirza Najaf Khán to re-enter his service, that he attached himself to Abdul Ahad Khán and that he attacked Bashir Khan, the lieutenant of Najaf Khán in charge of Hisar and Hansi [*Ibratnámá*, pp. 286-289]. But one mutilated sentence seems to throw doubt on the above statements of Khair-ud-din. Under the date 11th Ziqada 1189 A.H. (3rd January, 1776) we have the following fragment "*Khabar rashid ke Mullah Rahimdad Khán* HAMRAH-I-MIRZA NAJAF KHAN........." i.e., news reached that Mullah Rahimdad Khán in the company of Mirza Najaf Khán.........This perhaps warrants us in inferring that Rahimdad was *with* the Mirza—and certainly as a friend on that date i.e., 3rd January, 1776. So he must have been expelled from Deeg at some date prior to it.

The Siege of Deeg (May, 1775—April, 1776).

Deeg, the deserted capital of the Sinsinwar Jats, is now a sleepy provincial town of sombre look, situated 44 miles w. n. w. of Agra and 22 miles north of Bharatpur.   Though humiliated by the neglect of more than a century, and overpowered by enemies, she still keeps erect her Lakwa Burj lifting its head high into the sky like the haughty crest of Jawahir.   The town and its neighbourhood have lost their awe-aspiring martial look under British peace.   It is situated in a level plain, having nothing noticeable except its beautiful sheets of water which add to the charm as well as strength of the place making it almost inaccessible to the enemy, especially in the rainy season. Whatever human efforts could do to remedy the defects of nature were not spared by the Jat for strengthening this place.   The huge mud-wall with bastions encircling the town was so prodigious in height and breadth that it appeared at the first sight "like a long range of hillocks utilised for the purpose of enclosing the city" [*Le Nabob Rene Madec*, sec. 48].   A broad and deep ditch runs all around the city except near the Shah Burj which. commanded the main entrance.   This Shah Burj was almost a fortress by itself with

"an area of fifty yards square on the inside, for
the use of the garrison, and presenting four commanding bastions facing the four cardinal
points......About a mile from this place, and
nearly in the centre of the town, stands the
citadel, which is strongly built......The ramparts
are high and thick, furnished with bastions and
surrounded by a deep ditch faced with
masonry.* The approaches to the outer fort
were rendered extremely difficult by a number
of fortified outworks and small *garhis* strewn all
over the surrounding plain. Among these the
largest and strongest was Gopalgarh, a small
mud-fort which stood at a short distance opposite the Shah Burj. Though the countryman†
of Vauban could perhaps with justice ridicule
the engineering skill of the Jat, Deeg and
Bharatpur were then admittedly the strongest
and most carefully fortified cities in India.

Within these formidable fortifications was
a flourishing city, the wealth and magnificence
of which mocked the decaying grandeur of the

---

* *Memoir of the War in India* by Major William Thorn,
p. 414.

† M. Madec speaking about the fortifications of Bharatpur
remarks : "These people are so simple that they well believe
that they have found out the true manner of forfifying !"
[*Le Nabob Rene Madec*, sec. 47].

proud capitals of the Great Mughal, Delhi and Agra. The honour and wealth of the Hindus were considered nowhere more safe than at Deeg. Merchant princes and "nobles of the robe" of the Mughal Court built there large and handsome mansions for the better security of their treasure and families. Traders of all communities flocked there and turned Deeg into one of the main arteries of commerce by establishing their depôts of merchandise within its wall. The beautiful was not altogether neglected by the Jat in his pursuit of the useful. The architect whose skill was no longer in demand at the impoverished Court of Delhi sought the patronage of the wealthy Jat and transformed a robber-chief's retreat into a city of palaces worthy of the capital of a powerful nation. Thakur Badan Singh lavishly spent his great wealth in decorating Deeg with a splendid suite of palaces now known as the *Purana Mahal*. Rajah Suraj Mal, though unjust to himself like some pious and charitable Seths, did not grudge any expenditure towards the building of several noble edifices, such as Suraj Bhavan, Kishan Bhavan, and Gopal Bhavan, bearing the impress of a new style of architecture which experts are disposed to call the Jat style, characterised by a graceful combination of Jat solidarity with

19

Mughal elegance. Maharajah Jawahir Singh, envious of the inimitable grace and symmetry of the Kachhwah capital, sought to turn his own into a veritable paradise of his dreams. Large reservoirs of water for boating and beautiful gardens intersected by canals fed by artificial fountains immeasurably heightened the charm of the royal palaces. Such was the noble city of Deeg, great in beauty and strength, which was now coveted by the conqueror of the Jats to crown his victory.

Mirza Najaf Khan had withdrawn his main army to Farah (on the bank of the Jamuna, half-way between Mathura and Agra) from the neighbourhood of Deeg during the rainy season, leaving only a small detachment to watch the enemy. At the end of the rains he started to resume the siege and pitched his camp at a distance of one kos and a half from the Kama gate. He passed some days in reconnoitring the defences of the fort; his heart misgave him at the closer view of its strength. So numerous were the guns and matchlockmen manning its walls that Deeg appeared to him a living volcano, every inch of which seemed to emit fire and send forth an inexhaustible flood of molten lead. The fortifications were so extensive that his whole army was considered hardly sufficient to blockade effectively even one side of it. At last his soldier's eye descried the Achilles's heel in this apparently invulnerable monster of war. He assigned the task of erecting batteries against the Shah Burj (where the ditch terminated) to half his men, and himself with the other half besieged Gopalgarh* to cover their operations [*Ibratnama*, MS. p. 274]. The soldiers in their batteries dug trenches to protect themselves from the galling fire of artillery and musketry from the walls of Deeg. Several thousand Naga foot-soldiers were encamped in the intervening ground between Deeg and Gopalgarh. As they knew no fear or anxiety, their leaders would very often with a few of such followers boldly attack the Musalmans in the battery and drive off from the way the bullocks bringing grain to the army of the Mirza. This caused scarcity of foodstuffs in his camp and alarmed his troops. Shortly after Muhammad Beg Khan Hamadani and Najaf Quli who had been sent to reduce the surrounding country to order and obedience,

---

* It is interesting to observe that in 1804 Lord Lake also did exactly the same at the siege of Deeg : "On the right of our battery [against Shah Burj] was Gopalgarh an old mud-fort.........crowded with matchlockmen who by their constant firing annoyed working parties very much and did us considerable damage." [*Memoir of the War in India*—Thorn, p. 408].

returned to the camp with large convoys of grain and materials of war. The arrival of their victorious troops revived the courage of the besieging army. Mirza Najaf Khan having been thus reinforced, decided to drive away the enemy troops encamped in the open ground between Gopalgarh and Deeg.

One morning the Nawab, with his whole army arrayed for battle and his guns placed in front, marched to his chosen ground. All the Naga Gosains fully equipped for fight and carrying matchlocks in their hands came out to resist the Muslim army. Thousands of Jat soldiers poured in from every direction and rapidly formed ranks of battle. Ranjit Singh himself accompanied by all his brave and renowned chiefs descended from the fort and taking his post in one of the *murhalas* [redoubts] gave an order for attacking the enemy. At the same time the guns of Deeg and Gopalgarh kept on firing incessantly upon the troops of the Nawab, who were also exposed to a heavy fire of *zamburaks, jazail* and muskets from behind the redoubts. From all directions the Jat horse and foot began to press them hard and the furious Gosains dealt out martyrdom to many a Muslim. The troops of the Nawab were losing their ground; many were slain and the knees of others began to shake. The few who had hitherto tenaciously kept the field out of a sense of honour in spite of the deadly fire were at last about to flee. The Nawab, seeing the desperate condition of affairs, dismounted, and his choice companions and guards followed suit. At their head he charged the enemy with great intrepidity. His example spurred the disheartened Muslim troops to one gallant effort to break the enemy's lines. But Rajah Ranjit Singh, who had prudently kept himself beyond the danger zone, made no exertion to support his men, and he seems to have left the field at this critical moment. The Jat army, unable to stand the determined charge of the army of the Nawab, were forced to withdraw. The Gosains who had so long scorned the shelter of the fortifications of Deeg, entered the town with their baggage. Muhammad Beg Khan Hamadani pitched his camp on the ground formerly occupied by them.

Mirza Najaf Khan found that the capture of Deeg by force of arms was almost impossible. He ordered Najaf Quli to encamp with his troops, at a convenient place between Deeg and Kuhmir, and to be vigilant day and night in intercepting the food-supplies sent from Kuhmir to the besieged, and cutting off all communications between these two places. One night two thousand men and women carrying grain from the district of Kuhmir and escorted by a party of Jat foot-soldiers, fell in with the patrol of Najaf Quli's camp. At the sight of the enemy, they threw down their loads and fled to the jungles; a few were captured and sent to Mirza Najaf Khàn. His advisers suggested that these men should be deprived of their noses and ears and sent away to their homes, so that the people of Kuhmir might know the risk of such an enterprise. But the Mirza refused to punish the helpless and innocent people for the crime of one obstinate rebel. He set them free only with the warning that they should not make any such attempt in future [*Ibratnama* MS. pp. 266-267]. Najaf Khan's kindness proved more effective in disarming the hostility of the Hindu villagers than the usual frightfulness of mediæval warriors. His exalted character inspired confidence in the hearts of the mass of the Hindu people and his wise and humane policy removed for a while the general feeling of repulsion against Muhammadan rule, a legacy of the age of Aurangzib augmented by the bloody conquests of the Abdali.

M. Madec who had rejoined the army of Najaf Khan after his defeat by Rahimdad, proposed a night-attack upon one of the towers of the town where the guards were observed to have grown slack in their watch and duty. He offered to lead a party for the surprise, consisting of seven picked companies of grenadiers [*Sipahian-i-garandil*] with two guns; the Nawab was to stand ready in the camp with his army and was to start for the appointed place as soon as he should hear the sound of a volley of muskets which was to be fired as a signal by the storming party. M. Madec and the sepoys concealed themselves in the trench of the battery till midnight. When the guards appeared to have retired to rest, they silently made their way to the foot of the wall and began to ascend it making foot-holds in the wall with their bayonets and daggers. About one hundred men gained the top; M. Madec, owing to his nervousness and perplexity without waiting for others to climb up, ordered the sepoys to fire a volley of their muskets as signal for the Mirza. But it served no less as an alarm to the negligent watch who at once fell upon the sepoys on the wall without giving them time to reload their muskets. Most of them were killed and a few jumped down on the ground below to save themselves from the enemy's sword [*Ibratnama* MS. pp. 269-270]. As soon as the signal firing

was heard Mirza Najaf Khan rode with a loose
rein and stopped only at the foot of the tower.
By this time the day had broken, and the
garrison of Deeg throwing open the gates of the
fort attacked the troops of the Nawab who found
themselves caught at a disadvantage. The
army of Najaf Khan was exposed to a terrible
fire from the fort-guns and the matchlocks in
the smaller *garhis*. Veterans of the Nawab's
army fell down at every step; horses became
restive and threw down their riders. "Soldiers
and officers who had for years fought valiantly
in many a battle were unable to keep their feet
firm on that field of Resurrection and fled without a moment's thought, carrying confusion
even to their camp-followers. The defenders'
of the fort became bolder in their attack; it was
a strange sight to see one wretched Jat foot-
soldier armed only with a spear, rushing upon
ten troopers of the Nawab and the latter standing paralysed [with fear] and motionless like
pictures and statues, none having the courage
to resist the infidels." [*Ibid.*] The cruel-
hearted enemy seeing the plight of the army of
Islam gradually closed upon them. Out of
three or four thousand soldiers only a small
number of men held together fighting resolutely
around their brave general. When the Nawab

found even his companions inclined to turn
back, he wavered as to what course he should
take.   At this critical moment Somru with one
battalion of sepoys arrived with great speed to
the assistance of the Nawab and interposed his
detachment between the two armies. He
ordered his guns to be loaded with grape-shot
which dealt out death to hundreds at a time in
the ranks of the enemy. The progress of the
Jats was arrested and at last they were driven
into the fort. Mirza Najaf Khàn did not relin-
quish the ground so bravely won : he ordered
a battery to be constructed on that spot; [ibid
p. 281.]

Every day the prospect became more and
more gloomy for the besieged. The army of
Najaf Khán was being swollen daily by the
arrival of fresh troops. Rajah Himmat Bahadur
joined him with five or six thousand horse and
foot, and thirty guns. The Nawab Asaf-ud-
daulah sent Latafat Ali Khàn* with three
battalions of sepoys to the help of the Mirza.
Najaf Quli completely cut off the food-supplies
of the besiegers. It was not the task of feeding

---

* On the 8th of Muharram [1190 H; 28th February, 1776]
Latafat Ali Khan with three battalions [paltan] sent by Nawab
Asaf-ud-daulah, presented nazar to His Majesty, and receiving
khilat, went to the haveli of Safdar Jang [Waqa, 291].

a small garrison but providing food to every
soul in a populous city (of fifty thousand mouths.
at the lowest computation) that confronted Rajah
Ranjit Singh.   The inevitable came at last, and
the Jat was forced to yield but not a day too
soon.   Famine spread in the city and in its
train came epidemic and lawlessness.   "Every
street and lane was strewn with hundreds of
dead bodies of men and beasts.   The distressed
people made no distinction between clean and
unclean food.   Anything that came to hand was
thrown into the mouth by everybody without
hesitation."   [Ibid, p. 282*].   Under the
stress of such a calamity Ranjit Singh permitted
the citizens to go out, and a stream of wretched
humanity passed through the dismal gates of
Deeg towards the Muslim camp.   The officers
of Mirza Najaf Khàn urged him to drive these
refugees back into the fort by opening fire upon
them so that these people might increase the
horror of famine within and render the air of
the fort pestilential.   But the Nawab abhorred
this ruthless though clever device of stewing

---

* Khair-ud-din perhaps transgresses the bounds of credibility
when he says "Hanud āz hurmat gosht-i-gāo ighmāz kardah
dar zabuh-i-gao bā-Musalmānan ham-dast o iksar dar-manand-
gān   ba-khordan-i-murdah   bā-murdar-khawaran   hām-kassa
shudand." [Ibratnama, MS. p. 282].

the Jat in his own juice, and said "I do not
wish that these poor and destitute people should
be caught in adversity along with the rebels and
oppressors." He treated them very kindly and
provided for their comfort and security. He
planted an imperial standard [ālam] half
way between the city and his own encampment and issued a proclamation that those
who would take shelter under that standard
would in no way be molested. This welcome
message brought every day hundreds of
refugees to that standard. It so happened
that even rich merchants and money-lenders
wearing tattered dresses and concealing valuable
jewels and gold coins in their clothes began to
slip out in the company of the poor. The
camp-followers and wicked characters of the
Muslim army, who used to lie in wait and sometimes rob the refugees before they could reach
the standard, discovered this trick. When an
accidental search revealed jewels in rags, even
the Mirza's soldiers secretly joined them in this
business and deprived the poor refugees of every
piece of cloth on their bodies. This report
having reached the ears of the Mirza, he
summoned these soldiers and their officers and
severely reprimanded them for their ignoble act
of oppressing men in misery. From this time the

refugees were ordered to wait under the wall
of the fort, and when a large number of them
had assembled, the Mirza himself with his
guards escorted them to the imperial standard
and appointed a strong detachment of troops to
protect them. Within a few days almost all the
non-combatants left the city.

Insufficient food began to tell upon the
spirit and health of the Jat soldiers, who were
becoming weaker every day. Still Ranjit Singh
would neither evacuate the fort nor offer battle
to the enemy. The chiefs of his army and the
members of his own household became disgusted at his indecision and pressed him strongly
to make a choice between the two alternatives
now open to him : if he cared for honour, he
should at once lead them, half dead as they
were, against the Musalmans with the resolution
either to conquer or to die; or if he wished to
wait for any change of fortune by prolonging
the struggle he should retire to Bharatpur or
Kuhmir before it was too late. Ranjit Singh
descended from the fort one dark night, at a
spot near the battery of Rajah Himmat Bahadur
and eluding the pursuit of the enemy safely
reached the fort of Kuhmir. A considerable
number of Jats remained behind guarding the
women and children, and being resolved to die

in defence of the citadel.. Next morning, on the 10th Rabi-ul-awwal, 1190 A.H. (29th April, 1776), Mirza Najaf Khan entered the town. But the garrison, who had retreated with their families into the mansion of Badan Singh and the citadel, did not allow the Muslims to taste the joy of victory, rather "made it more bitter than the wine of death" [*Ibratnama* MS. p. 284]. They kept up an incessant and terrible musketry fire upon the troops of the Nawab, many of whom died in the attempt to dislodge them. The Mirza forbade the plunder of even the deserted houses of the town and posted strong guards everywhere. Impressed by the undaunted spirit of the Jat garrison, he expressed his willingness to grant them pardon and a safe conduct. They rejected his generous offer and persisted in their hostility. At length the Nawab ordered Somru to bombard these places by erecting batteries against them. Towards sunset breaches were made in the walls of the mansion and of the inner fort, rendering them untenable. In the darkness of the night the Jat grimly prepared himself for the last awful journey of life, steeling his heart against all sentiments of love and affection. His near and dear ones were sent ahead by the sword to a region where his own spirit, free

from earthly bondage, would seek theirs on the
morrow. With the first gleam of dawn the
warriors threw open the gates of the citadel and
fell upon the battery and the sepoys of Somru.
Whoever came in their path instantly fell
victims to their sword, sharpened by hatred and
despair. Somru's guns loaded with grape-
shots opened a destructive fire; but wound had
no pain, death no terror, nor life any charm for
these heroes, each of whom attacked thirty or
forty enemies and piercing the ranks of the
sepoys struck the guns with the sword in blind
fury. Glutted with the slaughter of their
enemies and covered with many wounds they
fell gloriously fighting to their last breath.
Deeg,* dyed crimson with the best blood of her

---

* Khair-ud-din has done full justice to the valour of the
Jats in this last phase of their struggle with Mirza Najaf Khan.
He says "Not a single man tried to save his life. If they had
fought unitedly they would have slain many more and safely
made their way [out of the fort]." No *johar* seemed to have
been lighted at Deeg; women and children were "put to the
sword" according to Khair-ud-din. M. Madec notices that three
wives of Nawal Singh prayed to the palace-eunuch to kill them
after the capture of the city by Najaf Khan. "They lay on
the carpet and he cut off the heads of all the three of them
one after another, and ended by killing himself on their
corpses" [*Le Nabob Rene Madec*, Sec. 48]. There is nothing
unusual in the slaughter of females by the Jats at Deeg. Speaking of the Jats in the reign of Akbar Manucci says "In order
to defend themselves these villagers hid in thorny scrub or

children and her foes alike, awaited her fate
at the hands of the conqueror.

———

retired behind the slight walls surrounding their villages. *The
women stood behind their husbands* with spears and arrows.
When the husband had shot off his matchlock, his wife handed
him the lance, while she reloaded the matchlock. Thus did
they defend themselves until they were no longer able to continue. When reduced to extremity, they cut their wives and
daughters' throats and then in desperation, they threw themselves against the enemy's ranks and several times, they succeeded in gaining the day by mere reckless courage." (*Storia
do Mogor*, tr. by Wm. Irvine, i. 134).

CHAPTER XV.

REIGN OF RAJAH RANJIT SINGH JAT
(1775—1805)

Afrasiyab's campaign in the Doab.

Rajah Suraj Mal had sown well the seeds of liberty and ambition in the heart of every Jat. If the parent-tree of the Jat State was withering in the land of Braj, its off-shoots grew up vigorously on newer soils and kept up the hope and faith of the people in their great political destiny. During the four years of the comparative neglect of the Doab by the Mughal Government since the battle of Dánkaur, several Jat leaders, on their individual initiative, had been carrying on war with the object of carving out small principalities for themselves. They had not only created a powerful diversion to draw off a part of the Mughal army, but also found means to "send secret help to the besieged at Deeg". [*Ibratnama*, p. 289.] Mirza Najaf Khan sent Afrasiyab Khan* to

---

* Khair-ud-din is not definite about the date. He says, "*It is said* that when the siege of Deeg was prolonged the Amir-ul-umra sent Afrasiyab Khan" [MS. p. 289].

subdue them and restore order and peace in the
Doab. Afrasiyab crossed the Jamuna with an
army of fifteen thousand horse and a pro-
portionate number of matchlockmen and guns.
After having expelled from that region all the
Jat officials who were the ring-leaders of disturbance and rebellion, he laid siege to Aligarh.
Jawahir Singh had spent a large sum of money
in strengthening its fortifications, given it the
name of Ramgarh (it having been known as
Sabitgarh before his time), and made it
the grand depôt of his military stores
and treasure. After Afrasiyab Khan had
reduced the garrison to great straits by a
siege of several months, Rajah Bhup Singh
of Mudsán and Hathras* commenced hostilities
in his rear. At the instigation of the Rajah the
peasants throughout the Doab refused to pay
taxes and resisted the authority of the Mughal
Government. Afrasiyab, finding himself unequal to the task, summond his master to his
assistance.

---

* Hathras on E. I. Ry., 25 miles east of Mathura; Mudsán
lies 8 miles west of Hathras. Another fort "Bawar" of the
Ibratnama cannot be indentified in the map. It may be a
mistake for Jowar, a large village 10 miles from Hathras and
4 miles north-west of Mudsán. But this village has no trace
of fortification. The first two places are situated between lat.
27°-40', and long. 78°-10'.

20

Mirza Najaf Khan's departure from Deeg.

Mirza Najaf Khan had strained his energy
and resources to the utmost in capturing Deeg,
in the belief that such a success would bring the
Jat down on his knees.   The fall of the capital
of the Jats sent a thrill of surprise throughout
India.   Titles and honours were heaped upon
the conqueror by the Court of Delhi.   But the
joy of the Mirza turned into gloom when he
found that in parting with Deeg the Jat did not
intend to part with his independence.   Without
suing for terms, Rajah Ranjit Singh prepared
for a more obstinate defence of his remaining
strongholds.   The Mirza spent the rainy season
in the Jat country and seemed to have contemplated a campaign against Jaipur.   But the
serious nature of the Jat rising in the Doab and
the failure of Afrasiyab Khan against the forts
of Rajah Bhup Singh Jat made him change his
mind.   However, before he departed from
Deeg he succeeded in planting a thorn to
torment both the Jat and the Kachhwah by
encouraging the aggressive views of Rao Rajah
Pratap Singh of Macheri, who gave them no
peace for several years from this time.

Mirza Najaf Khan started from Deeg with
ll his chiefs and a numerous army to subdue

the Jat rebellion in the Doab. A war-weariness seems to have come upon that veteran general, who had no more relish for this never-ending struggle with a people whom no odds could overawe, and no disaster could dishearten. He was inclined to peace, and signified his willingness to confirm Rajah Bhup Singh in his possessions as a feudatory of the empire if he would submit and come to his presence. But the Jat who never learns through the experiences of others, was not disposed to yield without a trial of strength with the conqueror of Deeg. He stood a siege at Mudsán and resolutely defended it for some time. Many brave soldiers of the Mirza were killed and wounded by the tremendous fire of guns, matchlocks and *huqqahs* [hand grenades] in their attempt to storm the fort. Rajah Himmat Bahadur who was with the Mughal army received a bullet-shot and was severely wounded. At last they succeeded in running several mines under the walls of the fort and forced the Rajah to evacuate* it. Mirza Najaf Khan gave the fort of Mudsán to Afrasiyab and himself undertook the siege of Hathras (eight miles east of

---

* Mudsán was captured between 9th Ziqada and 7th Zihijja of the year 1190 H. (20th December, 1776—17th January, 1777). [*Waqa*, MS. p. 297.]

Mudsán), whither the Rajah had fled. Pressed vigorously by the enemy, Bhup Singh sued for terms and sought an accommodation through Rajah Himmat. Bahadur. The Nawab gave back to him all his territories on the condition of military service and allowed him to retain those forts which he was holding at that time [*Ibratnama*, MS. p. 291]. He then marched against Ramgarh and, having captured it after a siege of twenty-four days, changed its name to Aligarh.*

About this time the Emperor summoned Mirza Najaf Khan to Delhi to punish the rebellious Ruhela chief who had slain Abul Qasim Khan (brother of Abul Ahad Khan), defeated an imperial army, and forcibly taken possession of many *mahals* of the crownland.

Mirza Najaf Khan's campaign against Zabita Khan.

Mirza Najaf Khan reached Delhi and was honourably conducted to the royal presence by Princes Jahandar Shah and Jahan Shah (4th

---

* Khair-ud-din says that Aligarh was captured by Afrasiyab Khan before he was confronted with the peasants' revolt in the Doab instigated by Bhup Singh. But considering his indifference to the sequence of events we cannot accept this against the testimony of *Imad-us-Saadat*, written at an earlier date.

Muharram, 1191 H. = 12th February, 1777).
Two months afterwards he accompanied the
Emperor in the expedition against Ghausgarh,
one of the strongholds of Zabita Khan. The
imperial army left Delhi on the 19th April (11th
Rabi I., 1191 H.) and arrived in the vicinity of
Ghausgarh on the 8th June. Zabita Khan with
his main army had already marched out of that
fortress to harass the imperialists by acting on
their supplies and attacking them from the rear.
Mirza Najaf Khan laid siege to the fort, but had
to suffer great hardships during the rainy season
which set in shortly after. He fought a pitched
battle with the army of Zabita Khan on the 18th
Rajab (22nd August). Though he succeeded
in beating off the enemy, the situation,
aggravated by the treachery of Abdul Ahad
Khan, was one of great peril for him. He
summoned Afrasiyab Khan from the Doab,
and was joined by that general on the 30th
Rajab (3rd September). Another great battle
was fought, and a decisive victory won on the
11th Shaban (14th September), mainly through
the fortitude and skill of Afrasiyab. On the
22nd Shaban (25th September) the Emperor
entered Ghausgarh in triumph, and on the 7th
Shawwal (8th November) the families of Zabita
Khan and other Afghan chiefs were sent to the

fort of Agra under the custody of Daud Beg
Khan and Afrasiyab Khan. Having left Najaf
Quli as governor of Saharanpur, the Emperor
and Mirza Najaf Khan hastily set out for the
capital to punish Rao Rajah Pratap Singh and
Ranjit Singh Jat.

Renewed activity of Ranjit Singh.

Ranjit Singh made a good use of the short
respite afforded by the embarrassment of Mirza
Najaf Khan at Ghausgarh. The Mirza had left
his incapable brother-in-law Saadat Ali in charge
of Hinduan and Biana (situated 70 and 50 miles
respectively south-west of Agra) with a good
deal of wholesome advice to behave himself
worthily and watch the movements of the Jats
cautiously. This noble, surrounded by a group
of carpet-knights, thought of anticipating the
Mirza in crushing the Jat, who seemed already
to be in his last gasp. He wrested several
parganas from Ranjit Singh and laid siege to
one of his forts. Ranjit Singh sent a Marathà
captain in his service with five or six hundred
horsemen to succour the besieged. They made a
long night-march, and at early dawn fell upon
the Muslim camp, immersed in sleep after
midnight gaieties. Saadat Ali and his companions woke up too late; before they could

put on their clothes, and get at their arms, the Marathas had forced their way into their tents. The Mughals fled and fled for more than 50 miles without turning back till safe within the walls of Agra. (*Ibratnama* MS. pp. 292-294).

Ranjit Singh, encouraged by this success, issued out of Kuhmir and re-occupied the greater part of the territories lost by Nawal Singh. Muhammad Beg Khan Hamadani started from Agra to check the activity of the Jat chief who was driven back into Kuhmir and forced to stand a siege there. But almost simultaneously the Rao Rajah assumed a hostile attitude towards the Mughal Government, and his aggression assumed such serious proportions that Mirza Najaf Khan had to order Muhammad Beg Khan Hamadani to raise the siege of Kuhmir and march against Macheri. Hamadani inflicted a defeat upon the army of the chief of Macheri in the month of Rajab, 1191 H. [August, 1777; *Waqa*, p. 302]. But this success hardly improved the situation in that quarter. The army of Hamadani was held at bay by the concerted hostility of Ranjit Singh and the Rao Rajah. The able and energetic Naruka chief aided by some powerful Maratha captains in his pay threatened to undo the work of Mirza Najaf Khan, snatching away the fruits

of his long and arduous campaigns against the
Jats. The condition of affairs was so desperate
that the Mirza had to leave the task of the subjugation of Zabita Khan half completed, and
only four days after his arrival at Delhi from
Ghausgarh he had to start for Agra to repel
the new danger [24 Shawwal = 25th Novr.,
1777; *Waqa*, p. 305].

Rao Rajah Pratap Singh conquers Mewat from the Jats.

Rao Pratap Singh, a scion of the Naruka
branch of the Kachhwahs started his career with
a patrimony of two villages and a half (Macheri,
Rajgarh and half of Rajpura), and closed it as
the founder of the Alwar Raj. His opportunity
came with the misfortune of the Jats, dating
from their disastrous retreat from the field of
Maonda. Taking advantage of the pre-
occupation of Nawal Singh in the civil war and
afterwards in his arduous struggle with the
imperialists, Rao Pratap Singh* seized with

---

* The *Rajputana Gazetteer* says "Taking advantage of the
depressed condition of the Jats, he [Rao P. Singh] between
Sambat 1832 and 1839 [1775—1782 A.D.], obtained Bahadurpur,
Dehra, Jhindoli, Bansur, Bahror, Barod, Rampur, Harsaura,
Hajipur, Hamirpur, Narainpur, Ghadi-Mamur and Thana
Ghazi." (1st edition vol. iii, p. 181). The Rao Rajah took
possession of the fort of Alwar on Mangsar Sudi 3
[Margasirsha], 1832 Sambat (25th November, 1775; see *ibid*).

ease all the parganas of Mewat. His crowning success was the capture of Alwar by bribing the Jat garrison, whose pay had long been in arrears. Mirza Najaf Khan, after his decisive victory over the army of Nawal Singh and his Jaipur auxiliaries, summoned the Rao Rajah to Deeg and asked him to join the Mughal army in a projected campaign against the Maharajah of Jaipur. The Naruka chief not only refused to bear arms against his suzerain but signified his firm resolve to join the army of Jaipur in repelling such an attack if made. Mirza Najaf Khan would have called him to account had not the rebellion of Rajah Bhup Singh Jat demanded his presence in the Doab. He made a virtue of necessity by conniving at the aggressive designs of the Rao Rajah as a desirable check upon his neighbours. The Rao Rajah fulfilled the expectation of the Mirza even to the extent of making him repent of it.

Siege of Kuhmir and the submission of Ranjit Singh Jat.

Mirza Najaf Khan established his head-quarters at Deeg and ordered Muhammad Beg Khan Hamadani to resume the siege of Kuhmir. His attention was mainly directed to the destruction of the formidable power of the Rao

Rajah by taking the help of the Maharajah of Jaipur,* Rajah Bhagwant Singh of Kanudah and other Rajput chiefs who had equally suffered from the aggression of the Macheri Rajah.

Ambaji Rao, Appaji Pandit, Bapuji Holkar and other Maratha allies of the Rao Rajah pressed him hard to make peace with Mirza Najaf Khan so that he might be able to prosecute war against his other enemies with greater success. The Rao Rajah started with a large and powerful army to meet the Mughal general at Deeg and pitched his camp near Asia [Rasia?] Pahari. On the 9th Ziqada, 1191 (9th Dec. 1777) he was admitted to an interview with the Mirza, who conferred upon him a very rich *khilat* and showed him every mark of esteem and favour. The negotiations for terms of settlement were protracted for many days, owing to the unyielding attitude of the Rao Rajah. If the agents of the Mirza pressed their demand too hard, he would silence them

---

* He had already sent, in response to an appeal for help from Maharajah Pratap Singh Kachhwah, a detachment of 1500 horse, two battalions of sepoys and four guns under Mir Muhammad Ali Khan and Zain-ul-Abidin [*Ibratnama* MS., p 348], possibly to assist at the siege of Rajgarh, a stronghold of the Macheri chief.

by directing his glance* to his vast encampment, as the most convincing reason of the correctness of his own contention. A plot was set on foot by some officers of the Mirza to make the Rao Rajah a prisoner; one day they surrounded his camp while the unsuspecting Rajputs were engaged in their daily ablutions and the Rao in performing his *pujah*. The cowards failed to entrap the lion-like Naruka, who with a gallant band broke through their toils of treachery and safely reached the fort of Lachman-garh.† The Muslim army besieged him there for four months without much success. One night the camp of Mirza Najaf Khan was surprised and his army badly defeated in a fight by the troops of the Rao Rajah. His enemies rejoiced over this reverse as ominous of the declining fortune of their formidable rival, and bestirred themselves to make a concerted attack upon him.

Muhammad Beg Khan Hamadani having

---

* "Chun karpardazán-i-sarkar dar bab i maamlah chize mi-goftand nazar bar sar kasrat-i-fauj o kanat zahir-i-khud namudah sar garani me-kard." [Ibratnama, p 340].

† This is situated 23 miles south-east of Alwar, on the border of the Bharatpur territory. Khair-ud-din says that Lachman-garh and wrested by the Rao Rajah from the Singh Jats. But local tradition, perhaps more authentic, says it was formerly known as Taur, taken from Swarup Singh Naruka.

been called away to reinforce the army of Najaf
Khan before Lachman-garh, Ranjit Singh issued
out of Kuhmir and again took to plundering
and burning the Mughal territories. By a bold
night-attack he killed the *Amil* of Farah (situated
half way between Mathura and Agra), and
ravaged the whole tract up to the walls of Agra
so thoroughly that lights ceased to burn in that
region.* The Emperor, urged by Abdul Ahad
Khan, decided to go towards Rajputana and
ordered the imperial camp to be pitched at
Tál Katora. The Sikh sardars were also won
over by the intriguing minister to the side of the
Emperor. Threatened by this dangerous league
of his enemies, Mirza Najaf Khan was cons-
trained to make peace with the Rao Rajah,
recognizing his title to Alwar and other
territories conquered from the Jats [Jamada II.
1192 H. July, 1778]. He sent back Hamadani
against Ranjit Singh and himself started for
Agra. In order to counteract the designs of his
enemies, he released the families of the Afghans
and restored Saharanpur to Zabita Khan
[Shaban, 1192 H. = September 1778; *Waqa,*
p. 310]. Shortly after this, he appeared before
Kuhmir with his whole army to finish the affair
of the Jats.

---

* *Ibratnama,* p. 345.

The siege of Kuhmir was prosecuted with great vigour, but the garrison in the hope of the arrival of the Emperor put up a stiff resistance. Mirza Najaf Khan grew impatient as the siege seemed to be dragging on to an interminable length. The imperial army broke up their camp at Tál Katora in the month of Shawwal and marched in the direction of Rewari. "The Amir-ul-umra out of the consideration of policy and general good sent a letter full of admonitions...........reminding him [Ranjit Singh] that there was yet time to secure pardon through submission and to atone for his past error by loyal service, without dragging several thousand men into destruction. When this letter reached Ranjit Singh his mind became distracted—he found neither strength in himself to offer resistance nor divine grace to guide his footsteps [to the auspicious presence of the Amir-ul-umra]. In the end, this excellent advice failed to find any place in his [obdurate] heart—he remained as haughty and obstinate as before" [*Ibratnama*, p. 346.] The besieging army redoubled their efforts and soon rendered the fort untenable. Despair seized the hearts of the garrison, "who found neither strength to go out nor place to stand upon." In their hour of supreme peril, they remembered the old queen Kishori, who had outlived the glory of the house of Bharatpur, and been pining in neglect and retirement after the death of Jawahir Singh. The wellwishers of Ranjit Singh advised him to send the old queen to the Mughal camp, because she enjoyed the respect and good-will of the high officers of the Amir-ul-umra, and might possibly by her intercession procure pardon for his past offences. But Ranjit Singh hesitated to act upon their advice lest the Mirza should compel him to surrender unconditionally by detaining her in the Mughal camp. One night he escaped with a few friends, leaving Kuhmir to its fate. Next morning the Muslim troops scaled the walls of the fort and overpowered the defenders. Rani Kishori fell a prisoner into their hands and was taken with all honour to the camp of the Nawab. "In obedience to his order, the officers of his Government erected lofty and secluded tents for her residence and expert servants were appointed to wait upon her, so that after a few days her grief might subside." [*Ibid*, MS. p. 347].

It was not with the suspicious and timid steps of a prisoner that she went to meet the conqueror when summoned by him, but rather in the hope and confidence of a mother in

distress who goes to see her foster child. "On
reaching the presence of the Nawab, she like
an affectionate nurse, walked round the person
of the Amir-ul-umra, and with a sincere heart
took away [on her own shoulders] all his evils.*
With tearful eyes, she narrated the pitiful tale
of her misery. When the Nawab Amir-ul-umra
learnt the distress of her heart, his own heart
overflowed with kindness and he very graciously
set her up as his own mother. He gave her
the fort of Kuhmir for her residence and the
mahals around it for her support. To please
her, he forgave the guilt of Ranjit Singh and
left to him the fort of Bharatpur with territories
worth seven *lakhs* of Rupees as jagir." His
magnanimity succeeded where the barbarous
ferocity of the Abdali had failed.

Death of Mirza Najaf Khan.

The Mughal empire now entered on its last
phase, illumined by a sudden effulgence of
glory, after a gloom of four distressful decades.
Rajputana once again bowed before the sceptre
of Delhi and a descendant of Timur for the last
time performed the impressive ceremony of

---

* *Basān daiya e mihrban girdash gardid o ba-sadaq dil bala
gardanash shud* [*Ibratnama* MS. p. 347] *Cf.* Babur's going
round the sick-bed of Humayun. This popular superstition
has not yet died out.

applying the *Raj-tiká* on the proud forehead of a Rajput prince.* The sword of Mirza Shafi taught the turbulent Sikhs to respect the imperial authority. Majd-ud-daulah was at last caught in the meshes of his own intrigue, and visited with well-merited disgrace,† and the fortune of Mirza Najaf Khan shone resplendent in solitary grandeur. People looked forward to a happy era of strong, just and tolerant rule, but Heaven sent them significant omens of evil days. In the afternoon of the 2nd Jamada II., 1192 H. (29th May, 1778), a meteor was seen trailing its ominous course through the sky for about one-fourth of a *ghari*, accompanied by a deafening sound like the boom of a large cannon such as was never heard by the oldest citizen of Delhi. Another‡ came three years

---

* At Narnol, on the 2nd Safar, 1193 (19th February, 1779), Maharajah Sawai Pratap Singh Kachhwah paid a *nazar* of one thousand and one *ashrafis* to the Emperor Shah Alam II., and received *Raj-tiká* from His Majesty's auspicious hand [*Waqa* MS. p. 321.]

† Majd-ud-daulah was made a prisoner and brought into the camp of Mirza Najaf Khan by Afrasiyab Khan on the 6th Ziqada, 1193 H. (November, 15, 1779). [*Waqa*, p. 313.]

‡ This occurred on one Monday between the 26th Jamada I. and 27th Jamada II, 1195 H. (20th May—20th June, 1781) "At noon [*do-pahar*] a strong wind began to blow. It became so dark that nothing could be seen. Then the sky became red and the storm blew more furiously. After a short time the day recovered its usual brightness" [*Waqa*, p. 333.] This may be

after, when a painfully dazzling summer noon became all on a sudden dark like a moonless night, portending, as it were, the eclipse of the glory of the empire and the violent extinction of the light of the Emperor's own eyes. A heavy bereavement had already come upon the royal family by the death of Prince Farkhunda Bakht (Mirza Jahan Shah); a heavier one was yet to befall the whole empire.

Mirza Najaf Khan had been suffering for some time from a disease which baffled the skill of the best physicians. From the Emperor to the meanest of inhabitant of Delhi, Hindus and Musalmans alike became anxious for the life of their beloved hero. When human efforts failed they turned to the heavenly powers and prayed for his recovery. A grand offering (bhet) was made at the shrine of the goddess Kalka Devi (near Oklah) in the night of 7th Rabi II.* [?],

---

a dust-storm so frequent in summer at Delhi. But there was certainly something unusual so as to deserve notice in the Waqa.

   * The Waqa says "About one pas and a half of the night still remained when Sheoram Das went to Kalka Devi for offering bhet on behalf of Nawab Najaf Khan............" [MS. p. 337]. There is some confusion about the date. The text writes 27th Rabi II. But according to a subsequent entry the Nawab died on 22nd Rabi II.; so the first date cannot be true. Therefore either 27th is a mistake for 7th or Rabi-us-sani is a mistake for Rabi-ul-awwal. 7th Rabi II. falls on Friday (22nd March, 1782) but 27th Rabi I. falls on Tuesday (12th March).

21

1196 H. on behalf of the Mirza, and the blessings of the deity were invoked for his restoration to health. The Nawab distributed sweets to Brahmans and little boys, and released cows meant for slaughter by paying their price in cash to the butchers with a strong injunction to the effect that none should seize or molest these animals. But all was in vain. His great soul passed away on Saturday, 22nd Rabi II., 1196 H. (6th April, 1782) and with it the last gleam of the glory of Islam departed from Hindustan.

Here this volume ends. We propose next to follow the fortune of the Jat of Gohud and of Amritsar, and see how the one heroically succumbed under the relentless might of Maharashtra, and the other, drinking *amrit* from the hands of the Guru, triumphed over all the warlike frenzy and resources of the Durrani empire, and saved the whole of Hindustan from a horrible rule of the Pathan Ghazis.

———

So the former is the more likely date because it *agrees with the day of the week.*

APPENDIX A.

THE THEORY OF THE INDO-SCYTHIAN ORIGIN OF THE JATS.

The Indo-Scythian theory, associated with the names of some of the greatest scholars in the field of Indian History and Ethnology, has so long held the field and stifled doubt by the force of authority. V. A. Smith, the last learned champion of this theory, says "When the numerous Bálá, Indo-Scythian, Gujar, and Huna tribes of the *6th century horde* settled, their princely houses were accepted as Rajput, while those who frankly took to agriculture became Jat."* Elsewhere he remarks, "There is reason for believing that the Jats entered India later than the Gujars, rather about the same time."†

The following points may, however, be urged against this theory :—

(1) Col. Tod's inscriptional evidence of the existence of a Jit ruling dynasty as old as 409 A.D.‡

(2) The traditional enmity between the Rajput and the Jat makes it extremely doubtful that they had entered India—if they did it at all—at the same time as comrades, but had afterwards become divided into two hostile groups. Everywhere we

---

* *J. R. A. S.* 1899, p. 534.

† *Ibid,* 1909, p. 63.

‡ Crooke's edition of *Rajasthan,* i. 128, foot-note 1. The editor expresses a doubt "whether the Jat Kathida is the Jat or Gaetae of Cathay."

find the earlier Jat occupant of the soil supplanted
by the new Rajput immigrants. The Pramar dis-
placed him in Malwa, and the Tunwar snatched
away Delhi from him.* The Rathor wrested
Bikanir and the Bhatti imposed his rule upon him at
Jaisalmir.

(3) The Scythians who were very probably men
with broad faces, and high cheek-bones, sturdy and
short in stature, are little likely to have been the
ancestors of a tall-statured and long-headed people
like the Jats.

(4) A great blunder committed by the enthusiastic exponents of the Indo-Scythian theory was to
overlook the line of migration of the people who call
themselves Jat to-day. The tradition† of almost all
the Jat clans of the Panjab (even including an
apparently extra-Indian people, the Babbar Jats of

---

*It is not unlikely that this famous city derives its name the
Dhillon or Dhillhon Jats, who are still found in large numbers
in Delhi district. Folk etymology connects the name Dhillon
with *dhila* or lazy.

† Only the Ghatwal, Kang and Malik Jats remember any
connection with *Gajni* or Gharh Gajni which, however, they
persist in placing *not in Afghanistan, but somewhere in the
Deccan*. (Rose's *Punjab Glossary*, ii. 56, 472; iii. 56). But
Sir H. M. Elliot goes on saying "Almost all the Jats of N. W.
Provinces who do not claim Rajput descent trace their origin
from the far north-west, and some of them as the Ganthwaras
point to Gajni or *Garh Gajni apparently that in Afghanistan*.
Here without any knowledge of the learned discussions about
the identity of the Jat and the ancient Gaetae we find tradi-
tionary legends of these tribes pointing to the *remote Gajni
as their original seat* !!!........." [*Memoirs of the N.-W.
Provinces*, i. 132.]

Dera Ghazikhan), points to the east or south-east—
Oudh, Rajputana and the Central Provinces—as
their original home. If popular tradition counts for
anything, it points to the view that they are an
essentially Indo-Aryan people *who have migrated
from the east to the west,* and not Indo-Scythians
who poured in from the Oxus Valley. Undoubtedly
a certain section of the Jats migrated outside India
along with the Bhattis and after several centuries
were swept back from the borders of Persia to the
east of the Indus. But they cannot be justly called
foreign invaders on that account.

It is perhaps against the rule of historical
evidence to identify the Jats with the Gaete, Yuti,
Yetha or other Indo-Scythian people simply for the
sake of the resemblance of sound between their
names, in defiance of the evidence of philology and
ethnology to the contrary. It is of little use to point
out the place of the Jatas or Su-jatas in the great
genealogical tree of the Yadu race, when doubt
hangs upon the very origin of the Yadus themselves.
Col. Tod made a rather desperate attempt to prove
the common origin of the Tatars, the Chinese and
the Aryan Kshatriyas of the Lunar race by a study of
the comparative genealogical trees of these three
races and the traditions of their origin. [Crooke's ed.
of *Rajasthan,* i. 71-72]. Wilson, who held the
Purans to be not older than 1045 A.D., also
suspected that the Hayas and the Haihayas of the
Hindus had some connection with the Hia,......"who
make a figure in the Chinese history......It is not
impossible, however, that we have confirmatory
evidence of the Scythian origin of the Haihayas as

Col. Tod *supposed''* [Wilson's *Vishnu Puran,*
p. 418, foot-note 20]. In short, it has been suspected
by many European Orientalists that a Central Asian
genealogy entered India with the Indo-Scythic races
and was cleverly engrafted on the Indo-Aryan
genealogical tree by the unscrupulous Hindu
ethnologist, who dubbed the descendants of the
barbarian invaders as Kshatriyas of the Lunar race.

Fictitious genealogies both of individuals and
peoples are among the commonest phenomena in
the history of all nations. But what is the *motive*
behind this? First, a successful upstart or a little-
esteemed tribe rising to importance which had no
brilliant past—wants to create one of fanciful
grandeur to serve as a worthy background of their
bright present and brighter future. Secondly, a
people adapt their genealogy to their newly-
adopted religion or to that of their more
powerful and more civilized neighbours. Such is
the case with the Muhammadan peoples outside
Arabia. Many tribes of Afghanistan, who were
idol-worshipping Buddhists as late as the time of
Sultan Mahmud Ghaznavi, are found to-day claiming descent from Khalid, a renowned contemporary
of the Prophet. [Dorn's trans. of the *Makhzan-i-
Afaghana*]. The Buddhistic Turks on their conver-
sion to Islam made similar changes to suit the Arab
tradition. It is notorious how Indian converts to
Islam set up ludicrous claims to Shaikh or Sayyid
origin. What Arabia was to the Muslim peoples
outside it, that India had been before the birth of
Christ to the Buddhistic peoples of the Middle and
the Far East. It is a known fact of history that

China and Tartary received Buddhism from the Indian missionaries. No Hindu has been ever known to claim a Chinese origin, but the people of China, as Sir William Jones* pointed out, claim a Hindu lineage.

The exponents of the Indo-Scythian theory must, in all fairness, admit that if the Central Asian Gaete could somehow become the Aryan Jadu or Jat, by a reverse process the Indian Jadu might as well degenerate into the Gaete in Central Asia. From the time of the conquest of the Indus valley by Darius to the dissolution of the Maurya empire (*cir.* 600 B.C.—200 B.C.), Indian tribes streamed out in continuous flow into other parts of Asia, under various circumstances. Just as the English Government encourage the Gurkha and Sikh mercenaries to found colonies in different parts of the Indian empire, specially in Burmah, and as the Russian Government a few centuries back established the hardy and warlike Tatar Cossacks on the Don and other exposed points of their empire, similarly, the Indian mercenaries or forced recruits who served the Persian empire from the day of Marathon and Thermopylæ to that of Arbela—were perhaps settled on the coast of the Black Sea where they became known as the *Sindis* and Kerketae.† Besides military service, commercial enterprise also possibly took the Indian peoples to different countries. The greatest impetus to this foreign

---

* See *Rajasthan*, i. 69, foot-note 1. W. Crooke remarks "the comparison of Mongol with Hindu tradition is of no value."

† See Elliot's *History*, i. 518.

migration was given by the extension of the Maurya
empire to the Hindukush, and the subsequent spread
of Buddhism throughout Central Asia and China.
The rapid Indianization of Turkistan, attested by
Fa-Hian and other Chinese pilgrims who passed
through that region to India, could not have been
achieved by a handful of missionaries only but also
perhaps by the Indian merchant and the Indian
mercenary. As with the spread of Islam, the Arab
was always a welcome emigrant among Muslim
peoples, so had been the Indian in the newly
converted Buddhistic countries. It can be legiti-
mately inferred that those Central Asian Buddhistic
kingdoms as well as the Greek principalities of the
Middle East encouraged the migration of the Indian
peoples into their own country in pursuit of a policy
like that of Peter the Great of Russia, who
recruited his official nobility from the Germans and
encouraged the migration of artisans from the
countries of Western Europe to westernise the
Oriental Russia. And the lead in the foreign
migration was given by the unorthodox and
enterprising Yadus who rapidly multiplied, absorb-
ing no doubt many · outlandish elements from the
Panjab tribes. That the race of Yadu migrated
outside India is supported by the tradition of the
Bhattis of Jaisalmir, who ruled Zabulistan till the
advent of Islam in that country. In their foreign
colonies only the aristocratic section of the Yadus,
such as the Bhattis, perhaps kept their blood
unadulterated; but the rank and file freely inter-
marrying with the alien races of Tartary had
produced a people of Turkoman type, speaking a

Turkish language. Alberuni mentions a Turkish tribe with an unmistakeable Indian name Bhatta-varyán.* Two other tribes of Central Asia who are supposed to be the ancestors of the Jats are the Dahae and Massagetae, (Great Gate), on the eastern coast of the Caspian [Rajasthan, i. 55]. The Dahae are said to be the same people as the Dahas of the *Vishnu Puran* (Wilson, *Vishnu Puran*, p. 192, foot-note 100) and the modern Dahiya Jats. This is a mere suggestion without any historical proof except the similarity of sound. On the same principle one may hold that the Dahae on the Caspian were a section of the Yadus, who bore in the time of Mahabharat the tribal name of *Dashāi*, easily reducible to *Dahai*.†

We are told that the Jats were called *Sus, Abars*, and by many other names. The fact is not that the

---

* "Leaving the ravine by which you enter Kashmir, and entering the plateau, then you have to march for two more days on your left the mountains of Bolor and Shamilán, Turkish tribes who are called *Bhattavaryán*. *Their King has the title of Bhatta-Shah*. Their towns are Gilgit, Aswira, and Shiltas, and *their language is Turkish*". [Eng. trans. Sachau, p. 207].

† Dahiyas : In the *Mahabharat* Shri Krishna is often addressed as दाषार्हं i.e., descendant of Dasharhá. Sisupal angrily designates his *Dasharha, unworthy of the title of King* (Sabha, chap. 39). In the list of peoples दषार्ण (*Dasharna*) comes before कुकुर (Kukura); but this seems to be a mistake for Dasharha (Bhishma, chap. 8; also Bana Parva, chap. 183). *Brihat Samhita* of Baraha-mihira mentions दाषार्ण: Dasharna as people inhabiting the south-eastern (आग्नेय) quarter (S. Divedi's Sans. text vol. x, p. 288), but in a following chapter this tribe is mentioned in the north-west along with the Kakayas and Gandharas [*ibid*, p. 314]. Though repetition is by no means unusual, the latter is perhaps a mistake for दाषार्हं।

Jats adopted the name of Su-Sakas or Abhirs but
that these latter peoples took the tribal designation
of the former, their more esteemed superiors.
Further we find "The Yuchi, established in Bactria
and along the Jihoon, *eventually* bore the name of
Jeta or Yetan, *i.e.*, the Gaetes." [*Histoire des
Huns*, i. 42]. What on earth could induce all these
conquering tribes, the Saka, the Yuchi, the Hun,
and other Turkish peoples to assume such desig-
nations as Yeta, Gaete, and Bhattavaryán? This
leads one naturally to suspect that there must be
some fascination, some great tradition of nobler
blood and higher civilization associated with this
name, having as much attraction for these Central
Asian tribes as the proud name "Rajput" has for
all the martial Hindu tribes of India. These
descendants of the ancient Indo-Aryan colonists
settled on the banks of the Oxus and the coast of
the Black Sea stood in the same relation to Aryandom
as the descendants of the present generation of the
Indian emigrants in the far off Fiji and in the wilder-
ness of Africa will stand to ours after a century or
two when their Indian nationality will hardly be
recognisable owing to admixture of blood, and
religious and linguistic differences from their parent
stock.

APPENDIX B.

THE LEGEND ABOUT THE YADU TRIBE.

In the Rig Vedic age the Yadus lived in the land of Sapta-Sindhu and were characterized by adventurous habits and heterodox beliefs. Indra* is said to have crossed the ocean and brought back to the shores of Sapta-Sindhu, Yadu and Turvasu who used to live on the farther shores of the ocean as unanointed kings, probably in a new colony of their own. After their return, they performed many sacrifices on the banks of the Saraswati. But they relapsed to heresy again; owing to their heterodoxy and indifference to the worship of Indra, they are denounced in a hymn of the Rig Veda [Rig. x. 62, 10] as unbelieving Kshatriyas in the same way as the orthodox Pandit of to-day would condemn a non-conforming Hindu as a Mlechha. Yadu, the legendary progenitor of the tribe, was the eldest son of King Yayāti† who disinherited him and cursed

---

* Rig. VI. 120, 12 and IV. 30, 17.

† Mr. R. P. Chanda notices the two conflicting legends in the *Harivamsa* about the origin of the Yadus, *viz.*, one from Yadu, the son of Yayāti, and the other from another Yadu, son of Haryasva of Solar Iksvaku race. (*The Indo-Aryan Races*, pp. 28-30). His preference of the second legend tracing the descent of the Yadus from the son of Haryasva has not been perhaps very judicious and scientific, because it militates against the whole tradition of the Lunar Race recorded in the *Mahabharat* and all the *Purans*. Besides *the second one is not the main version* of the *Harivamsa* but an incidental narration of a legend by Bikadru to Shri Krishna.

his line for disobedience, saying "Wicked and without dominion shall be thy progeny." Yayāti made his youngest son Puru his successor on the throne of Aryandom proper, and gave Yadu an appanage in the far south—some say south-west, where the race of Yadu multiplied and prospered, and carried on a sort of hereditary feud with the descendants of Puru for recovering the birth-right of their eponymous ancestor. They seemed to have formed republican military aristocracies, often very tyrannical. We perhaps catch a glimpse of it in the *Mahabharat** where a rebellion *en masse* of Vaishyas and Shudras, headed by the Brahmans against the powerful Haihaya Yadavas—of whom the Jatas or Su-jatas were a branch—is alluded to. The Brahmans, displaying *kusha* grass on their standard,

---

This appears to be an extempore fabrication of the genealogy of Shri Krishna like that of the Sayyid origin of Tipu Sultan by his ambassadors at Constantinople. If the legend has any truth it shows that a branch of the Solar Race became engrafted upon the Lunar Race descended from Yadu, son of Yayāti. It is strange that Mr. Chanda has overlooked the words of Madhu to his son-in-law Haryasva, "My darling! in the course of time your race shall mingle with the Yadu Race, descended from Yayāti; and, though you are of Solar Race, your clan would become subordinate to the Lunar Race" [*Harivamsa*, chap. 93.] Mr. Chanda evidently prefers this self-contradictory Solar origin of the Yadus because it conveniently makes the Kathiawar peninsula the original home of the Yadus whom he is eager to prove *Aryan emigrants from Mesopotamia with a good deal of Semitic blood.* [*The Indo Aryan Races*, p. 33.]

    * See *Udyoga Parva*, chap. 154, and *Shanti Parva*, chap. 49.

marched with a motley host of Vaishyas and Shudras against the Kshatriyas.

A great avenger arose among the Brahmans in the person of Parashuram who exterminated the Kshatriya race twenty-one times. The few who escaped his battle-axe took shelter in mountains and among the lower classes; some were protected by kind-hearted Brahmans. Without instruction and without ceremonials they grew up like Shudras. *Rishi Kashyapa reclaimed them* and restored them to the rank of Kshatriyas again. This was perhaps the first creation of a class of Neo-Kshatriyas of adulterated blood claiming descent from the Lunar race.

Another important feature of the history of the Yadus was their hereditary feud with the kings of the Solar race. The sons of Yadu made a great attempt to overthrow their more cultured and orthodox rivals by forming a confederacy with the Saka, Palhava, Parada, Yavana, Kamboja and Barbara tribes against the father of the famous king Sagara. This king Sagara annihilated nearly the whole of the Haihayas, and would have destroyed their Mlechha allies also but for the intercession of Rishi Vashista.* From this time the decline of the

---

*"Sagara in compliance with the injunction of his spiritual guide, contented himself therefore with imposing upon the vanquished nations some humiliating conditions. He made the Yavanas shave their heads entirely; the Sakas he compelled to shave the upper part of their heads; the Paradas wore their hair long; and the Palhavas let their beards grow, in obedience to his commands......Them also, and *other Kshatriya races*, he deprived of the established usages of

political power and social ascendancy of the Yadus began.

The Yadus never recovered completely from the shock of their disastrous defeat and degradation at the hands of king Sagara. They seem to have since been fast sinking into something like the present Jat status, considered socially inferior and not entitled to regal honour by their erstwhile compeers.* About the time of the *Mahabharat*, they occupied the Surasena or modern Mathura country. Eighteen clans lived · together, obeying the command of Ugrasena, the head of the leading clan of the Bhojas (who being descended from the Haihayas represented the eldest line of Yadu). Ugrasena was called King only by courtesy. He was the Grand Patriarch of the whole tribe by sufferance,

---

oblations to fire and the study of the Vedas."—Wilson's translation of the *Bishnu Puran*, p. 376.

* The following passage in the *Bishnu Puran* perhaps faithfully reflects the attitude of monarchical tribes like the Kurus to the Yadavas. The Kuru chiefs who looked upon the Yadu Race as not entitled to regal dignity angrily retorted against the imperious tone of Balaram—who came to demand the release of Shri Krishna's son captured in an attempt to carry off the daughter of Duryodhan—"What shall the Yadava give orders to the chiefs of the family of Kuru? If Ugrasena issued his mandates to the Kauravas, then we must *take away the white umbrella that he has usurped* and which is only fit for the kings.......................The *homage that is due to us, their superiors,* by the Kukkura and Andhaka tribes, may not be paid by them, but whoever heard of a command issued by a servant to his master?" The Yadava envoy with his instinctive republican contempt for princes and thrones cried out furiously, "Fie upon the pride that boasts of a throne, the leaving of a hundred mortals." [*Bishnu Puran*, p. 603].

without any pretension to despotic authority ; real
power was vested in a Council of Elders, consisting
of the most influential persons of the different
gotras. His position was, so to say, like that of
the recognized head of a Jat *báráh* or *chaurasiyá*,
i.e., a group of twelve or eighty-four villages inhabited mainly by the same people. But an
Aurangzib was born to Ugrasena—the cruel and
resolute Kansha, who imprisoned his father and
usurped despotic authority over the Yadus with the
help of some powerful mercenary fighters. The
upstart, having married two daughters of the powerful Magadha Emperor Jarasandha, swelled up with
pride and was half ashamed to call himself a
Yadava. He reduced the junior clans of the
Yadavas to the position of subjects and his tyranny
drove many of them to cattle-rearing* as a means
of livelihood, which could no longer be earned by
the sword and as members of the ruling aristocracy.
Shri Krishna killed the wicked Kansha and restored
Ugrasena to his authority. Eighteen times did the
haughty prince of Magadha renew his attack upon
the Yadavas to avenge the death of his son-in-law ;
as often was he forced to retire discomfited. At
last worn out in an unequal conflict, the Yadava
chiefs decided upon the evacuation of the Mathura
region, where their powerful enemy gave them no
peace.

The Yadus were indifferent in their allegiance
to the Vedic gods and the Brahmans, nay more,

---

* Vasudeva, father of Shri Krishna is described as "living
as a tributary [*karada*] of Kansha at the hill of Govardhana,
attached to the cows" [*Harivamsa*, Chap. 55.]

positively hostile, if we are to believe the Pauranic traditions. They insulted their *purohit* [family-priest] Gargya, who vowed vengeance upon them and did penance to *Rudra* in order to get a son* "capable of humbling the pride of the Andhaka and Brishni clans" [*Harivamsa*, chap. 114]. They owed their final destruction at Prabhas to the curse of Rishi Durvasa, upon whom their wicked young sons played an indecent prank. Shri Krishna himself abolished Indra-worship in the land of Braj, even when he was a mere boy, and after his accession to power he humiliated the pride of the king of gods by forcibly taking away the heavenly flower tree [*Páriját*] from the Garden of Paradise. The ancient Haihayas worshipped Dattatreya, while their descendants in the time of the *Mahabharat* are found worshipping Shiva. The most striking feature of the Yadava people was their great republican confederacy upheld by extreme clannish spirit. Though divided into numerous branches, and often so remote from one another as to permit intermarriage, they continued to hold together as sons of the same father, presenting a united front to the common enemy, sharing the common weal and woe, and living and moving as one body. While left to themselves, petty jealousies and family feuds marked their lives. Drinking, gambling, and gay festivities enlivened their society. The *Hari-vamsa* gives a very animating picture of their social life. They go out for excursion ; men and women,

---

* The son was the Black Yavana prince whose enmity drove the Yadavas to seek refuge on the western sea-coast.

young and old, all joining in the mirthful sports
either in the pleasant shady woodland or on the
smiling beach. Balaram, always in a state of
intoxication, begins singing aloud, with his wife
keeping tune with the clapping of his hands. His
younger brother Shri Krishna, with his wife, his
sister, *and his friend*, follows him and sings
in chorus. The younger people, quite unabashed,
catch the contagion and sing tumultuously. Next
a water-sport (sprinkling water at one another while
bathing) is proposed by Shri Krishna. They divide
into two parties ; one under Balaram consisting of
one half of the Yadavas and the sons of Shri
Krishna with their wives ; the other half under Shri
Krishna with Balaram's sons and their wives.
Heavily drunk, they plunge into the water, taking
off their clothes and ornaments, and begin throwing
water at one another. So excited do they become
that the playful emulation assumes the turn of a
serious fight regardless of the presence of the ladies.
The cool-headed Shri Krishna sees the danger, and
puts a timely stop to the sport. They come out of
the water, dress themselves, and sit at their meals.
Pomegranates and other fruits, different preparations of meat and a roasted buffalo-calf are served.
After their meals they drink various kinds of wine
in the company of their wives. There were, however, some vegetarians and teetotallers among
them, such as Uddhava and Bhoja, who content
themselves with rice-pudding, curds and sweetmeats. Such sporting and feasting of the young
and old, men and women together, so repugnant
to the more refined section of the Aryans, prevailed

22

perhaps among the Yadavas only, though we hear
of such tribal festivities in the country of Magadha
in the earlier years of the great Emperor Ashoka.
The author of the *Harivamsa* tells us explicitly that
"placing love above everything else, the Brishnis,
Andhakas, and Dasharhas *used to behave to their
sons as friends** (*i.e.*, without the reserve usually
due to age and parental relation.)

In the twenty-sixth year of the reign of
Yudhisthira (*i.e.*, after the battle of Kurukshetra), a
terrible catastrophe came upon the race of Yadu
and destroyed it almost root and branch. They had
become wicked, arrogant, cruel, and disrespectful
to their elders and to the venerable Brahmans.
The most influential heads of the tribe, Balaram,
Shri Krishna, Babhru, and Ahuka met in a council
to devise means for the reformation of the morals
of the Yadavas. They issued a proclamation in
the city that any person drinking wine even alone
and in privacy should be put to death with his
whole family. But such Puritan severity could
hardly succeed in a city of Epicureans. Shortly
afterwards, they made a grand pilgrimage with their

---

* See *Harivamsa*, ch. 145, 146. It is interesting to notice
that this सखिभाव between father and son still seems to
prevail among almost all sections of the rural population of
western India. A father generally addresses his son not as
Bawa or *Beta* but as *Bhai*. When sons grow up in age they
follow literally the moral injunction of Chanakya " प्राप्तेतु
षोकशेवर्षे पुतंमित्र वदाचरेत्" *i.e.*, a son should be treated as a
friend when he attains his sixteenth year. It is not unusual
to hear little daughters and sons of educated Sindhi gentlemen
addressing their father as *Dada* [elder brother].

'wives to the sea-coast of Prabhas. Putting aside
all restraints, they held drinking parties, enlivened
by the songs and dances cf courtesans and the per-
formances of expert actors. The younger folk, in
a state of intoxication, gave to the monkeys fcod
prepared for feeding the Brahmans in order to see
how the animals fought ! Kritavaima, Satyaki, and
even the sons of Shri Krishna emptied their wine-
cups in his very presence. A quarrel broke out
between Satyaki and Kritavarma, who had fought
on opposite sides at the battle of Kurukshetra.
Satyaki suddenly rushed upon Kritavarma and cut
off his head. Their friends, and members of the
different *gotras* soon ranged themselves into two
parties and a deadly conflict ensued. Mad with
wine and the spirit of revenge the warlike Yadavas
fought to their last breath. When weapons became
useless they plucked up sea-reeds and attacked one
another desperately ; none thought of saving himself
by turning back or by standing aloof.

Several days afterwards Arjun came to Dwaraka
and led back towards Hastinapur the woeful
remnant of a mighty tribe, consisting mostly of
widows, orphans and old men. One day he halted
near the Panjnad river, at a place *rich in cattle and
agricultural produce*, and inhabited by Abhira
Dasyus (pastoral robber tribes). A large convoy of
females with a slender escort was too great a
temptation for them ; with no other weapon than
their quarter-staves they fell upon the rear of
Arjun's line of march. The victor of Kurukshetra
lost a part of his convoy and found it extremely
difficult to conduct the rest through the land of the

sturdy robbers. He left the Bhojas under the son
of Kritavarma in a colony in the city of *Mártikavati**
in the western Panjab. A second colony of the
Yadus was founded by him on the banks of the
Saraswati where he established the son of Satyaki
with the old men and the boys of his family. He
crowned Vajra, the grandson of Shri Krishna, as
king in the old Pandava capital of Indraprastha.
Thus the seeds of the race of Yadu became scattered
over the Land of the Five Rivers and the valley of
the Jamuna.

---

* The city is mentioned both in the *Mahabharata* and
the *Harivamsa*. *Brihat Samhita* [ed. S. Divedi, Sans. text,
vol. x. p. 294] mentions it along with Takshashila, Gandhara
and Pushkalavati, *i.e.*, cities of the north-west. Col. Tod
evidently identifies it with the hill of Jud or Yadu-ka-tila.

APPENDIX C

THE JAT RISINGS DURING AURANGZIB'S REIGN.

Professor Jadunath Sarkar has recently secured from the Jaipur State archives copies of many hundreds of official letters and news-sheets (*akhbarat-i-darbar-i-muala*) sent to Rajahs Bishun Singh and Sawai Jai Singh by their agents at the imperial Court. These came to hand after my History had been printed, and hence I can give here only a brief summary of the new facts thus brought to light about the activity of the Jat rebels during the last two decades of the reign of Aurangzib.

In these letters, the audacious Jats are invariably designated *Jat-i-badzat* (the Jat of evil breed.) This clearly indicates the impotent fury of the Mughal Government, which knew not how to suppress them. The sphere of the marauding activity of the Jats, as these letters illustrate, extended from Mathura to the border of Jaipur, and from the hills of Miwat to the bank of the Chambal. Peace and order fled from this region. The roads became so unsafe that Rs. 200 used to be demanded as escort-hire for accompanying a caravan only from Agra to Dholpur. Merchants and wayfarers could travel only under passes bought for a heavy price from the freebooting Jat leaders. Among the strongholds of the Jats in that period Sinsani, Sogor, Sonkh, and Wair are often mentioned.

The Mughal administration, we find again and again, was hopelessly corrupt ; local officials and soldiers alike connived at the rebellious activity of the Jats and even entered into collusion with them for sharing the plunder of their own master's subjects. One example may be given here from a news-letter : Fazil Khan, an officer posted at Agra, was ordered to escort some imperial treasure to the Chambal. He gave secret notice of his journey to the Jats, who replied that their ammunition had run short. Fazil Khan then secretly sent them a supply of it, and the pre-arranged highway robbery of the treasure was carried out as per plan !

On 28th March 1688, Mir Ahmad, the custodian of the tomb of Akbar, reported to the Emperor that at might a party of Rajaram's men had fallen upon the tomb and carried off its carpets, vessels, lamps and other decorations. Another report was to the effect that Rajaram had sacked eight villages assigned for the support of Shah Jahan's tomb near Agra.

The extant news-letters do not mention the burning of Akbar's bones by the Jat rebels, for which the only authority hitherto known is Manucci. But Aurangzib's inexorable wrath towards the Jats and his repeated orders for the *general* massacre of the Jat people, which these letters mention again and again, lend support to the belief that the current rumour about the burning of Akbar's bones was probably based on truth.

Several letters to Bishun Singh (Rajah of Jaipur) from his Court agent Kesho Rai tell us of the Emperor's constant anxiety at the growing menace

of the Jat rising and his impatience at the delay of
Bishun Singh in taking the field against them. The
Rajah was repeatedly told that he would be most
highly rewarded if he could subdue the Jats and
capture Sinsani before the arrival of Prince Bidar
Bakht for the same purpose. But he delayed. At
last he joined his forces with those of the prince
and laid siege to Sinsani. Bidar Bakht having been
soon afterwards recalled, Bishun Singh was left in
supreme command of the Jat expedition. The
Jaipur general Hari Singh conducted the siege of
Sinsani and carried on punitive operations. In one
encounter with the rebels, Hari Singh was severely
wounded, and a rumour even spread that he had
been killed. The Jats, probably under pressure of
scarcity within the walls, secretly evacuated Sinsani
and the Jaipur troops occupied it after a show of
assault! This was the version of the affair that
reached Aurangzib, and naturally he refused to give
any reward to Bishun Singh. The Jaipur agent at
the imperial Court tried hard to contradict this news
as a malicious fabrication of his master's enemies,
and at the same time wrote to Bishun Singh to
placate the local *waqianavis* with rich bribes and
induce him to magnify the heroic services of the
Jaipur troops!

BIBLIOGRAPHY

The Jats have no written history of their own. Their political history is interwoven with the general histories of the empire of Delhi, and these have necessarily been laid under contribution in the present work. I shall confine myself to the discussion of the merits of only the most important works frequently referred to in the text.

PERSIAN

1. The *Waqa-i-Shah Alam Sani* [MS.] Professor Jadunath Sarkar who possesses the only copy of this work, rescued it from deplorable neglect in the house of a Kayeth family at Patna. It is a skeleton diary of Delhi occurrences and news, the leaves still surviving run with many gaps from 1739 to 1799. Prof. Sarkar who styles it the *Delhi Chronicle during the Anarchy*, thus remarks of it, "It is of priceless importance and constitutes a record of supreme value to the critical historian of this perid. Here we have an absolutely contem porary chronicle of the events and rumours of Delhi, written down immediately afterwards by an inhabitant of the city, without any embellishment, garbling or artificial arrangement of a later date...... ......While studying it, I have often been tempted to liken it to the old *Anglo-Saxon Chronicle* during Danish incursions. The artless truthfulness, the exclusion of emotion or comment, and accuracy of record are the same in both works." [See pp. 5-6

of the proceedings of the third meeting of the
Indian Historical Records Commission at Bombay.]
I subjected this *Chronicle* to a strict comparison with
the Persian as well as Maratha and French sources
which can also claim contemporary value. Now I
have been so far convinced of its accuracy that in
cases of conflicting dates and statements in other
histories of this particular period, I accept its
testimony in preference to theirs. The *Waqa-i-
Shah Alam Sani* has been the touchstone for judging
the value of all Persian histories of the latter half of
the eighteenth century.

2. The *Ibratnama* [MS.] of Khair-ud-din
Muhammad Allahabadi [1751—1827].* He was an
influential official in the employ of Prince Jahandar
Shah, son of Shah Alam II, and an eye-witness of

---

* For an account of the life and works of Khair-ud-din,
see Dr. E. D. Ross's article in *J. R. A. S.* 1902, pp. 136-138.
Though it is fuller than that of Prof. Dowson, some errors
have crept into it : *e.g.* "He (Khair-ud-din) then attached himself to the fortunes of the Shahzada Jahandar Shah, the
eldest son of Shah Jahan [?] whom he assisted in his attempt
to seize upon the throne [?] of Delhi." Shah Jahan in the
text is evidently a mistake for Shah Alam II. Khair-ud-din
assisted the prince not "in seizing upon the throne of Delhi"
as Dr. E. D. Ross would make us believe, but in trying to
secure possession of the citadel and imperial treasure lest they
should fall into the hands of Ghulam Qadir and Ismail Beg
Khān. He was made the prince's supreme agent [*ibid*, 60] and
in this capacity visited Begam Samru at her camp near Delhi.
He procured for the prince her powerful support against
Ghulam Qadir and Ismail Beg [MS., p. 63; for fuller details,
see Brajendranath Banerji's *Begam Samru*.] The prince praised
the author for his eminent services and wise counsels.

many of the occurrences described in the latter part
of the work. The author in the opening pages of
the *Ibratnama* tells us that he was impelled to write
this "Book of Warning" by the shocking atrocities
of Ghulam Qadir whom he curses with honest indignation, as *nimak-haram* (false to his master's salt.)
He mentions with gratitude and respect the name
of Sir George Henry Barlow, Governor-General who
encouraged his historical studies.

As regards the value of this work Dr. E. D.
Ross quotes with approval the opinion of Dr.
Charles Rieu "*Ibratnama* is *the fullest and most
accurate* account we possess of the chequered
career and troubled times of Shah Alam, and *it has
all the value of contemporary record*, penned by
one who had taken an active share in some of the
principal transactions of the period and was person-
ally acquainted with some of the most prominent
actors on the scene." Those who may have an
occasion to study this history in the light of the more
authentic records of the period would possibly dis-
sent from this view. Though it is undoubtedly the
fullest history of the reign of Shah Alam and is
indispensable to students of this period of Indian
history, it is by no means the most accurate one.
Up to the 12th regnal year of Shah Alam II, this
work does not throw more light on Delhi history
than what is supplied by the *Siyar-ul-Mutakhkharin*.
Khair-ud-din no doubt gives us useful details for
the period between the 12th and 20th regnal years,
but almost all his dates are wrong and inaccurate.
From the 20th year onwards, however, *Ibratnama*
has certainly great value.

His graphic details often produce the effect of a melo-drama, and this very fact often leads us to suspect his accuracy. My admiration for this history decreased with the progress of my studies in and around this period. However, we have no option but to accept as true all his statements which have not been definitely contradicted by more reliable authorities.

3. *Chahar Gulzar-i-Shujai* of Harcharan Das* (Prof. Sarkar's MS.) The author was in the employment of Nawab Qasim Ali Khan, a nobleman of Delhi. He migrated to Oudh with his master's family in the first year of the reign of Alamgir II. and began the study and writing of history to enliven the dreary days of his exile and penury. He says that he reached his 80th year in 1194 A.H. *i.e.*, 1180 A.D. He writes in a simple style and his facts and dates are generally accurate. But the memory of the old man seems to have failed him sometimes. We need not be surprised if he commits mistakes here and there and confuses names and dates. The following will serve as a typical example. "Jawahir Singh Jat, after the death of his father Suraj Mal, laid siege to the citadel of Agra. But having despaired of taking it by force of arms owing to the bravery and faithfulness of the imperial commandant Fazil Khan, he had recourse to intrigue. He secured entrance into the fort by bribing Muyyid Beg who was in charge of the gates—with three *lakhs* of Rupees. When the fort was captured after its evacuation by the Muslim garrison in 1174 H. (1761 A.D.) Jawahir

---

* For an account of his life, see Elliot, viii. 204—206.

Singh threw the traitor Muyyid Beg into prison, and
as a reward for the fidelity of Fazil Khan granted
him a monthly pension of three hundred Rupees."
The real facts are different, *viz*:—The fort of Agra
was captured in 1761 by Suraj Mal and not by
Jawahir Singh. Father Wendel tells us nothing about
such an incident in his valuable sketch of Jawahir
Singh's reign. It is, on the other hand, not likely
that the whole story is altogether false. The details
may be true of the capture of Agra by Suraj Mal.

4. *Tarikh-i-Muzaffari* (MS.) of Muhammad
Ali Khan. The author Muhammad Ali belonged to
a distinguished family of Panipat. His grandfather
Lutfullah Khan held the rank of a *haft-hazari* [7,000
horse], and during the reign of Muhammad Shah
served as governor of Kabul and Multan. One of
his uncles Shakir Khan was the author of a history
called *Tarikh-i-Shakir Khani* (Prof. Sarkar's MS.)
The author left Panipat for Bihar in search of
employment and became the darogha of the Faujdari
Adalat of Tirhut and Hajipur through the patronage
of Muhammad Reza Khan Muzaffar Jang, the *Naib
Nazim* of Bengal. The *Tarikh-i-Muzaffari* was
composed about 1800 A.D., and named after the
patron of the author. Prof. Dowson says, "This is
one of the most accurate general histories I know
............The history of the later empire is particularly
full." (Elliot, viii. 316). There was a learned
discussion over the historical value of this work in
the second meeting of the Indian Historical Records
Commission, held at Lahor (1920). Prof. Jadunath
Sarkar remarked, "We possess three nearly contemporary and fairly long histories of the Delhi

empire during the second half of the 18th century, viz., the Siyar-ul-Mutakhkharin, the Ibratnama of Fakir Khair-ud-din Allahabadi, and the Tarikh-i-Muzaffari. Of these the second is the longest, most accurate, and (in his opinion) the best, as the author lived at or near the Court of Delhi, while writers of the other two works lived in Bengal and Bihar and had no access to the imperial Court records and other original sources of information. For the period before 1760 (covered by the first volume of the Tarikh-i-Muzaffari), this book is a mere compilation from earlier works and therefore cannot claim to be considered as a primary authority. The second volume (covering the years 1760-1809) was composed later than the Ibratnama and is much inferior to the latter. In short, the Tarikh-i-Muzaffari, in most parts, is neither an eye-witness's report nor a summary of State-papers." Chaudhuri Abdul Hamid maintained that the author of Tarikh-i-Muzaffari belonged to a "family of historians and high officers of the Mughal Court, and as such he presumably had access to State-papers" [Proceedings, Indian Historical Records Commission, 1920, p. 23.]

But the fact is that none of the three histories bears any trace of the use of State-papers. All the three authors relied mainly upon what they had heard from others. Even Khair-ud-din often cites as authorities little known persons such as Mir Muhammad Yaqub who found the date of the battle of Barsana in the chronogram "larza bar ek o sang az in fathe haidari" which is found wrong [vide text]. It is perhaps unjust to pronounce a verdict against an author merely on theoretical grounds,

without patiently examining the contents of his work.
A test-study of the period between the accession of
Ahmad Shah and the battle of Panipat as dealt with
in all these three histories in the light of independent
sources convinces me of the originality and trust-
worthiness of *Tarikh-i-Muzaffari*. The civil war
between Safdar Jang and Ahmad Shah, and the
diplomatic activity of the Abdali before Panipat have
been described with greater accuracy and fuller
wealth of details in this book than in the other two
more popular histories.* Some minute details given
by the *Tarikh-i-Muzaffari* warrant us in inferring
that the author derived his information from reliable
eye-witnesses, perhaps some members of his family
who lived so near the capital. The following
instance bears out the truth. The *Waqa-i-Shah
Alam Sani* which is the diary of events kept by an
inhabitant of the capital says, "On the 21st Jamada
I., 1165 H., Nawab Safdar Jang, having taken leave,
started [from the city] *while it was raining............*
and pitched his camp at the garden of Ismail Khan"
[*Waqa*, p. 76]. The *Tarikh-i-Muzaffari* also says,
"The Nawab started from his palace and proceeded
by the road running along the bank of the river
[Jamuna]. When he was passing opposite the
imperial citadel, he alighted from his horse, and
made the customary salute towards it. At that time
a shower was falling from the sky and drops of tears
too appeared in the eyes of the Nawab" [MS.
p. 69]. The *Ibratnama* and *Siyar-ul-Mutakhkharin*

---

* Khair-ud-din gives us only a brief summary of these
two episodes, devoting not more than 15 lines to each.

do not take notice of these minute details. The only history from which *Tarikh-i Muzaffari* may have borrowed this is *Chahar-Gulzar-i-Shujai,* which says: "At the time of his departure, *it was raining heavily.* While he reached near the Auspicious Residence [the citadel], he alighted from his elephant and did obeisance towards." The *Tarikh-i-Muzaffari* gives some valuable information which we miss altogether in every other regular history of the 18th century. The following passage gives us the only recorded indication of the fact that the Mughal Government also had some Jat mercenaries who fought against Suraj Mal. "Ghazi-ud-din Imad-ul-mulk............with his own troops and *His Majesty's Jats [firqa-i-Jat Badshahi]* exerted himself in the defence of the city [against Nawab Safdar Jang and Suraj Mal]."* This is indirectly supported by the unassailable testimony of the *Waqa:* "On the 22nd Ziqada, 1165 H. [20 September, 1753] ....*men of the Jat contingent went inside the citadel* and created disturbance for their pay. They obstructed the audience chamber of the Emperor and the *deohris* [out-apartments] of the Begams. His Majesty came to the Diwan-i-Am" [MS., p. 70].†

---

* *Tarikh-i-Muzaffari,* MS., p. 69.

† The *Waqa* contains another passage telling us about the unruly character of the Emperor's Jat mercenaries: "On the 19th Rabi II., 1166 H. (13th February, 1754), the soldiers of the Ali Shahi, Walah Shahi, and the Jat regiments assembled in the mosque of Quddus-ul-Ahad for their pay, raised a tumult and prevented men from going inside the fort......took away the turbans and clothes of the passers-by and blocked the *Shah Rah* [Royal road]" (MS., p. 85.)

5. *The Siyar-ul-Mutakhkharin*, the most popular and widely known history of the period, hardly
requires any comment. The English translation of
this book by Mustafa is generally accurate; but he
seems to have taken a liberty like that of Briggs in
his translation of Ferishta to add here and there a
phrase or two of his own unwarranted by the text.
Though the author, Ghulam Husain lived in Bengal,
his father and uncles served at Delhi and as his history is based on information supplied by them, the
chapters dealing with the history of the Delhi and
Oudh Courts have been found useful and trustworthy. He does not give us anything of value
about Jat history after the death of Suraj Mal.

6. *Imad-us-Saadat* by Mir Ghulam Ali. (Persian
text, Newal Kishore Press, Lucknow). This work
was composed about 1808 at Lucknow whither the
author was forced to flee from Delhi, when that city
was in agony from the atrocities of the accursed
Ghulam Qadir. Though this work is mainly a
history of the Oudh Nawabs, it throws interesting
and useful side-lights upon the affairs of Delhi.
The book reads like a string of entertaining stories,
which are the typical product of Lucknow. But
a careful study reveals the inquisitiveness of the
author and his habit of taking pains to know the
truth. Sometimes he contradicts popular stories and
enters into a critical examination of them. He
almost always gives us the names of his informants.
Though his history is neither full nor methodical, it
amply repays perusal.

7. *Bayan-i-Waqa* [MS.] by Abdul 'Karim
Kashmiri. The account of the reign of Ahmad

·Shah and incidental notices about the Bharatpur Jats down to the murder of Ratan Singh are very valuable and accurate.

8. *Calendars of Persian Correspondence*, published by the Imperial Records Department, Calcutta. We have three volumes of these valuable Calendars covering the period between 1767-1772. These contain English translations of the Persian letters issued by the Government of Bengal to their officials, agents, and foreign notables along with the answers and news-letters received from them about occurrences in Upper India. These may be regarded as *primary sources* of the history of this period. They stand next to the *Waqa-i-Shah Alam Sani* in importance and very often prove valuable supplements to the latter. Their destruction would have been an irreparable loss to the students of Indian history.

MARATHI

1. Though the Marathi *bakhars* or chronicles were generally composed at a much later date than the events they relate and hence are not considered by scholars to be sound material, yet the *Bhao Sahibchi Bakhar* (in the scholarly edition of Kashinath Narayan Sane) is an exception. I have found it most useful and reliable for my period. The writer, Krishnaji Shyam Rao, resided at Indraprastha near Delhi. He seems to have been well versed in Hindi and acquainted with the affairs of the Jats, Rajputs and Ruhelas. The speeches put by him into the mouths of the different historic personages may not

23

have been true word for word, but they undoubtedly represent the spirit of the actors.

Minor mistakes are not infrequent. *E.g.*, he says that during the Mathura expedition of Ahmad Shah Abdali, "8000 Bairagis took up arms at Brindaban and died fighting...The Ghilzai [=Abdali] butchered several pious Bairagis who resided at Gokhri [=Gokul]" (p. 32). We know from the Persian sources (cited in my text) that it was at Brindaban that the *Vaishnav* Bairagis were massacred. G. S. Sardesai (*Panipat Prakaran,* p. 77) quotes a letter from Krishna Joshi of Delhi, which tells us that Gokul was saved from the Abdali by the *Naga* monks, two or three thousand of whom died in its defence.

2. *Dilli-yethil Rajkaranen* or letters of the Maratha envoy at Delhi, published by D. B. Parasnis, in two volumes. Of first-rate importance as regards dates and events (except hearsay reports of distant occurrences.)

3. Marathi historical documents, mostly published by the Bharat Itihas Samsodhak Mandal of Poona,—esp. in its annual reports, Sammelan reports, and recently started quarterly journal. No student of the history of the Delhi empire during the second half of the 18th century can afford to neglect the ever-increasing mass of contemporary Marathi records and letters brought to light by a band of devoted Maratha workers. But the sifting of sound historical material out of them requires as much skill and labour as are demanded in collecting particles of gold from sand.

A letter from Antaji Mankeshwar (published in the Mandal's *Journal*, vol. III. Nos. 2—4, 1924 A.D.) throws interesting side-light upon the civil war between the imperial Paymaster and Safdar Jang. This is perhaps the only evidence to show that Maratha auxiliaries took part in the first stage of the struggle and that the success of Ghazi-ud-din was partly due to their valour. Antaji would naturally exaggerate the services of the Marathas, but be it said to his credit, he does not ignore the heroism of the Jat chief Suraj Mal on the enemy's side. This letter adds flesh and skin to the dry bones of the narrative of the battle of Faridabad given in the *Waqa*, and therefore we translate both of them here.

Waqa-i-Shah Alam Sani:—"Sunday, Zihijja 1165 A.H. (=June 1752 A.D.) News arrived [at Delhi] of a battle having taken place near the tank of Faridabad between the Bakhshi-ul-mulk and the troops of Nawab Safdar Jang. The latter was defeated and put to flight" (p. 81 of MS.)

Letter from Antaji Mankeshwar to Babu Rao Baba, from Indraprastha, Bhadra Badi Ekadashi :—"Mansur Ali and Suraj Mal were at Faridabad and the imperial army encamped at Kalika-ji (near Okla) ...Daily skirmishes, marching and counter-marching took place. After that, on Shravan Badi 11, Friday, Mansur Ali with the Jat advanced in readiness for battle. A fight took place at Faridabad. The Jats fought obstinately, but were defeated. Suraj Mal displayed great valour, and a personal encounter took place between him and ourselves, in which he received a spear-thrust. The Jats have retreated beyond Ballamgarh, to which the Mir Bakhshi has laid siege. We are plundering the Jat territory in the neighbourhood."

4. *Marathi Riyasat*, by G. S. Sardesai, Vol. II. (1707-1740), Vol. III. (1740-1760), and Vol. IV. (Panipat Prakaran).

Every student of the history of India in the 18th century owes a heavy debt of gratitude to Mr. Sardesai, who has nearly completed the stupendous task of sifting the vast mass of printed materials available in Marathi, critically testing their value, and presenting a synthesis of them in an attractive garb. What we admire in this great historian is his fearless love of truth and freedom from bias, even more than his unsurpassed industry and critical power. So far as Marathi sources are concerned, we can confidently rely on his valuable works. But it should be remembered that his failure to use the Persian sources has left his narrative one-sided and defective at some places, just as the Persian chroniclers on their part have missed out many facts concerning Maratha affairs. For example, Sardesai makes no mention of Suraj Mal's participation in the war between Madho Singh and Ishwari Singh. [Vol. II. 65-70.]

FRENCH

1. *Geographie de l' Indoustan*, by Joseph Tieffenthaler. This celebrated Jesuit missionary came to India in December 1743 and visited Deeg, "the residence of the prince of the Jats" next year. He has left brief descriptive notices of Deeg, Kuhmir, and Bharatpur as they then were.

2. *Le Nabob Rene Madec*, par Emile Barbe. An extremely valuable documented history of this celebrated French mercenary general's career in India. The long extracts from his memoirs and those of certain other Frenchmen who came into direct contact with Jat and Delhi affairs, printed by M. Barbe, have been fully utilised by me, as the evidence of "eye-witnesses."

3. *Memoires de l' origine, acroissement, et etat present de puissance des Jats dans l' Indostan.* [*Orme MSS. O.V.* 216 No. 2, pp. 86+86 ; a second copy in *India* XV. No. 11, pp. 150.]

Mr. S. C. Hill ascribes its authorship to Father Francois Xavier Wendel, who lived in India from 1751 till his death in 1803, and resided for several years at Agra. He is frequently referred to in the *Calendar of Persian Correspondence* (of the English E. I. Co.) He was in high favour with the Bengal Government and sincerely devoted to the English interests.* We find him acting as the agent of the English at Lucknow after the flight of Mir Qasim from Bengal.

We do not know what made the Reverend Father repair to the Jat country, accept service under Jawahir Singh as his political adviser, and stay at Deeg till the death of that Rajah. The fact that he went there shortly after the flight of Samru to the Court of Jawahir Singh leads us to suspect that he was in the pay of the English and that his real object was to keep the Bengal Government informed of any

---

* See esp. his letter from Lucknow, 12 Nov. 1763, in *Pers. Corr.* i. 263.

hostile designs of the powerful and ambitious Jat
Rajah who held the balance of power in Northern
India between the Abdali and the Maratha.

The Father set about collecting information
about Jat history administration and manners at
Deeg, and wrote this long account, which is of
priceless value as regards the fulness and authenticity
of its information on most points. My chapters on
Suraj Mal and Jawahir Singh owe their detail and
freshness to this French manuscript.

The most astonishing assertion which he makes,
—apparently on hearsay,—is that Suraj Mal was not
at all the son of Badan Singh. He has also cast
some doubt on the birth of Jawahir Singh, which was
probably based on a mischievous rumour started by
the malicious Jat nobles who wanted to set the
eldest prince aside from the throne of Bharatpur.

4 and 5. *Memoire sur l'Empire Mogol* by Jean
Law and Gentil. These have yielded very little new
information.

INDEX

ADDITIONS AND CORRECTIONS

P. 13 footnote †, *should be considered altogether deleted*
,, 25 footnote line 4 *add* is *after* which
,, 26 l. 5 *for* Paban *read* Pahan
,, 35 l. 11 *for* दिल्लिश्वरो *read* दिल्लीश्वरो
,, 45 ,, 12 ,, younger brother ,, son of the the younger brother
,, 63 ,, 29 ,, Shura ,, Sura
,, 67 ,, 11 ,, barve ,, brave
,, 81 ,, 11 ,, Ismail Beg Khan ,, Ismail Khan Kabuli
,, 84 ,, 18 ,, poisoned ,, murdered
,, 99 ,, 15 ,, accused ,, accursed
,, 115 footnote 3 *for* करावाचा ,, माराठ्याचा
,, 120 l. 24 ,, Rao ,, Rai
,, 123 ,, 11 ,, *add* one of *after* of *and change* army *into* armies
,, 123 ,, 12 *for* two lakhs *read* half a lakh
,, 123 ,, 10 and 14 *for* brother ., cousin
,, 125 ,, 6 *for* mosques ,, a mosque
,, 125 ,, 26 ,, Shahan-i-Shah ., Shahan-Shah
,, 128 ,, 21 ,, brother ,, cousin
,, 136 ,, 4 *for* had passed away *read* remained
,, ,, footnote l. 4 *after* gives *add* on the authority of Kashi Rai
,, 137 f. l. 20 ,, no ,, no other
,, 159 l. 12 ,, the women ,, women
,, 162 ,, 12 ,, peasant ,, a peasant
,, 170 ,, 2 ,, a small ,, the small
,, 182 ,, 21 ,, field of ,, fief of
,, 191 ,, 24 ,, Renell ,, Rennell
,, 193 ,, 21 ,, was added ,, were added
,, 194 ,, 1 ,, interests ,, interest
,, 194 ,, 15 ,, gain by ,, gain by the
,, 196 ,, 5 ,, heavy ,, the heavy
,, 196 ,, 9 ,, to the ,, on the

P. 199 l. 14 *for* the English   *read*   English
, 210   *f.*   1. 10 *for* नाहृव   ,,   नाहर
,, 217 l. 10 ,, traditions   ,,   tradition
,, 221 ,, 26 ,, by means   ,,   by no means
,, 222 ,   13 ,, etiquette   ,,   etiquette of
,, 222 ,, 27 ,, of very   ..   of the very
,, 256 ,, 11 ,, awul   ,.   awful
,, 256 ,, 12 ,, of native   ,,   of the native
,, 267 ,, 22 ,, in course   ,,   in the course
,, 315 ,, footnote l. 6 *for* and   ..   was
         ,, the Singh Jats   ,.   Ranjit Singh Jat
,, 329 ,, 26 *for* designates his   ,,   designates him

SHER SHAH

A critical study based on original sources.

BY

K. QANUNGO, M.A.

464 pp. One full page illustration. Rs. 4.

"Sher Shah is one of the world's worthies to whom History has not done justice.........Hitherto the world has been content to take Sher Shah as portrayed in the few translated extracts given in Elliot and Dowson or Ferishta.........My task has been to seek *all* the sources on Sher Shah—primary, secondary and third-rate, without any omission, to study them in the original Persian texts, and then to reconstruct the life-story of Sher Shah on a fresh original and.........exhaustive basis.

The result of this original study of Sher Shah has been to place his character in a new light and fix his fame on the basis of concrete and well-ascertained facts, and to correct the innumerable mistakes about his life and times into which my predecessors writing general histories had fallen......I have given the reasons and evidence for any conclusions. "Professor Jadunath Sarkar placed at my disposal all the materials collected in his splendid library, rich in rare Persian MSS., books of reference, learned journals maps and gazetteers. He has read this book in MS. and in proof." (Author's Foreword.)

In addition to nine chapters on the history of Sher Shah from his birth to death, two chapters are devoted to an exhaustive study of his instructions and comparison of them with Akbar's (60 pages) and his character (20 pages). There is also a full and critical bibliography (22 pages) on the Persian sources and European writers on the subject.

OPINIONS ON SHER SHAH

W. Foster, C.I.E.—"I am favourably impressed by the volume. The author has evidently caught.........the spirit of patient research and scrupulou; impartiality, and I congratulate Prof. Jadunath Sarkar on having found so apt and able a disciple."

W. Crooke, I.C.S.—"You have succeeded in satisfactorily clearing up what has hitherto been one of the most obscure periods in the history of India, and the work does great credit to your learning and industry."

Editor, Modern Review.—"It is an excellent work......... Mr. Qanungo has given us a correct idea of everything which Akbar.........owed to the constructive statesmanship and the administrative genius of Sher Shah.........In this his first work, the author has displayed such grasp of his subject, such a severely critical historical spirit, and such sense of proportion, —in one word, given evidence of such maturity of powers, that we may well hope that what he may accomplish in his maturer years will be hailed as the work of a master-builder."

' Calcutta Review.—"At last the forgotten Afghan ruler has come into his own, and this is entirely due to Mr. Qanungo's efforts............The uniformly high standard of Mr. Qanungo's work. He has read and studied with care the various Persian authorities dealing with the period."

H. Beveridge.—"This is a careful and well-written life of the famous Afghan ruler of India in the 16th century. It is a cheerful evidence that the spirit of research is abroad among the Bengalees and that the East is no longer to be put off with rhetoric and exaggeration....

Prof. Kalika-ranjan has executed his task with great labour and thoroughness, and he has told us much that is not generally known." *(J.R.A.S.)*

Sir R. C. Temple.—"I started to review Prof. Qanungo's admirable *Sher Shah*, but it ended in my writing for the *Indian Antiquary* a resumé of that remarkable man's career based on the latest researches for which we all owe so much to the younger Professor. It will appear sometime during the course of this year.

The monograph on Sher Shah suggests to me the want of similar monographs based on original documents on at least three remarkable rulers of the earlier Muslim days in Delhi—Alauddin Khilji, Feroz Shah Tughlaq and Sikander Lodi. I write to suggest that you turn on your pupils to study these men and to produce monographs on them of the same kind as that so well done by Prof. Qanungo." [Letter to Prof. J. Sarkar.]

———